C000297764

BORDERS

A GUIDE TO SPRING, SUMMER
& AUTUMN COLOUR

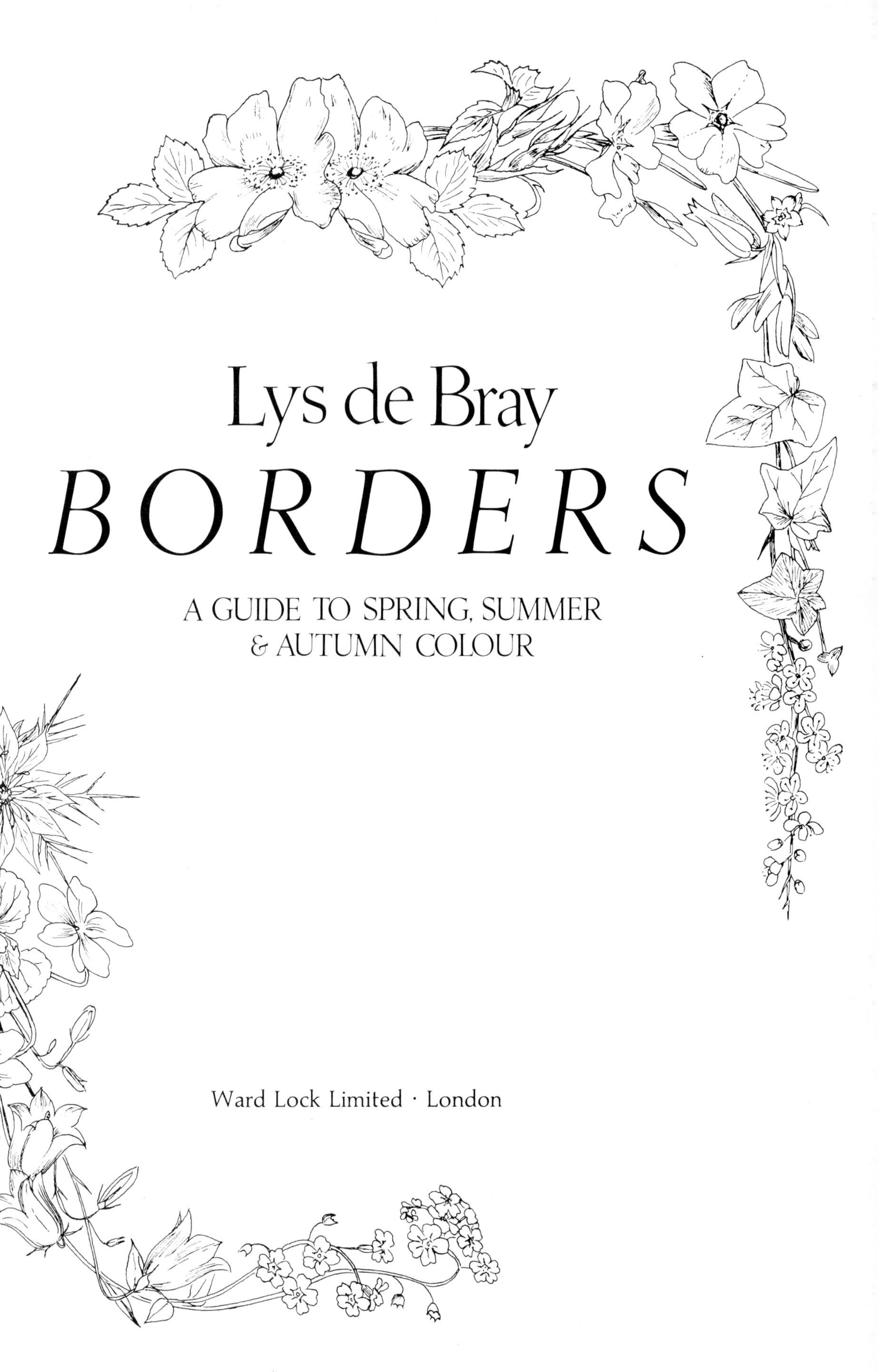

Lys de Bray

BORDERS

A GUIDE TO SPRING, SUMMER & AUTUMN COLOUR

Ward Lock Limited · London

Acknowledgements

The publishers are grateful to the author for granting permission to reproduce the ten colour paintings. All the colour photographs were taken by Bob Challinor and the line drawings were drawn by the author.

The publishers are especially grateful to the following garden owners for allowing us to photograph their gardens: Mrs M. A. Bampton (pp 7, 15 and 30); Mrs H. A. Bampton (pp 18 and 26); Mrs P. Hickman (pp 31, 38 and 39); Mr and Mrs R. Raworth (pp 43 and 47); Mrs R. H. B. Arkwright (p 111); Pusey House Gardens (pp 114, 115, 118 and 123); Major and Mrs M. T. N. H. Birchall (p 127); The Hon. Michael Flower (pp 2, 131, 134, 135, 170); the National Trust (Bodnant) (pp 134 and 166); Beth Chatto (pp 138, 146, 158 and 166); and Christopher Lloyd Esq. (p 154).

First published in Great Britain in 1987
by Ward Lock Limited, 8 Clifford Street
London W1X 1RB, an Egmont Company

House editor Denis Ingram
Designed by Clive Dorman
Text set in Monophoto Palatino
by Latimer Trend & Company Ltd, Plymouth

Printed and bound in Italy
by New Interlitho SpA

British Library Cataloguing in Publication Data

De Bray, Lys
Borders.
1. Plants, Ornamental 2. Flower gardening
I. Title
635.9 SB404.9

ISBN 0-7063-6522-4

(frontispiece)
The elegance of mellow brick and a wide grass walk emphasize the thickly-planted and summer-long interest of the oldest border in the country. In foreground *Atriplex hortensis rubra* (Crimson orache) is valuable for its unusual colouration, while poppies, *Lychnis coronaria* (rose campion) astilbes, alliums, and delphiniums are seen at their best.

Contents

PREFACE

Most people think of borders as 'herbaceous' borders but in general this is not strictly true. The glorious and billowing ebullience of a mid-summer border in full bloom is usually a carefully planned collection of plants that are structured around the more solid shapes of the appropriate shrubs and some essential roses. This book is primarily about the herbaceous plants that should constitute the greater part of any border, but it takes into account that there are many months of the year when such plants are not at their best, or not even visible. Therefore, bulbs are featured, as are appropriate shrubs, some useful climbers, and a comprehensive section on roses—both old and new.

Border-planning is vital (though it must not show) and this book has many suggestions and seasonal reminders. Foliage is also far more important tha it was formerly, and can and should play an important part in a well-designed border.

A good border is artful—though it should appear artless—and therein lies the art.

L. de B.

1

Which Kind of Border?

The term 'border' has come to mean a long flower bed of greater length than width, containing different types of plants that bloom harmoniously together at their appropriate flowering times, which may be from spring until late autumn. The type of border that you have—or hope to have—is usually dictated by the size, shape and aspect of your garden and the fixed features in it, by your gardening knowledge and interests and, lastly, by the amount of time that you are prepared to devote to it without neglecting the rest of the garden.

Oddly enough, cost is not always the chief priority—gardeners are generous folk and gifts or exchanges are normal,

Bright colours are softened by the plants' own foliage and form a traditional setting for an old church tower; lupins, delphiniums, pyrethrums, phlox and sweet peas.

while many plants can be propagated either from cuttings or from seed. To help you decide on the type of border that you would like I have defined and described several very different kinds, with planting diagrams and suggestions for each. The flowering chart (Ch. 10) is a quick reference and should provide many more ideas.

THE FORMAL BORDER

A formal border is often the simplest to plan, plant and maintain. It should be symmetrical in shape and should follow the line of near-by garden features, which may be a wall or walls, drives, paths, patios, terraces, paving, hedges or fences. The width of the border should remain constant and proportionate to its length and immediate surroundings, and the planting scheme can be planned on paper very much more easily than for other types of border; this scheme can be changed or improved upon each year. A formal border can be a ribbon of colour from early spring until autumn because its secret lies in the choice and massed planting of easy, undemanding but effective and reliable annuals, bulbs and low shrubs together with foliage, herbaceous and edging plants. Such a border requires regular weeding and dead-heading in order to stay neat, while some (but not all) of the bedding plants will benefit from feeding, and regular watering may be essential in dry seasons. I mention these four points because they are an important consideration when planning a formal border whose manicured appearance will depend on them.

The site of this border should be open and sunny, well away from the shade, overhang or roots of trees, and the situation should not be too windy. Choose plants that have a neat, firm growing habit, or those that can be disciplined unobtrusively. Aim to cover as much of the soil as possible with your choice of plants rather than Nature's, to avoid unnecessary weeding. Measure the length and width involved and calculate the number of plants needed in maturity. It is a good idea to have some extra 'standbys' in reserve in case of fatalities.

Decide on the time-scale of the border—whether it is to burst into life and beauty from early spring onwards (Fig. 1) or whether it is to be a summer border only (Fig. 2). (The first is more work, expense and a greater challenge.) If it is to include the spring season, then bulbs should be planted at the appropriate time in the autumn, and pansies, double daisies, forget-me-nots and polyanthus should be ordered or grown. Wallflowers make a wonderful band of scent and colour, but must be set out in autumn and lifted in time for the summer bedding plants,

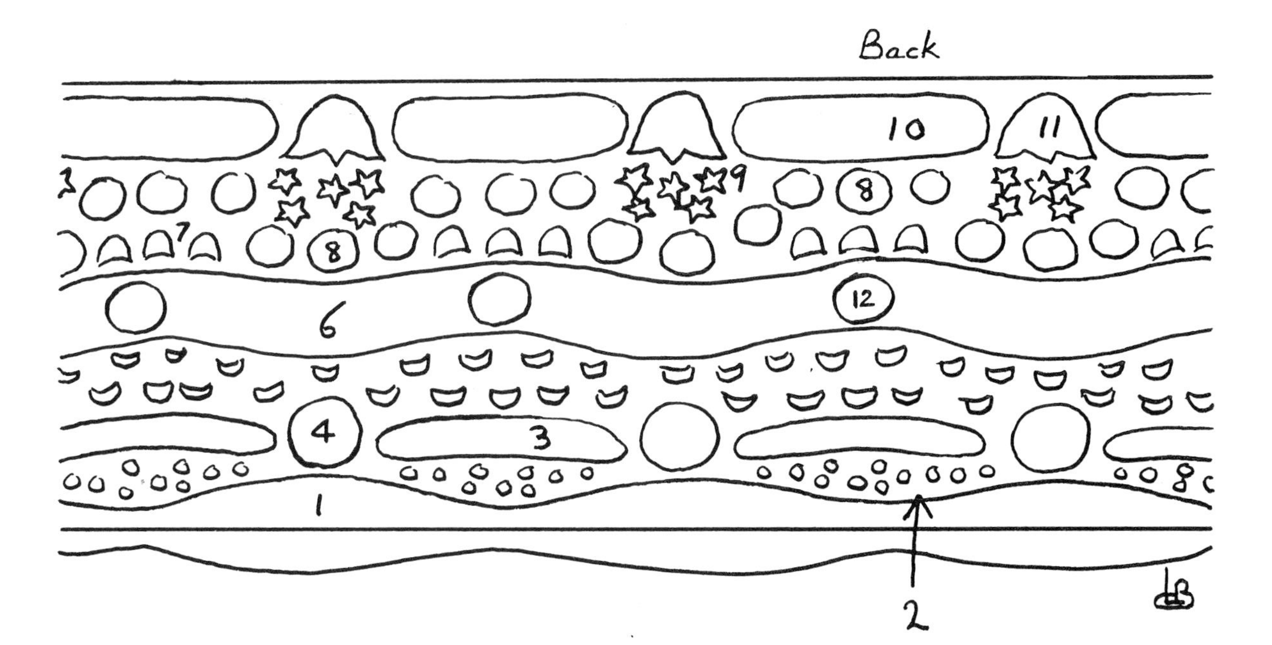

1. White Arabis or *Alyssum saxatile or Ajuga reptans*
2. *Puschkinia scilloides* *
3. Pink or blue or white *Anemone blanda* *
4. Mossy Saxifrage, pink, red or cream *
5. Early (species) tulips, white and yellow or yellow and red *
6. Forget-me-nots **
7. Tall late tulips, red, yellow or orange. Purple-black with mixed or pale yellow wallflowers **
8. Wallflowers: mixed, crimson or other single colours **
9. Late Narcissus such as *N.* 'Actaea' **
10. Senecio greyi or box or golden privet
11. *Euphorbia wulfenii*
12. Iris

* Replace when over with white, blue, yellow, purple and crimson pansies.
** Remove when over and replace with summer bedding plants

FIG. 1 Formal border, spring into summer

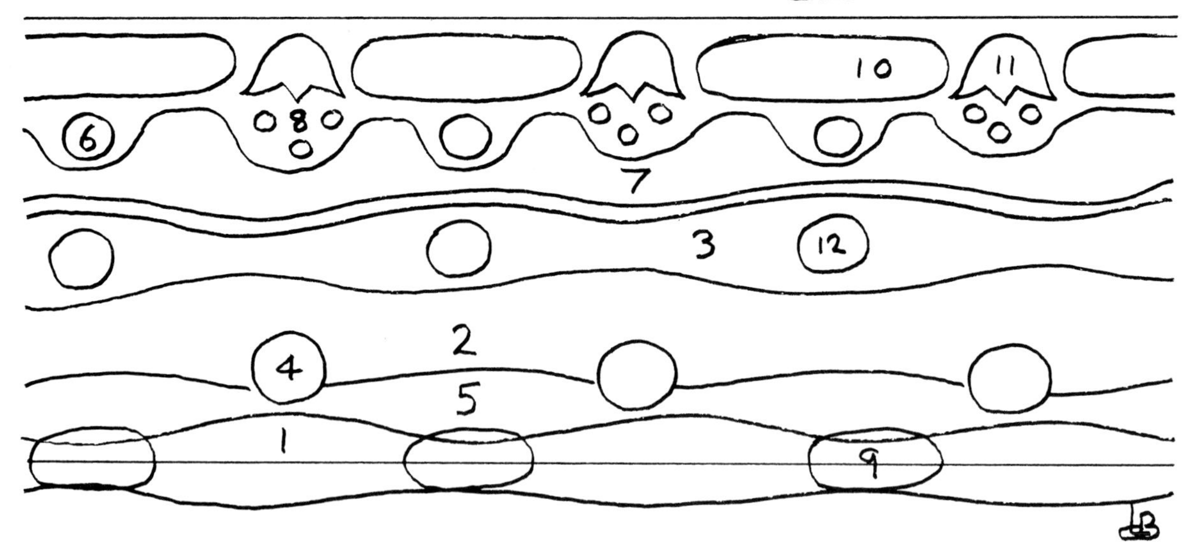

1. Arabis, clip back hard
2. Single colour or mixed pansies, remove for Ageratum
3. *Begonia semperflorens*, pink or crimson, bronze leaves
4. Variegated-leaved pelargoniums or Coleus
5. Lobelia, blue or crimson
6. *Lavatera trimestris* – pink or white
7. Antirrhinums, one colour
8. *Allium giganteum*
9. Sweet alyssum
10. *Senecio greyi* or box or golden privet
11. *Euphorbia wulfenii*
12. Iris (or Cannas or Gladiolus)

FIG. 2 Formal border, summer

which are often ready before the wallflowers have finished flowering. These annual bedding plants are an essential part of a formal scheme because of their long and colourful flowering season, usually until the first frosts. Plant them evenly and rather more thickly than usual, having checked their respective heights. To set off the often brilliant and uniform colours, use a central band of low, neat-growing shrubs and foliage plants which can be chosen for their contrasting, or restful, leaf shapes and colours. It will be found that grey or silver-leaved plants look well with almost any colour scheme, and, though apparently unobtrusive, they add a touch of elegance and distinction. Finally, standard roses cast little shade and these can be spaced evenly along the central part of the bed; if mixed varieties and colours are chosen they should flower simultaneously, but it is often less worrying to select an appropriate number of one kind.

Such borders as this, when carefully planned, planted and maintained, can be quite spectacular. They look even more pleasing when seen from above as in a terraced garden or from the gardener's own bedroom windows.

THE INFORMAL BORDER

This is the kind of border that most of us have; it is often inherited, it varies in width (often considerably), as well as direction, and its site may have all kinds of problems. Part of it may be in shade, while part may be in strong sunlight. It may turn a windy corner abruptly to follow a house wall or path; it may at times be double-sided, becoming single-sided a little further on, and it almost always has a collection of flowering shrubs or mature roses or even a tree or two that are there to stay. Strangely enough, this is the easiest kind of border to look after because each section of the bed is governed by a different set of problems which must be separately solved.

It is as well to examine the area as a whole before any planting begins. Do this in early spring or late autumn when it is easier to be ruthless. Draw a large rough sketch plan of the shape of the bed—only you need see it—and mark in all the plants, shrubs or trees that are to remain in one colour, say red. You may decide to move some of these, so draw them in, in their new positions. Evaluate all the problems honestly (shade; roots; poor or exhausted soil; sour, mossy soil; thin sun-baked gravel; wind, a dreadful view, etc.) and take comfort in the knowledge that there are plants which will do well in all of these situations, and help to conceal the last all-too-common problem. These plants may not be rare or exciting but their performance is guaranteed, and they will cover the soil and almost always give flowers. In the case of poor, exhausted, sour or animal-polluted soil the remedy is to improve or replace it. This is dull, often hard work and may be expensive but need only be done once, though it must be done properly. Mark in these problem areas with hatching in a second colour (together with your analysis and solution to each difficulty); these areas may have to be 'furnished' with a more limited range of plants.

The remaining parts of the border can now be planned to take as many favourite flowers as space allows. Consult the flowering chart for planting distance or sideways spread, because the temptation to overplant an apparently empty border is very strong. See Fig. 3 for brief lists of easy and obliging plants for difficult situations.

THE TRADITIONAL BORDER

This is the hardest form of gardening there is, and a mature mixed border in full summer glory is the result of years of care and regular attention to seasonal tasks. Most mixed borders are at their best from late spring to late summer though it is perfectly possible to prolong colour at each end of this time-scale.

Again, start with a large sketch-plan (to scale if possible), and draw in the border or borders, which can be double, with a wide path between. Put in the points of the compasss as an aide-memoire—irises like to face due south, for example—and all shrubs, roses and other large permanent plants that you may have, and wish to keep. Self-control plays a large part in the planning of this type of border because when perfectly planted and growing well, the flowers have an artless look to them which is a total deception. They have been chosen for their colours, heights and flowering times and the wrong plant (popped in because there seems to be space for it) can quite spoil your careful scheme in mid-summer.

Decide on your colours first—you may wish to avoid red altogether, or bright yellow, or magenta. It is a good idea to get some sheets of appropriately coloured wrapping paper, from which you can cut out irregular blobs to represent specific plants. These can be pushed around until they look right, and notes can be made on them about height and spread, or sprawl, which is a very important factor to remember. Low plants are very useful for the front of the border, but they need not all be the same height. Plant in irregular groups of three, five or seven when setting out medium-sized plants; never dot these about singly or their impact will be lost. Many of the better herbaceous plants are quite expensive, but, nevertheless, buy a

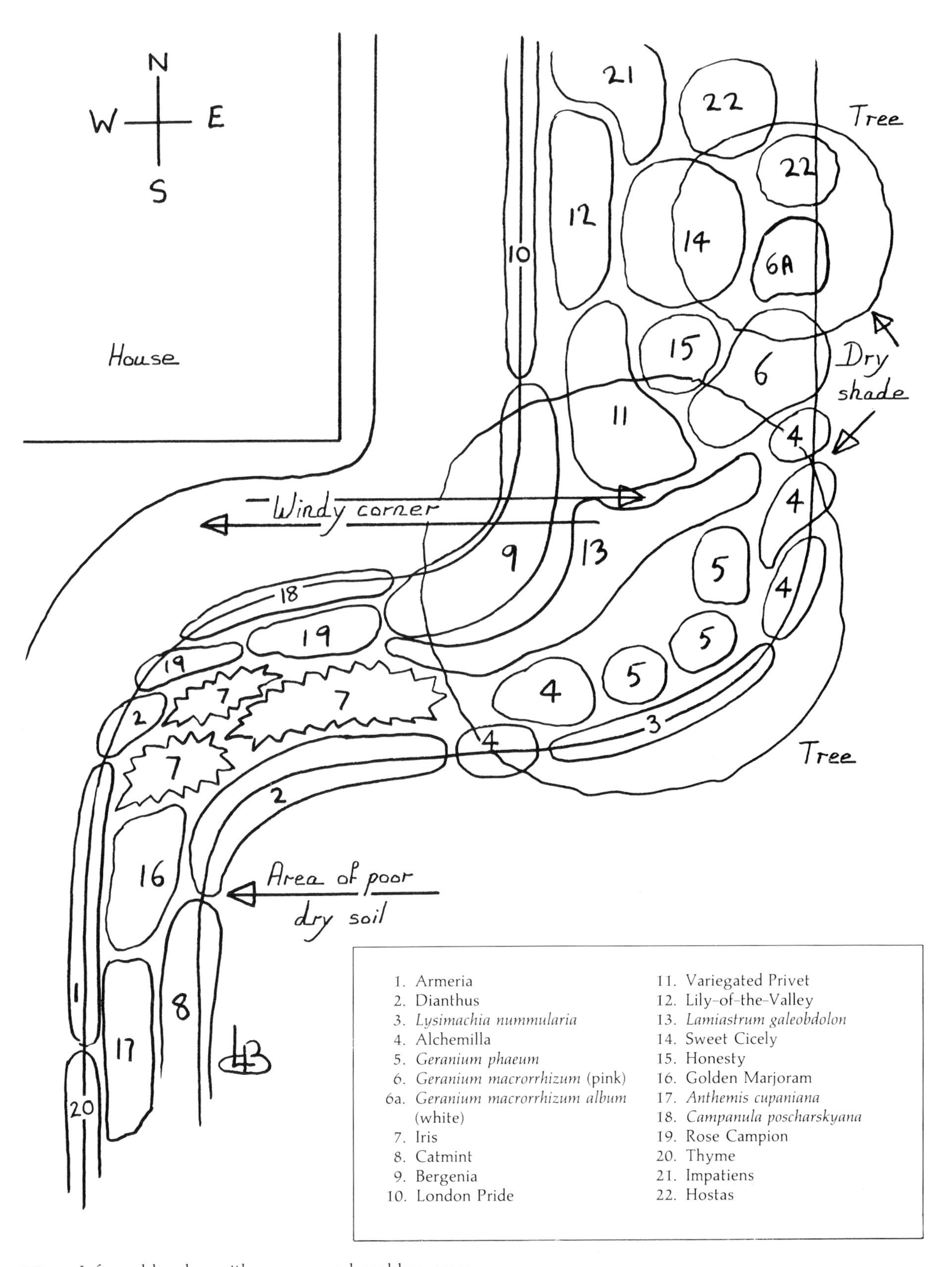

FIG. 3 Informal border, with average and problem areas

1. Campanula – *Campanula lactiflora* (in shades of blue and lilac)
2. Tradescantias – *T. virginiana*, 'Osprey', 'Isis', 'Blue Stone'
3. Gysophilas (pink or white) – *G. paniculata*
4. Catmint – *Nepeta faassenii*
5. Geranium – *G. endressii* or *G. pratense*
6. Pinks – Dianthus
7. Ajuga – *Ajuga reptans*
8. Anthemis – *Anthemis cupaniana*
9. Galtonia – *Galtonia candicans*
10. Shirley Poppies, mixed – *Papaver rhoeas*
11. Anchusa – *Anchusa azurea*
12. Geranium – *G. macrorrhizum*, pink
13. Pansies – Violas
14. Love-in-a-mist, sown successively – *Nigella damascena*
15. Anemone, planted successively – *Anemone coronaria*
16. Clematis – *C. integrifolia*
17. Deep pink Snapdragon – Antirrhinum
18. Cleome – *Cleome spinosa*
19. Geranium – *G. sanguineum*
20. Rock rose – Helianthemum
21. Heuchera – *Heuchera sanguinea*
22. Busy Lizzies (lilac) – Impatiens
23. Musk Mallow (white) – *Malva moschata alba*
24. Lavatera – *Lavatera trimestris*
25. Phuopsis – *Phuopsis stylosa*
26. Salvia – *Salvia horminum*
27. Salix – *Salix argentea*

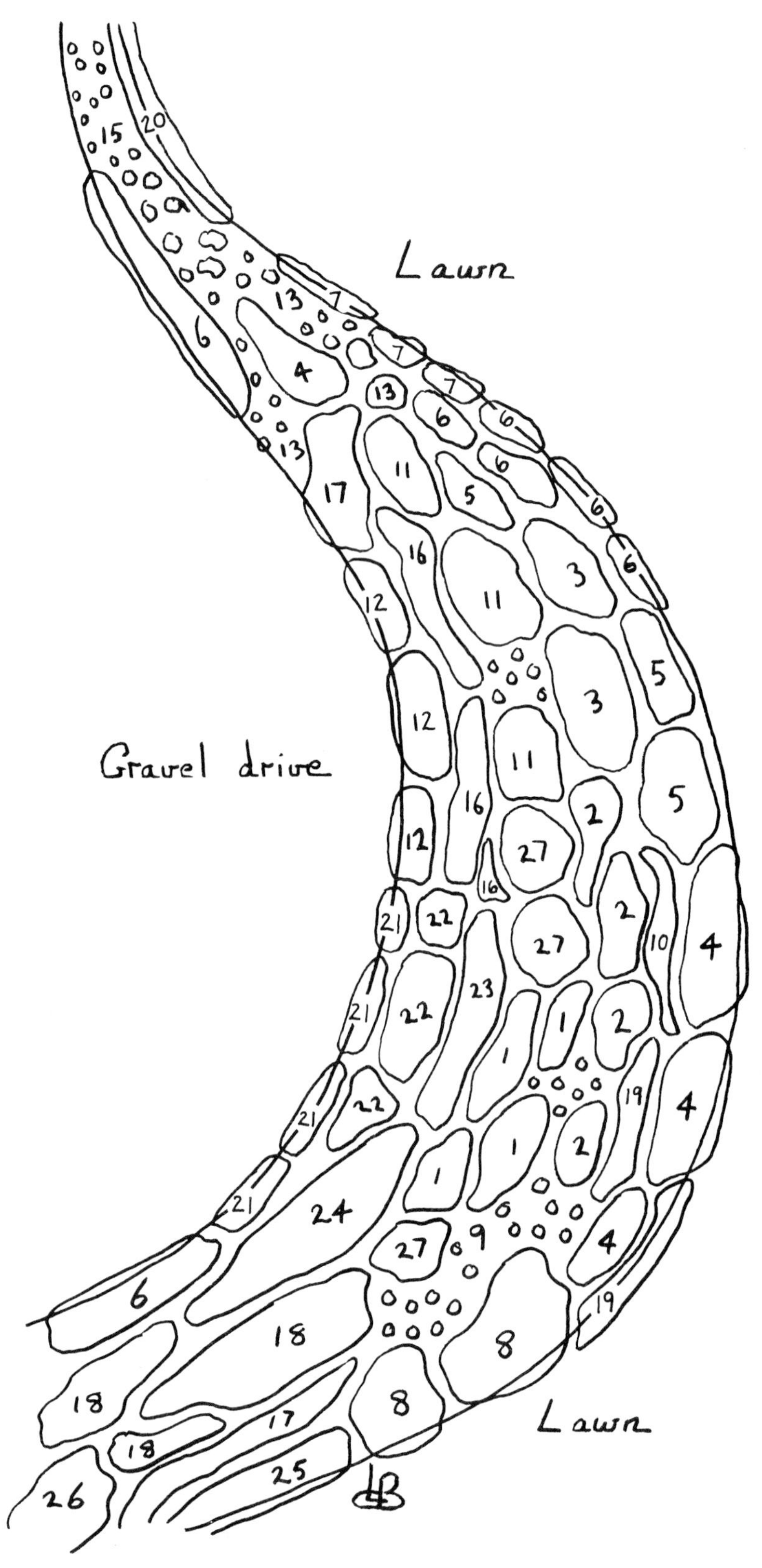

FIG. 4 Plants for double-sided summer border

minimum quantity of three for maximum effect, except for really large and spreading plants such as acanthus, aruncus, peony and *Euphorbia wulfenii*. A mixed border of this kind cannot be made quickly and there will be plenty of time for later acquisitions. Fill in the gaps with well-known and some unusual annuals, as well as with the faithful bedding plants, until you have worked up a stock of perennial plants by seed or division, and in the meantime you will gain more and valuable knowledge of the requirements of the plants that you already have. Always buy the best that you can afford—pedigree pot-grown plants that look healthy and well formed will transfer into your border with no problems and will give you pleasure for years to come. Those empty spaces will fill up all too quickly and there will come a time when you will find yourself passing on wheelbarrow-loads of your own surplus. Figure 4 gives suggestions for a double-sided border which is at its peak in early to late summer.

THE COTTAGE GARDEN BORDER

These borders used to line the path that led from the cottage garden gate to the front door. The path was almost always

A colourful border enhanced by background greenery: pansies, pinks, pyrethrums, iris and lupins.

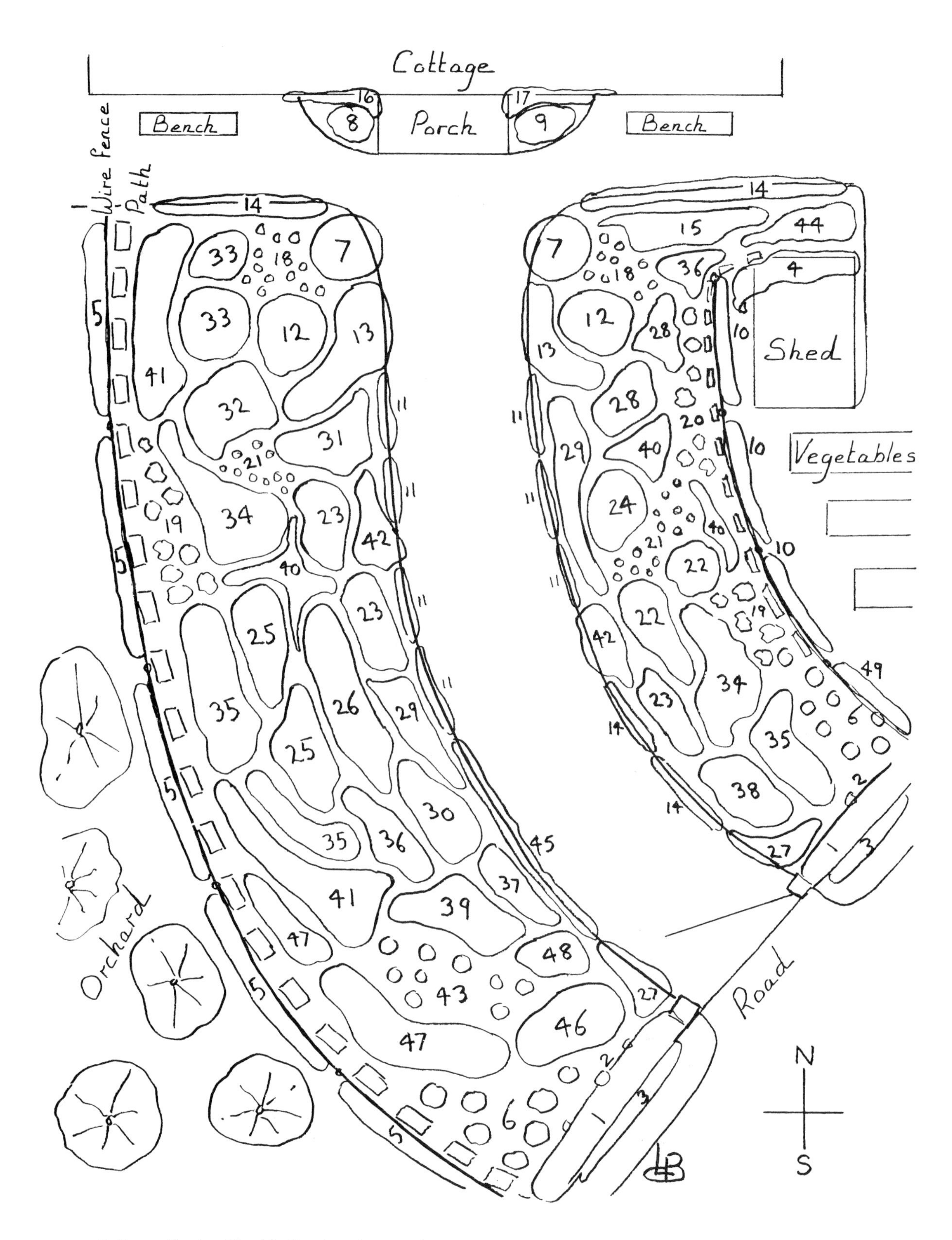

FIG. 5 Cottage Garden Double Borders (summer)

1. Lavender hedge – Lavandula
2. Everlasting pea – *Lathyrus latifolius*
3. Red and white Valerian all along – *Centranthus ruber*
4. Clematis – *Clematis montana*
5. Espalier apples – Malus
6. Foxgloves – *Digitalis purpurea*
7. Clipped Box or Rosemaries – Buxus or Rosmarinus
8. Myrtle – *Myrtus communis*
9. Jasmine – *Jasminum officinale*
10. Honeysuckle, clg. roses or Runner beans – Lonicera, Rosa or *Phaseolus multiforus*
11. Thrift (pink, white, red as appropriate) – Armeria
12. Peonies – Paeonia
13. Catmint – *Nepeta faassenii*
14. London Pride – *Saxifraga umbrosa*
15. Lily-of-the-Valley – *Convallaria majalis*
16. Clg. Rose – Rosa
17. E. Honeysuckle – Lonicera (early flowering)
18. Lilies – Lilium
19. Hollyhocks – *Althaea rosea*
20. Delphiniums – Delphinium
21. Lilies – Lilium
22. Love-in-a-Mist – *Nigella damascena*
23. Godetia – Godetia
24. Gypsophila – Gypsophila
25. Canterbury Bells – *Campanula medium*
26. Stocks – Matthiola
27. Violets – Violas
28. Shasta Daisies – *Chrysanthemum maximum*
29. Lobelia – *L. erinus*
30. Ageratum – Ageratum
31. French Marigolds – *Tagetes patula*
32. African Marigolds – *Tagetes erecta*
33. Anchusa – *Anchusa azurea*
34. Snapdragons – Antirrhinum
35. Lupins – Lupinus
36. Cornflowers (blue) – *Centaurea cyanus*
37. Snow-in-Summer – *Cerastium tomentosum*
38. Pyrethrums – *Chrysanthemum roseum*
39. Californian Poppy – *Eschscholzia californica*
40. Shirley Poppies – *Papaver rhoeas*
41. Dahlias – Dahlia
42. Pinks – Dianthus
42. Gladiolus – Gladiolus.
44. Dame's Violet – *Hesperis matronalis*
45. Sweet Alyssum – *Lobularia maritima*
46. Sweet Sultan – *Centaurea moschata*
47. Phlox – *Phlox paniculata*
48. Mignonette – *Reseda odorata*
49. Sweet peas – *Lathyrus odoratus*

(above) Key to FIG. 5

straight and therefore so were the edges of the borders. The back of the bed often partially concealed a small orchard on one side and a vegetable plot on the other, all thriving because of the excellent natural product afforded by the lack of main drainage.

Such flower beds were a sentimental collection of old-fashioned flowers and shrubs such as lilac, myrtle, rosemary, relaxed lavender bushes and, of course, roses, all garlanded with honeysuckle. This delicious mixture would have had much sentiment—linking each plant with someone special—a fuchsia from a sailor son, a fine clump of pinks from an old aunt, or some rare auriculas from relatives in the grimy coal towns in the north of England; and, of course, the myrtle came from great-grandmother's wedding posy.

This kind of border is almost the easiest of all. Just plant everything that you like best, as long as there is sufficient light and space for it to grow. Again, take note of the eventual spread of the plants and set them out accordingly (Fig. 5). In late spring there will be a great many neat tuffets of varied green, with (apparently) too much bare soil between. By mid-summer you will be glad that you did leave that space for the plants to grow into, because they will have.

2

Aspects

I have touched briefly on certain 'aspects' that you, and your border, have to live with.

The ideal 'aspect' is that facing due south (or north in the southern hemisphere) with a high, sheltering wall at the back. The next best thing, visually, is a high, sheltering hedge of yew, holly or beech (not privet or that terrifying conifer x *Cupresso-cyparis leylandii*. The first is too greedy, though just about manageable for the strong in heart and thew, while the second will escape from captivity if allowed and will soon tower over the chimney-pots, as it grows to 15 m (50 ft) in maturity. In the first situation you are indeed blessed and can grow just about

Here shrubs of all kinds form an excellent frame for *Geranium sanguineum*, petunias, salvias and other oncoming flowers of summer.

anything that loves the sun. The next and all-too-common aspect is a shaded border. The cause of the shade should be analysed—that caused by the canopy of trees will prevent the sun-loving plants from flourishing; and where 'drip' exists (from the leaves of the trees) many plants will not give of their best. Here it is better to plant some of the subjects listed in Fig. 6.

Where there are trees there are roots, which will mop up moisture like sponges as well as consuming (where surface-rooting) a great deal of the usually expensive nourishment that you have laboriously made or purchased. The other kind of shade is that cast by walls and buildings, and this is easier to cope with—some plants actually thrive in such situations. It should be remembered that this shady area (usually facing north) can get quite dry and should be regularly watered.

Windy gardens are interesting (to a gardener who has not to endure the constant rush and eddy of turbulent air). Many shrubs will take a very long time to grow to a minimum height; for example, I know of a magnificent free-standing *Garrya elliptica* growing in a woodland garden which is some 4.5 m (15 ft) high and is big enough to take tea under; I know of another which has been buffeted by Atlantic gales whose constant worrying has dwarfed its habit to a midget height of 60 cm (2 ft). The answer here is to plant only short, strong and resilient plants (those with Mediterranean origins are good—many have scented or aromatic leaves which give off constant fragrance on sunny days) as well as the more obvious ground-huggers. Plant the taller, more luscious-leaved things in the lee of substantial shrubs like hydrangeas, griselinia and escallonia, all of which thrive in coastal gardens. In inland areas where wind is a problem it is best to visit neighbouring gardens, where possible, to see what is doing well. Many so-called 'rockery' plants have origins in the mountainous regions of the world and these thrive in a sunny, exposed position, provided there is plenty of downward root-room. It is a question of planting something that will do well, not of attempting an unsuitable subject in an environment that it cannot cope with (Fig. 7).

Very dry soil can be another problem if looked at one way, but an absolute boon for gardeners who want to grow plants which thrive in such situations (Fig. 8).

Damp soil is the other end of the spectrum. If caused by natural springs, then many bog-loving treasures will be happy for ever, though they will have to endure dreadful privations when the ground freezes in winter. If the damp is caused by poor drainage, where the rain-pools lie on the surface for too long, then land drains are, alas, the only solution if you want to have anything of a garden.

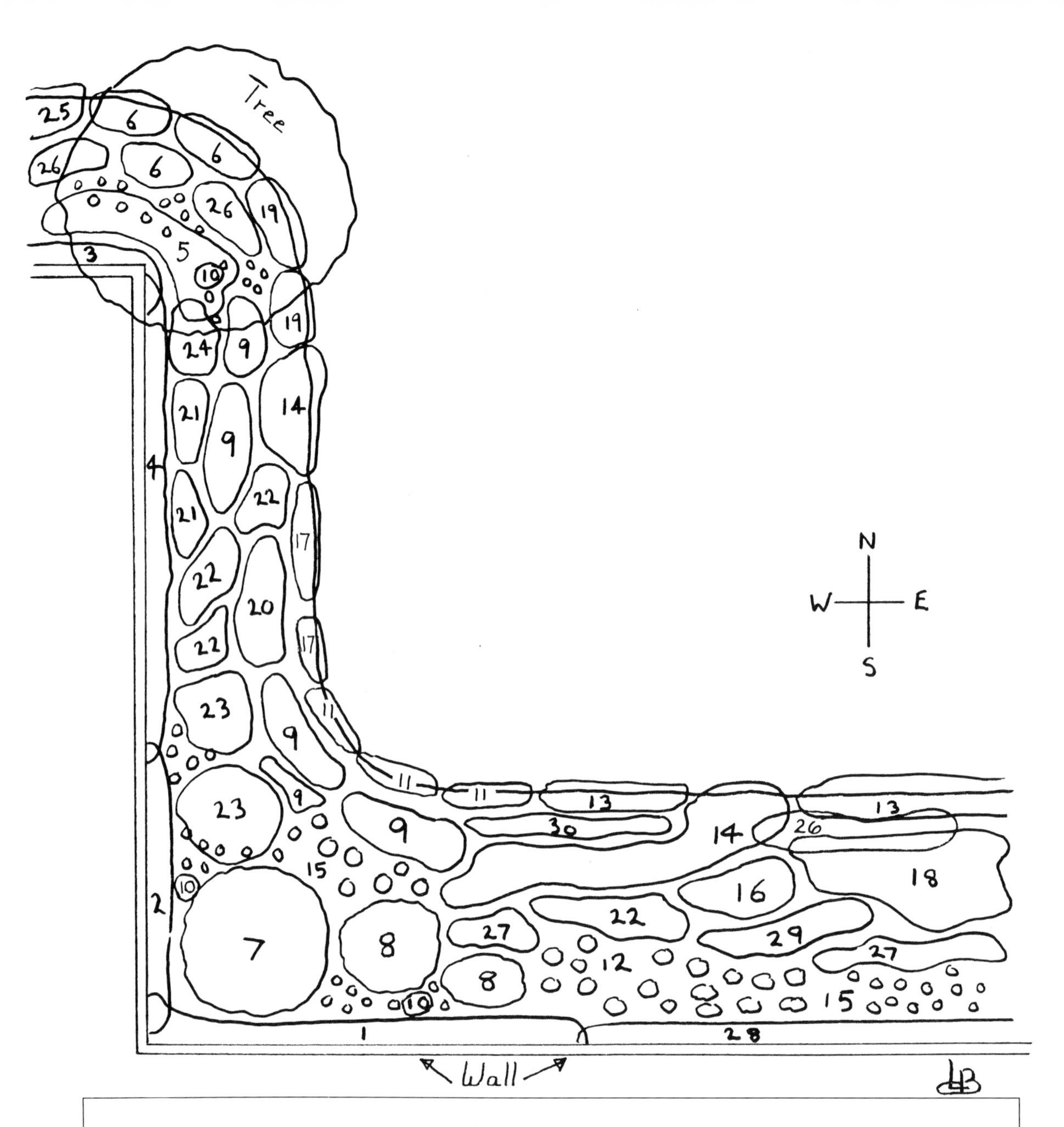

1. Hydrangea (clg.) – *Hydrangea petiolaris*
2. Ivies – Hedera
3. Vine – *Vitis henryana*
4. Golden Hop – *Humulus lupulus aureus*
5. Dead Nettle – *Lamiastrum galeobdolon*
6. Bergenias – Bergenia
7. Fatsia – *Fatsia japonica*
8. Goat's-beard – *Aruncus sylvester*
9. Hostas – Hosta
10. Narcissus to flower same time as *Clematis armandii*
11. Campanula – *Campanula poscharskyana*
12. Foxglove – *Digitalis purpurea*
13. London Pride – *Saxifraga umbrosa*
14. Busy Lizzies (blocks of one colour) – Impatiens
15. Lilies – Lilium
16. Rue – *Ruta graveolens*
17. Coral Flower – Heuchera
18. Lily-of-the-Valley – *Convallaria majalis*
19. Lady's Mantle – *Alchemilla mollis*
20. Epimedium – *Epimedium*
21. False Spikenard – *Smilacina racemosa*
22. Geranium – *Geranium macrorrhizum*
23. Monkshood – *Aconitum napellus*
24. Dame's Violet – *Hesperis matronalis*
25. Corydalis – *Corydalis lutea*
26. Welsh Poppy – *Meconopsis cambrica*
27. Columbine – *Aquilegia vulgaris*
28. Clematis (white) – *C. armandii*
29. Dame's Violet – *Hesperis matronalis*
30. Pansy – *Viola cornuta*

FIG. 6 Dry Shade and Some Drip

Sloping gardens can be a delight or a difficulty. Inevitably, they are expensive to lay out properly in the first place, often needing professional help in the construction of terraces, paths and sloping drives. Such gardens (often windy as well) are always well drained, however, and therefore the plants will thrive, though they will often be shorter than average. Take heart and remember the Hanging Gardens of Babylon. Sheltered 'bays' can be artfully planted, using wind-tolerant shrubs to protect more delicate-leaved subjects.

We now come to the actual shape of border, by which I mean single- or double-sided. To explain this more fully, it means that a border may be 6–9 m (20–30 ft) long by 1.5–2.4 m (5–8 ft) wide. If it is set against a wall, hedge or fence and viewed only from the front and along its length it is single-sided. A border wider than 2.4 m (8 ft) is difficult to attend to for maintenance, and it is best to have a 'service path', or row of large stepping stones at the rear from which the gardener can reach back into the border for weeding or other work. In any case, if this particular single-sided border is against a wall, hedge or fence, the wall (or fence) should be part of the planting with climbers and roses forming a curtain of leaves and flowers in their season. These climbing or 'leaning' plants will need attention and maybe a step-ladder, so the 'service path' should be substantial and firm enough to accommodate this. Hedges will need clipping or shearing, and the clippings have to fall to the ground, not on to the plants in the border, so, in addition to the step-ladder (and the gardener) there must be sufficient space for the clippings. Even a 1.2 m (4 ft) single-sided border may be too wide to lean over in comfort, so to avoid damaging the plants the same small path can be made at the back if there is space. The path will vanish completely in summmer, and a further good reason for having it is that it provides ventilation between the back of the tall plants and the wall or hedge.

When planting single-sided borders, set the tall plants at the back, but not in a serried rank of hollyhocks, sunflowers, giant campanulas or moon-touching mulleins. Intersperse these and others of a similar height with slightly lower plants, and allow one or two of these groups to come further forward into the border, to break the line with lower-growing things.

A double-sided border is much harder to plan and plant, since it is viewed from all round. At the beginning stick to those plants that you are familiar with—you will by now know their habits. For example, the leafy stems of *Geranium pratense* 'Johnson's Blue' extend during and after flowering. Where space permits, they can be left to sprawl, but where they are likely to smother their neighbours, they can be sheared back after

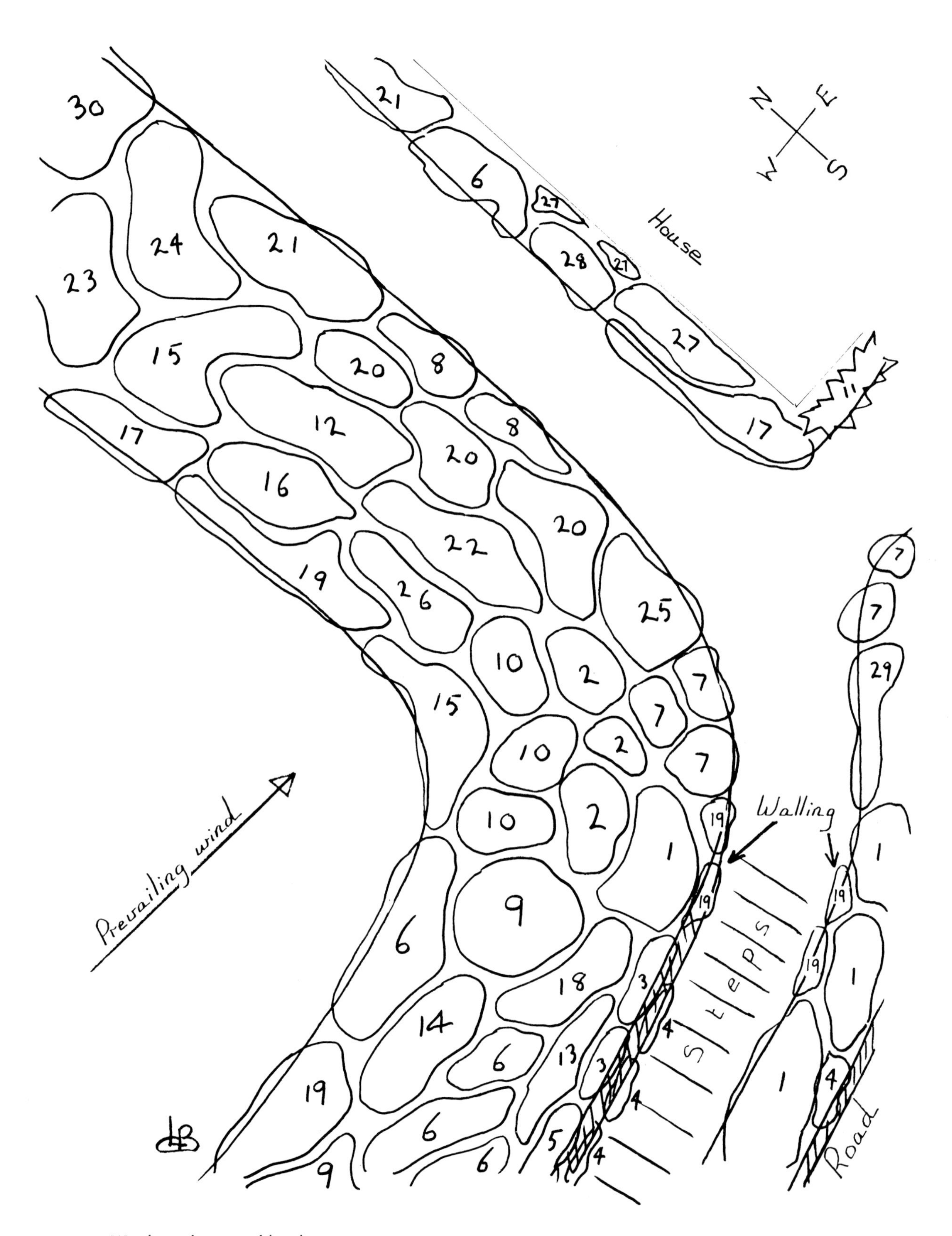

FIG. 7 Windy and exposed border

1. African Daisy – *Dimorphotheca barberiae*
2. Rosemaries – Rosmarinus
3. Aubrieta – Aubrieta
4. Valerian – *Centranthus ruber*
5. Arabis – *Arabis albida*
6. Thrift – Armeria
7. Yuccas – Yucca
8. Lady's Mantle – *Alchemilla mollis*
9. Potentilla – *P. fruticosa*
10. Phlomis – *P. russelliana*
11. Iris (dwarf) – Iris
12. Jacob's Ladder – *Polemonium coeruleum*
13. Livingstone Daisy – *Mesembryanthemum criniflorum*
14. Pinks – Dianthus
15. Everlasting flower – *Helichrysum petiolatum*
16. Sedum – *Sedum spectabile*
17. Snow in summer – *Cerastium tomentosum*
18. Hebe – *Hebe* 'Carl Teschner'
19. Campanula – *Campanula portenschlagiana*
20. Dwarf lavenders, shades of violet and pink – Lavandula
21. Clustered Bellflower (dwarf vars.) – *Campanula glomerata*
22. Scotch Rose – *Rosa rubiginosa*
23. Sea Holly – *Eryngium maritimum*
24. Euphorbia – *Euphorbia polychroma*
25. Montbretia – Montbretia
26. Rose Campion (pink) – *Lychnis coronaria*
27. Nerines – *Nerine bowdenii*
28. Anthemis – *Anthemis cupaniana*
29. Prostrate Rosemary – *Rosmarinus lavandulaceus*
30. Red Hot Pokers – Kniphofias

(*above*) Key to FIG. 7

flowering; the plant will re-grow in a few weeks and remain neat (and smaller) for the rest of the season. Another example is the very attractive light green leaves of *Hemerocallis* 'Dumortierii' which grow ever longer after flowering; not content with this, they then lie down to rest for the remainder of the season, completely smothering smaller plants within a 1.2 m (4 ft) radius. The same treatment can be given to this plant, and it will likewise refurnish itself. But do this to most other plants and you will kill them.

It is best not to grow very tall subjects in a double-sided border, since these will generally need staking and in this situation it is difficult to conceal the stakes; without these, summer gales and hailstorms will do great damage. Tall plants will create shade if the border runs east and west, so for these reasons it is better to choose plants of low to medium height, such as *Alchemilla mollis* (lady's mantle); *Anaphalis triplinervis*; *Anthemis cupaniana*; armeria (thrift); callistephus (China aster) (take a chance with these—they are so colourful and long flowering though not really weather-proof); low-growing campanulas, low-growing centaurea; *Cerastium tomentosum* (snow-in-summer); dianthus (pinks); *Dimorphotheca barberiae*; some erigerons; eryngiums; geraniums (but not *G. psilostemon*, it is too tall and floppy); geums; helianthemums; helichrysum; iberis; *Lupinus arboreus* and so on (this is where the chart will help) interspersed with those that have tall, thin (but strong) flower stems, such as alliums, centaurea (cornflower); dierama (angel's fishing rod) and *Echinops ritro* (globe thistle).

A long border can be carefully planned so that the colour comes (a) all at once, (b) in a progression, starting at one end

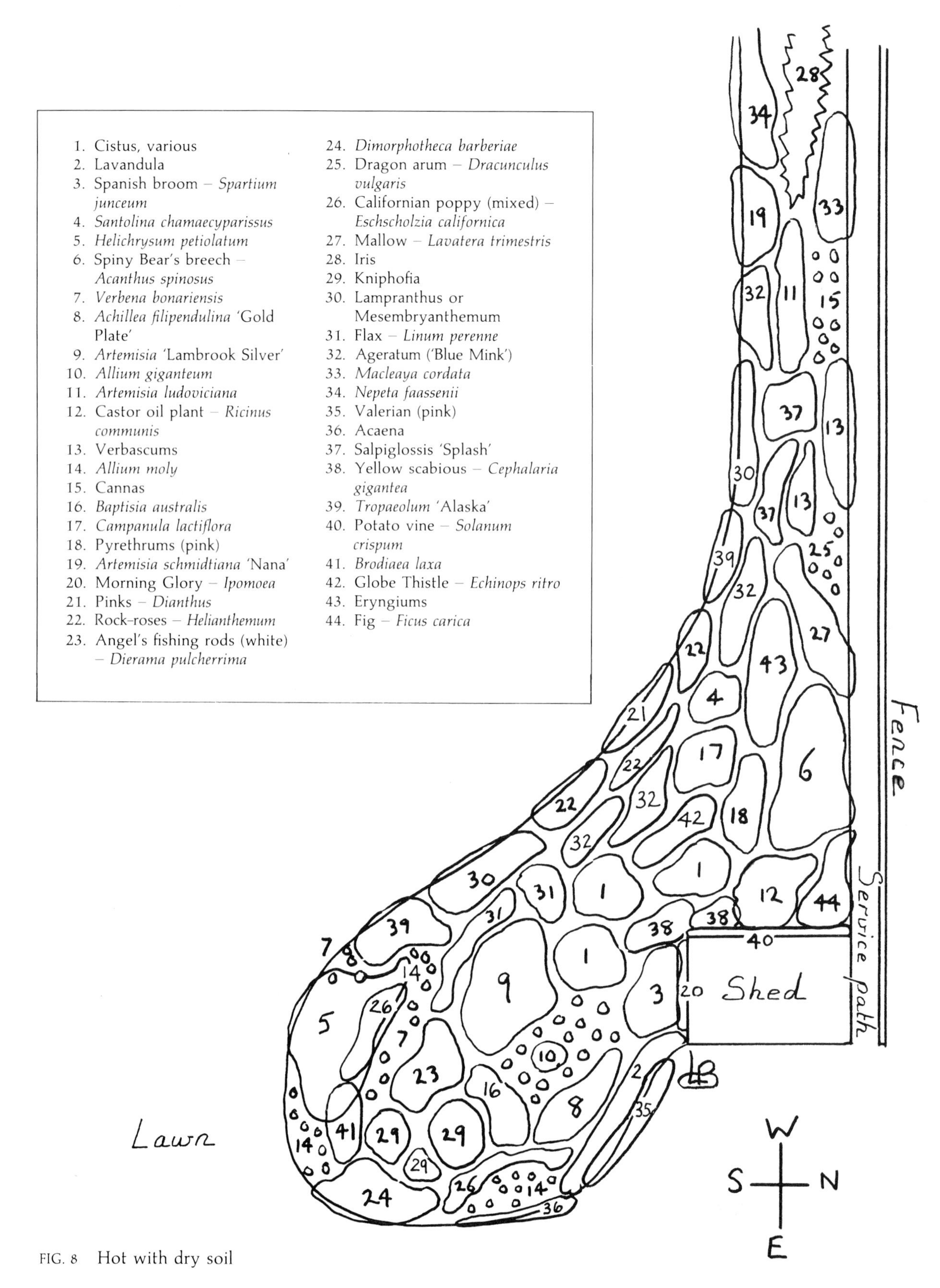

FIG. 8 Hot with dry soil

and finishing at the other, or (c) in definite groups: this last is often the easiest to manage. Individual dots of colour should be avoided where possible, as they lose impact when surrounded by a sea of greenery even though this may be full of interest to the gardener himself.

Short borders are the most usual and require the most strength of mind on the gardener's part. There really is not room nor space for all his favourite flowers and therefore a choice must be made and adhered to, with sufficient planting space for each. If those extra treasures are sneaked in, as so often happens, either the treasure will grow large and smother all about it, or it will be forgotten, to vanish for ever under the lusty summer growth of its neighbours. Remember that the border can be changed or modified each year, with less successful plants being discarded in favour of new and different ones. Plant the treasure elsewhere in the garden to grow larger for a season until it is time for the autumn game of general-post.

Narrow, single-sided borders are much easier to plant as they will generally have something substantial such as a wall, hedge or fencing at the back which will shelter the plants. However, do not grow really tall things such as althea (hollyhock) or helianthus (sunflower) because, though they are attractive to look at in mid-summer, by the time they begin to flower their nether regions are seldom pleasing to look at. In a wider border all this is further away from the eye and can be easily hidden by other plants but in a narrow border there is no getting away from the coarse stems and withered leaves. Exceptions to this are the beautiful-leaved macleayas, which should be planted where they can be viewed as a whole; their leaves and stems remain cleanly good-looking for the entire season.

3

Backgrounds and Foregrounds

When looking at a well-planned and maturely beautiful border in full bloom your eye will, subconsciously, take in the background as well as the foreground; this is the setting for your border and it is very important.

Beginning with the ideal again, a wall is almost perfect because it is (usually) warm and sheltering while pleasing climbers or 'leaners' can be grown up against it to harmonize with the border flowers. However, an east-facing wall has to be planted more carefully (with extra-hardy climbers) because these can perish in very cold, wet winters (see Ch. 6 for some suggestions for wall plantings). Walls have one drawback; they are dry at the base and most (but not all) plants will need extra watering in hot summers and, strangely enough, during dry winters as well.

Fences can be of various types from substantial wooden affairs made of overlapping panels (more privacy with these) to interwoven ones (less privacy), post-and-rail, white-painted picket, and the simplicity of chain-link. All wooden fences (and their posts) must be treated with preservative before or during installation, and this preservative should be of a type that will not kill climbing plants. Creosote was much in favour at one time (because there was not much else), but this is a real destroyer and should never now be applied where vegetation is intended to flourish. Choose the best and strongest fencing that is available; it has to last many years and it will often have to support a considerable weight of climbing plants which will be doing their best to destroy it from the start.

Maintain the fence with regular coats of preservative (or paint) applied during dry periods in the winter or spring and replace broken slats or woven strips as they occur. Many fences have trellis on top to give them extra height for clematis, roses and other climbers and this is often an addition to the original fence, having been added at a later date. The expanding wooden type of trellis is not to be recommended as it has a very short life and will, inevitably, collapse horrendously in the

(Opposite)
Curving edges enlarge any garden, however small: anchusa in the foreground.

middle of a wet and windy night because of its cumulative weight of vegetation. Choose instead strong plastic-coated wire trellis in a neutral brown (never green—the colour is an unnatural one) or beige which will be invisible even in winter. Support it with separate posts or angle-irons and run a wire along the top edge of the trellis to keep this as taut as possible under the very considerable summer weight of the climbers, especially when wet.

Chain-link fencing, together with its concrete posts (though at first sight unattractive) is exceedingly strong and can be relied upon to last for many years with little attention. Leafy annual and perennial twiners or climbers can be planted against it, and these will conceal it in the first summer, though more permanent shrub plantings should be planned at the same time.

Hedges are excellent as they are the most natural background for the soft or gay colours of a flower border. *Taxus baccata* (yew) grows much more quickly than supposed, though it, like all hedging plants, must be kept low to begin with so as to form a thick base with no gaps. Holly (a mixed holly hedge is delightful but is distracting as a background) is excellent though painful to clip; but if it is to be a boundary hedge then a certain amount of suffering is tolerable for the excellent security such a hedge affords. There are many other types of hedging to choose from, according to your locality. *Fagus sylvatica* (beech) is good on chalk and free-draining soil; privet is neat and quick-growing but desperately greedy, and, as with all hedges, an access and maintenance path is even more essential because this will distance the border to some degree from the hungry roots of the privet. Espalier apple trees are a traditional background to lower-growing border plants (which must not be taller than the lowest fruit-bearing branches). These trees are surprisingly leafy in mid-summer and very beautiful when the fruit begins to ripen and turn colour. Again, access from both sides is essential for pruning and the maintenance of the supporting wires along which the tree-branches are trained.

In front of the border there may be a choice, and grass immediately springs to mind. It is, of course, the most perfectly restful foreground that one could have, but it has its limitations and difficulties. For example, many plants billow more largely over the lawn than they should, for various reasons such as the excellence of the gardener's own compost at one end of the scale and the fact that they have been planted too near the edge of the border at the other. This leaves a semi-circular bare patch at the edge of the lawn or path during winter (when the grass does not grow much) and by late spring when the grass begins to cover the patch, the plant is doing exactly the same thing again except that it is a season older, and, generally, larger. For this reason paved edges of brick, stone or carefully chosen cement slabs are excellent, and this then also does away with the hard work of lawn-edging and trimming for ever. The plants spread and spill most naturally and attractively over these edges, benefiting from the advantages of reflected warmth and a cool root-run. The one drawback to this is that the border will now remain a fixed size and no more gradual and secret encroachments into the lawn area are possible.

Paths of all kinds are very appropriate, especially where they would make a better foreground to the flowers than worn grass. In addition, the plants will seed themselves into the cracks and chinks between the slabs, and such an environment is most suitable for ground-hugging mat-formers such as thymes, helianthemums and acaenas, though these are best not encouraged in areas of heaviest traffic. Well-made gravel paths are always dry underfoot but have the disadvantage of being so perfect a home that many 'edging' plants prefer to live in them rather than in the comfortable softness of the border. Weeds are a constant problem and this is one place where weed-killers should not be used for fear that they will leach into the surrounding soil.

Brick paths laid in traditional patterns are beautiful, especially in the summer, but winter frosts may eventually damage them and in shaded areas mosses and algae will grow quickly, making them very slippery. However, in an open sunny situation where the winters are not too cold they can make an extra feature in the garden though complex designs should not be laid as these will distract the eye from the border flowers. Narrow paths should never be less than 90 cm (3 ft) wide (remember the width of the laden wheelbarrow in autumn) and for comfort and sociability, 1.5 m (5 ft) or wider is a better width where space permits. Always use frost-resistant paving-bricks which will last for many years. It is very tempting to utilize demolition house-bricks, especially if these are cheap, but though they are initially very effective (and often have a ready-made antique look to them) the frosts will begin their gradual work of destruction in the first winter. Chips will break off corners, flakes will lift and the carefully laid path will in time become hazardous and will need to be completely replaced in the end. However, if saving the cost of paving-bricks is a consideration at this time, then use the old, permeable ones for now, always recognizing that replacement will be essential in the not-too-distant future.

Edges are important; there needs to be a clear line beyond which the plants are actually trespassing, even if allowed or encouraged to do so. Grass paths or lawns should be kept

Low-growing plants of many textures spill over the edge of this border, with tall macleayas at the back. The sculptural angelica is set off beautifully by *Rosa rubrifolia*.

sharply edged, even if most of the border seems to be billowing, flopping, trailing or otherwise attempting to colonize it. Use one or two garden forks pushed firmly into the ground to hold back the skirts of the plants while cutting the edge, and move the forks as you go. (This is also a good time to find and destroy slugs and snails.)

Opposite
The luxuriance of high summer must be carefully planned during the winter months. Here are traditional lupins, iris, pyrethrums.

4

Colours, Scents and Shapes

Colour

Where the garden is a small one it may be best to plan a good mixed border, choosing the plants for height, colour and flowering time with the aid of the chart in Chapter 10. A pleasing colour scheme can be planned with blue flowers and blue and grey-toned foliage at the nearest end, or ends, of the border(s). These can shade through pale blue to white; with light yellow or cream flowers and a scattering of pale pink, followed by rose-pink and carmine which can have groups of darker-toned crimson flowers. After this can come brighter reds, again interspersed with white, grey or glaucous-leaved plants and more pale yellow, which can then lead on to deep and brilliant yellows, golds and oranges. Again, mix the orange with white and grey or deep crimson foliage plants. More and different reds can be used, giving way to softer crimson, then rose and finally purple, violet and lavender. This is where the colour magenta can be used safely and effectively, with a little more, if liked, at the blue end of the border.

The following diagrams show the positions of plants chosen for this scheme. Inevitably, even in the best regulated borders, gaps will occur. If these are at or near the front, fill them with suitable replacements from a garden centre, or small foliage plants that do not clash with the carefully planned harmony. If the fatalities are at the back it may not be necessary to do anything at all and the nearby plants will probably be grateful for the extra breathing space.

White and silver borders

Where the garden is a larger one, or the gardener is really dedicated (or, better still, both) then pleasant experiments can be made with colour and one of the most restful and beautiful combinations is a white and green or white and silver border; the botanically minded gardener will find that many coloured flowers have white varieties not generally mentioned in the catalogues. Half the fun of this type of planting lies in the pursuit (and acquisition) of these rarer treasures. White flowers have many subtle shadings or contrasting markings and it is unusual to find a flower that is entirely and purely white. It may be preferred to collect the white varieties and plant them next to their coloured counterparts throughout the border, until space runs out. These white varieties are sometimes difficult to recognize because they are not so often seen, so siting them next to the familiar and, therefore, better known plant is helpful both to the gardener, and, more particularly, to his visitors.

In an all-white border it should be remembered that most white flowers have yellow or golden stamens which provide a glint of colour to the scheme. In a white and green border the colour green is naturally provided by the plant's own leaves, while other foliage can be introduced for extra interest and green flowers such as *Moluccella laevis* (bells of Ireland), euphorbias, *Tellima grandiflora* (best in shade), the lime-green *Zinnia* 'Envy' and the green-flowered variety of *Amaranthus caudatus* called 'Viridis'.

In a white and silver border the 'silver' is supplied by white or grey-foliaged plants, many of which are shrubs. *Artemisia absinthium* is silver in the sun, and *A.a.* 'Lambrook Silver' is even more so. *A. ludoviciana* (Turkish sage) has willow-shaped leaves and grows from ground-level winter dormancy to 1.2 m (4 ft) by mid-summer. It is beautiful as a contrast plant but is very invasive; flower-arranging friends will love you for rooted portions of it in early spring but it is best to be truthful about its character. Another artemisia, *A. schmidtiana* 'Nana' is better behaved, being a low growing, silky, strokable plant that stays put. It springs from the ground each spring to a height of 20 cm (8 in) and a spread of about 30 cm (12 in), though it can be worryingly late after a particularly hard winter. Leave the old branches on the plant as a protection until the new growth is well up.

A larger background shrub is the deciduous *Elaeagnus commutata*, syn. *E. argentea* (silver-berry), which grows to 2.4 m (8 ft); this has very elegant silver-green leaves and silver berries and is good against a wall.

The stiffly branching shrubby *Helichrysum splendidum* has silver-white stems and branches resembling coral; it grows to 38 cm (14 in) and spreads to about 90 cm (3 ft). This shrub should be cut hard back in spring and it will then remain neat for the rest of the season; its yellow flowers (in mid- to late summer) may not suit the scheme and can be cut off if not wanted. *H. petiolatum* is a very lovely, but tender, foliage plant more usually seen trailing wispily from large raised urns,

This border is planted for interest — *Crambe maritima* (Sea Kale) will soon froth with tiny blossom beside the silvered spikiness of *Onopordum acanthium* (Scotch Thistle) and brilliant blue geraniums.

The shapes of plants are important all season long: prunella is in foreground beside the handsome leaves of *Helleborus argutifolius,* while the flower-spikes of digitalis are always instantly recognizable; Centaurea sprawls at the edge of the border.

troughs or tubs. It has silver-felted heart-shaped leaves and occasional and unremarkable flowers. It should be planted out in late spring and will form a flattish tangle of silvered stems and leaves that will extend rapidly and it will need regular pruning to keep it within its allocated area. It grows to 23 cm (9 in), unless assisted upwards, which is not its habit, and will trail to over 1.2 m (4 ft).

Santolina chamaecyparissus, syn. *S. incana* (cotton lavendar) is much used for dwarf (and aromatic) hedging in herb gardens. It grows to 60 cm (2 ft) with a similar spread if left unclipped. It has golden-yellow tansy-like flowers in mid-summer which can be snipped or sheared off if not needed.

Another very tender but beautiful dwarf shrub is *Convolvulus cneoreum* which has pewter-silver foliage with pink-toned white trumpets for most of the summer. *Hebe pinguifolia* 'Pagei' is a neat dwarf shrub with white flowers and attractive small, greyish evergreen leaves. It grows to 23 cm (9 in) and spreads to about 90 cm (3 ft), but it has a tendency to open out in the middle in old age which spoils its appearance. Should this happen, scrap the plant and replace it with a container-grown specimen, or take cuttings from early to late summer, and next year when these are large enough the parent plant can be removed.

A tiny treasure to grow in groups in gritty soil is *Euryops acraeus*, which looks like a miniature silver palm tree, though with un-palm-like yellow flowers. It grows to a height of 20 cm (8 in), with an eventual mounding spread of 30 cm (12 in). It is tender except in mild areas, and cuttings should be taken as insurance.

For the front of the border there are grey-leaved helianthemums (sun roses, or rock roses) such 'Mrs Croft' (which has pink-orange flowers) and 'The Bride' with creamy-white ones. most helianthemums are only about 15 cm (6 in) high (or less) but spread satisfactorily to about 60 cm (2 ft). The old-fashioned *Stachys lanata* (lamb's ears or saviour's flannel) has softly furry leaves and rather lanky flower stems of pale mauve flowers; many gardeners cut these off as being too tall when the plant is grown for edging, or the non-flowering variety 'Silver Carpet' can be planted instead. Both need an airy, open situation as they are prone to mildew. Both, and more particularly 'Silver Carpet', dislike cold, wet winters and a few reserve plants should be kept in a frame.

Cerastium tomentosum (snow-in-summer) is whitely silver and is a satisfyingly thorough carpeter—too much so at times, and in small gardens the smaller variety *C.t.* 'Columnae' will be found more suitable. The silver-grey leaves of dianthus make an

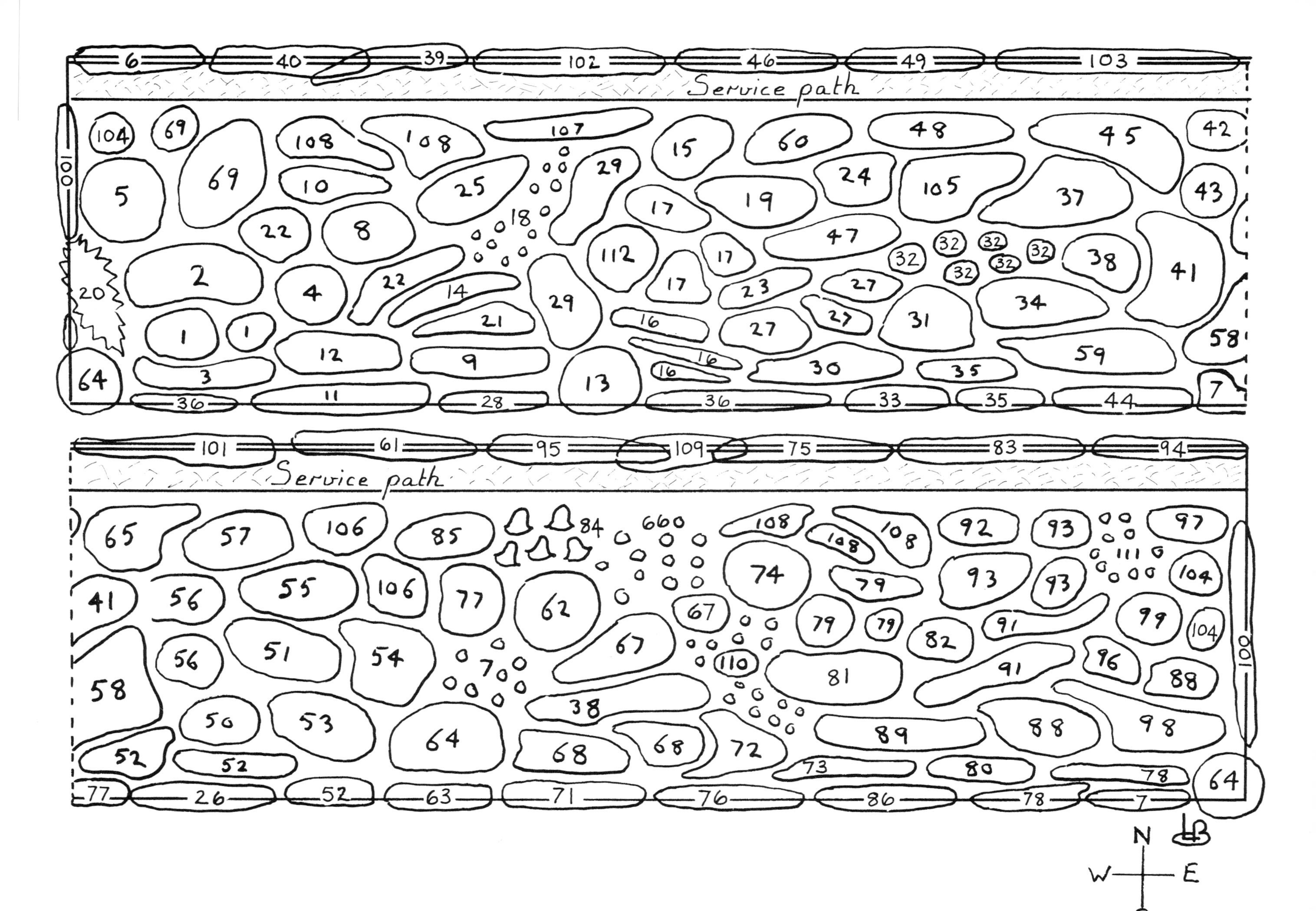

Service path
Service path
N
W
E
S

1. Geranium 'Johnson's Blue'
2. *Centaurea montana* (blue)
3. *Geranium sanguineum* (magenta)
4. Geranium 'Mrs Kendall Clarke'
5. *Artemisia absinthium* 'Lambrook Silver'
6. *Caryopteris × clandonensis*
7. Dwarf Snow-in-Summer – *Cerastium tomentosum* 'Columnae'
8. Jacob's Ladder – *Polemonium coeruleum*
9. *Gilia capitata*
10. Shasta Daisies
11. *Helianthemum* 'The Bride'
12. Ageratum, pink
13. Gypsophila, white
14. Santolina
15. Inula 'Hookeri'
16. Satin Flower – *Sisyrinchium striatum*
17. *Campanula aliariifolia*
18. Madonna lily – *Lilium candidum*
19. Tree Lupin (creamy-yellow)
20. Iris (white)
21. Flax – *Linum perenne*
22. Musk mallow (white)
23. Musk mallow (pink)
24. Sidalcea (pink)
25. *Campanula lactiflora* (pale blue)
26. Heuchera (red)
27. Stocks (pink and carmine)
28. Helianthemum (pink)
29. *Monarda didyma* 'Melissa' (pink)
30. Begonia semp. (red-crimson)
31. Pelargonium (carmine)
32. *Lobelia cardinalis*
33. Armeria (pink)
34. *Artemisia ludoviciana*
35. Armeria (red)
36. Armeria (white)
37. Cosmea
38. *Ruta* 'Jackman's Blue'
39. Morning Glories
40. *Ceanothus* 'Gloire de Versailles'
41. Antirrhinums (red to dark crimson)
42. *Artemisia abrotanum*
43. *Potentilla fruticosa* (cream)
44. Lobelia (red-purple)
45. *Rosa rubrifolia*
46. Rose 'Alberic Barbier'
47. Antirrhinums (white)
48. Sidalcea (red)
49. Clg. rose (red–crimson)
50. *Anaphalis triplinervis*
51. *Argemone mexicana*
52. Lobelia (white, bronze foliage)
53. *Calendula officinalis* (pale yellow or cream)
54. *Calendula officinalis* (orange)
55. Coreopsis
56. *Oenothera fruticosa*
57. Fennel (Bronze)
58. *Salvia splendens*
59. *Phlox drummondii* (red and crimson)
60. *Cephalaria gigantea*
61. *Elaeagnus commutata*
62. *Centaurea macrocephala*
63. Helianthemum (yellow)
64. *Artemisia schmidtiana 'nana'*
65. Verbascums (cream to salmon)
66. Cannas (red, bronze foliage)
67. *Campanula latiloba* 'Alba'
68. Pelargonium (scarlet)
69. *Echinops ritro*
70. Cannas (orange, green foliage)
71. Dianthus
72. Candytuft (red)
73. Virginian stock
74. Rose 'Iceberg' or 'Virgo'
75. Clematis (white, late-flowering)
76. Thymes
77. Jerusalem Cross – *Lychnis chalcedonica*
78. Lobelia (blue)
79. Cornflower – *Centaurea cyanus*, tall;
80. *Campanula latiloba* (white)
81. *Campanula lactiflora* (lilac – pale blue)
82. *Baptisia australis*
83. *Clematis* 'Jackmanii'
84. Tiger lilies
85. *Lavatera trimestris* (white)
86. *Campanula carpatica* (blue – mauve)
87. *Ageratum* 'Blue Mink'
88. *Monarda didyma* 'Prairie Night' (purple)
89. Pansies
90. *Nigella damascena* 'Moody Blue'
91. *Liatris callilepis*
92. Purple Loosestrife – *Lythrum salicaria*
93. *Phlox paniculata* (lilac)
94. Everlasting Pea – *Lathyrus latifolius* (pink)
95. *Clematis orientalis* 'Lemon Peel'
96. *Salvia virgata*
97. *Melianthus major*
98. Petunias
99. *Perovskia atriplicifolia*
100. *Ajuga* 'Metallica'
101. *Clematis* 'The President'
102. *Clematis* 'Hagley Hybrid'
103. Everlasting Pea (white)
104. *Geranium psilostemon*
105. *Polygonum amplexicaule atrosanguineum*
106. *Achillea* 'Gold Plate'
107. *Ricinus communis*
108. Delphiniums
109. Canary Creeper
110. *Galtonia candicans*
111. *Camassia* (dark blue)
112. *Rose* 'Constance Spry'

FIG. 9 Summer-flowering border with planned colour-scheme

excellent permanent edging and white-flowered varieties like the sweet-scented 'Mrs Sinkins' can be chosen.

The courageous gardener may like to plant the sculpturally interesting *Onopordon acanthium* (Scotch thistle) whose whitely silver leaves are best in its first year, forming large rosettes 3ft or more across. This plant is a biennial, and in the second year it will shoot upwards, forming an angular, prickly, silvered framework. It is a large plant about 8ft high, needing to be grown in groups of three or five, therefore it needs a large border to keep everything to scale. Its presence may provoke scathing comments from less appreciative visitors but to their remarks the gardener can turn a deaf ear. It is, after all, *his* garden and *his* border.

Senecio maritima has several varieties with silver-white leaves, such as 'Diamond' (or 'White Diamond') and 'Silver Dust' which is whiter and has the more finely dissected leaves. All have rather untidy yellow flowers which are best removed. The plants are surprisingly hardy and can be left in the border, though generally grown as annuals, but they will not be so neat-growing in successive years.

The foregoing is a small selection of foliage plants to grow in association with white flowers , and collecting these 'silvers' for their own sake can be dangerously addictive. On the whole they should be regarded as more tender than green-leaved plants or shrubs, and when ordering small, new plants by post from a nursery always specify spring delivery if you live in a cold area. When they arrive do not plant them out in the open border if the weather is still cold and wet, but instead, plant them into pots of your own soil and keep them under cover in a cold greenhouse, frame, conservatory or porch. Order the plants well in advance if buying from a garden centre and tell them that you will not be collecting them until late spring. These plants will usually be container-grown and there will be less or no disturbance to their root systems if they are carefully planted. It is as well to take no chances. There are a great number of white flowers to choose from and some suggestions are shown in Table 1; the plants are arranged in three height groupings and are in flower from late spring to late summer or later. Check the chart again for more exact heights and spread, planting distances and flowering times. They are not all in flower at the same time. Those with the most impact are marked with an asterisk.

It will be found that while some flowers close up at night (or earlier) those that remain open are luminously lovely in the dusk.

Occasional height adds charm and interest: a standard wisteria weeps blossom in spring, while in the foreground pale pink helianthemums (rock roses) luxuriate in the sun beside the good contrasting blue of veronica. Centranthus (Valerian) is in flower for months.

Blue borders

White, silver or grey-leaved plants look equally and differently beautiful when grown with blue flowers. This can be very interesting because there are so many shades of blue (though some of them need to be kept well separated). In a blue border the darkest blue tones may verge on violet or indigo which makes for pleasing colour contrasts.

Table 2 shows a selection of blue-to-violet flowers arranged in the same height groupings, flowering from late spring to late summer or later. Those marked with an asterisk (*) are particularly effective. They do not all flower at once, so consult the chart again for actual times and heights.

Red borders

From the calm tranquillity of blue, white, silver and grey one might turn to the opposite extreme and the excitement of scarlet. A red and crimson border (particularly against a white, pale-coloured or grey stone wall) gives a great lift to the spirits.

This kind of one-colour border need not be a large one, though once you begin to collect the various red flowers you will be surprised at the many different shades that exist. It will be found that there are several crimson, plum or bronze-leaved

TABLE 1. SOME FLOWERS FOR A WHITE BORDER

Low 5–30 cm (2–12 in)	_Medium_ 30–105 cm (12 in–3½ ft)	_Tall_ 105 cm–2.4 m (3½–8 ft)
*_Anthemis cupaniana_	*_Achillea ptarmica_	
Arabis	_Agapanthus_	
Armeria	*_Anaphalis_	
	*_Anemone_ × hybrids	
	Aster	
Bellis		
*_Campanula_ spp.	*_Campanula_ spp.	*_Campanula_ spp.
*_Cerastium_ spp.	*_Centranthus ruber_	
	Chrysanthemum spp.	
Delphinium hybrids	*_Delphinium_ hybrids	*_Delphinium_ hybrids
	Dianthus	_Digitalis_
	*_Dicentra_	
	*_Dimorphotheca_	
Endymion		
	*_Geranium_ spp.	*_Galtonia_
	**_Gypsophila paniculata_	
	Hesperis	
*_Iberis_		
*_Iris_	*_Iris_	
Lobularia	*_Lavatera_	*_Lilium_ spp. and vars.
	Lychnis	
	*_Malva moschata_	
	Matthiola spp. & cars.	
	Monarda	
	Nicotiana	
	*_Paeonia_	
	Papaver orientale	
	Petunia	
	Physostegia	
	*_Platycodon_	
Thymus	*_Thalictrum_	
	*_Tigridia_	
	Tradescantia	
Vinca	_Verbascum_	_Verbascum_
Viola spp.	_Veronica_	
	Zantedeschia	

shrubs which will give greater body and substance to this planting scheme, while several red flowers have handsome crimson foliage which sets off their intense colouration admirably. These are the tall _Lobelia cardinalis_ or _L. fulgens_, antirrhinums

TABLE 2. SOME FLOWERS FOR A BLUE BORDER

Low 5–30 cm (2–12 in)	*Medium* 30–105 cm (12 in–3½ ft)	*Tall* 105 cm–2.4 m (3½–8 ft)
Ageratum *Ajuga*	*Agapanthus* spp. *Allium caeruleum* **Anchusa* *Aster*	*Aconitum* spp.
	Baptisia *Brodiaea laxa* *Brunnera*	
Centaurea cyanus *Convolvulus tricolor*	*Camassia* *Catananche* **Centaurea* spp. *Clematis heracleifolia* *Clematis integrifolia*	**Centaurea cyanus*
Delphinium ajacis **Delphinium* hybrids	*Delphinium consolida* **Delphinium* hybrids	**Delphinium* hybrids
Endymion	*Erigeron* spp. *Eryngium* spp.	*Echinops* *Eryngium* spp.
	**Geranium ibericum* **Geranium pratense* 'Johnson's Blue' **Gilia capitata*	
Iris	*Iris*	
**Lobelia*	*Limonium* **Linum* spp.	
Myosotis		
	**Nigella*	
**Phacelia*	**Polemonium*	*Perovskia*
	Scabiosa spp. *Tradescantia* vars.	
Veronica spp. *Viola* vars.	*Veronica* spp.	*Veronica* spp.

(snapdragons), *Dianthus barbatus* (sweet-william), dahlias and bronze or crimson-leaved varieties of *Begonia semperflorens* which make a compact block of low, rich colour when thickly planted. The border or bed can be planted up from among the following flowers, again divided according to height.

From Table 3 it will be seen that there are fewer tall red flowers, so this lack can easily be filled with appropriate coloured roses, either as bushes, standards, ramblers or as climbers. There is an excellent annual foliage plant with plum-purple leaves called *Atriplex hortensis rubra* (crimson-leaved

TABLE 3. SOME FLOWERS FOR A RED BORDER

Low 5–30 cm (2–12 in)	*Medium* 30–105 cm (12 in–3½ ft)	*Tall* 105 cm–2.4 m (3½–8 ft)
*Anemone coronaria vars.	Amaranthus	
Antirrhinum	*Antirrhinum	Antirrhinum
	Astilbe vars. (damp soil)	
*Begonia semperflorens vars.		
	*Crocosmia	*Canna (choose those with bronze or crimson foliage)
Dianthus chinensis	*Dahlia	*Dahlia
	Euphorbia griffithii	
	Gaillardia	
	Geum	
	Gladiolus	
Helianthemum nummularium vars.	Hemerocallis	
	Heuchera vars.	
	Iberis umbellata	
	*Impatiens (for shadier borders)	
	Kniphofia	
Lampranthus	*Lobelia cardinalis	
	*Lobelia fulgens	
	*Lilium spp.	
	*Lychnis chalcedonica	
Mesembryanthemum	Monarda	
	Nicotiana	
	*Pelargonium	
	Penstemon	
	Petunia	
	Phlox drummondii vars.	
	Phygelius	Polygonum amplexicaule atrosanguineum
	Potentilla	
	Salpiglossis	
	*Salvia	
	Sidalcea	
	*Tigridia	
Tropaeolum	Tropaeolum (climbing)	
	*Zinnia	

orache), which adds great richness of colour, and the following shrubs have crimson or wine-coloured foliage. *Cotinus coggygria* (smoke bush) has oval leaves and grows to a height of 2.4 m (8 ft) with a similar spread (there are even darker-leaved

A well-planted border using old-fashioned and easy-going plants: cerastium (Snow-in-Summer) *Stachys lanata* (Lamb's ears) digitalis, nepeta (catmint) and roses.

varieties such as *C.c.* 'Foliis Purpureis' and 'Royal Purple'. *Berberis thunbergii* 'Atropurpurea' (or its variety *B. t.* 'Atropurpurea Nana', 30–45 cm (12–18 in) high for small gardens) grows to 1.2 m (4 ft) with a spread of 1.8 m (6 ft). Both these are deciduous, as is *Weigela* 'Foliis Purpureis' which is obligingly slow-growing, to an eventual height and spread of about 1.8 m (6 ft). The small-leaved *Leptospermum scoparium* 'Nicholsii' has dark purplish-bronze foliage and carmine flowers, but it is tender, as is *Pittosporum tenuifolium* 'Purpureum', which has pale green leaves changing to deep bronze-purple. The sharp accent of the sword-shaped leaves of *Phormium tenax* 'Purpureum' provides a rigid and wind-proof outline, though young plants in exposed positions may succumb in bad winters. Green-leaved red flowers can be set against the dark richness of *Fagus sylvatica* 'Purpurea', syn. Riversii (copper beech), which can be grown as hedging, as can the berberis; the latter will become a completely leafless though still prickly skeletal structure in winter, whereas the beech will keep most of its leaves.

Yellow borders

Other single-colour borders can be designed, for example, using all the yellow and golden tones, complemented by yellow or yellow-variegated foliage plants (some of which are evergreen). This would have an always-bright and cheerful appearance, even on the wettest and most thunder-dark days of summer. There are a great number of yellow flowers, so the selection may be pleasingly difficult if space is limited. Choose larger quantities of one type for greater impact rather than ones or twos of everything which can easily become a shapeless muddle when the flowers are regenerating. A group of ten similar plants will always have flowers whereas even the most hard-working single plant must recover itself periodically and during this time it goes into an eclipse.

SCENT

Scent is so much an accepted part of a garden that while being enjoyed, it is often taken somewhat for granted. Where a seat already exists in a tranquil part of the garden it might be an idea to re-think the area and plant scented flowers and shrubs so that their deliciousness is condensed in one place rather than being dissipated throughout the whole garden (Fig. 10). If the seat is set against a wall then it may already have perfumed roses, *Lonicera* (honeysuckle) and *Jasminum officinalis* (summer-flowering white jasmine). At each side and all around, plant some of the following as space allows, remembering to plant the night-scented ones (marked 'NS' on the list below) nearest to the seat if you are in the habit of relaxing in the gathering dusk of an early summer evening. Here is a short list of the more familiar perfumed flowers and shrubs—some are more aromatic than sweet, but this makes for a better bouillabaisse, so to speak.

Flowers for scent

Anthemis nobilis (chamomile)
Artemisia abrotanum (southernwood)
Centaurea moschata (sweet sultan)
Cheiranthus cheiri (wallflower)
Choisya ternata (Mexican orange)
Clematis flammula
Clematis montana
Convallaria majalis (lily-of-the-valley)
Dianthus spp. (pinks)
Dianthus barbatus (sweet-william)
Foeniculum vulgare (fennel)
Galtonia candicans (summer hyacinth)
Helichrysum angustifolium (curry plant)
Hesperis matronalis (NS) (dame's violet, sweet rocket)
Iris spp.
Jasminum spp. (NS) (jasmine)

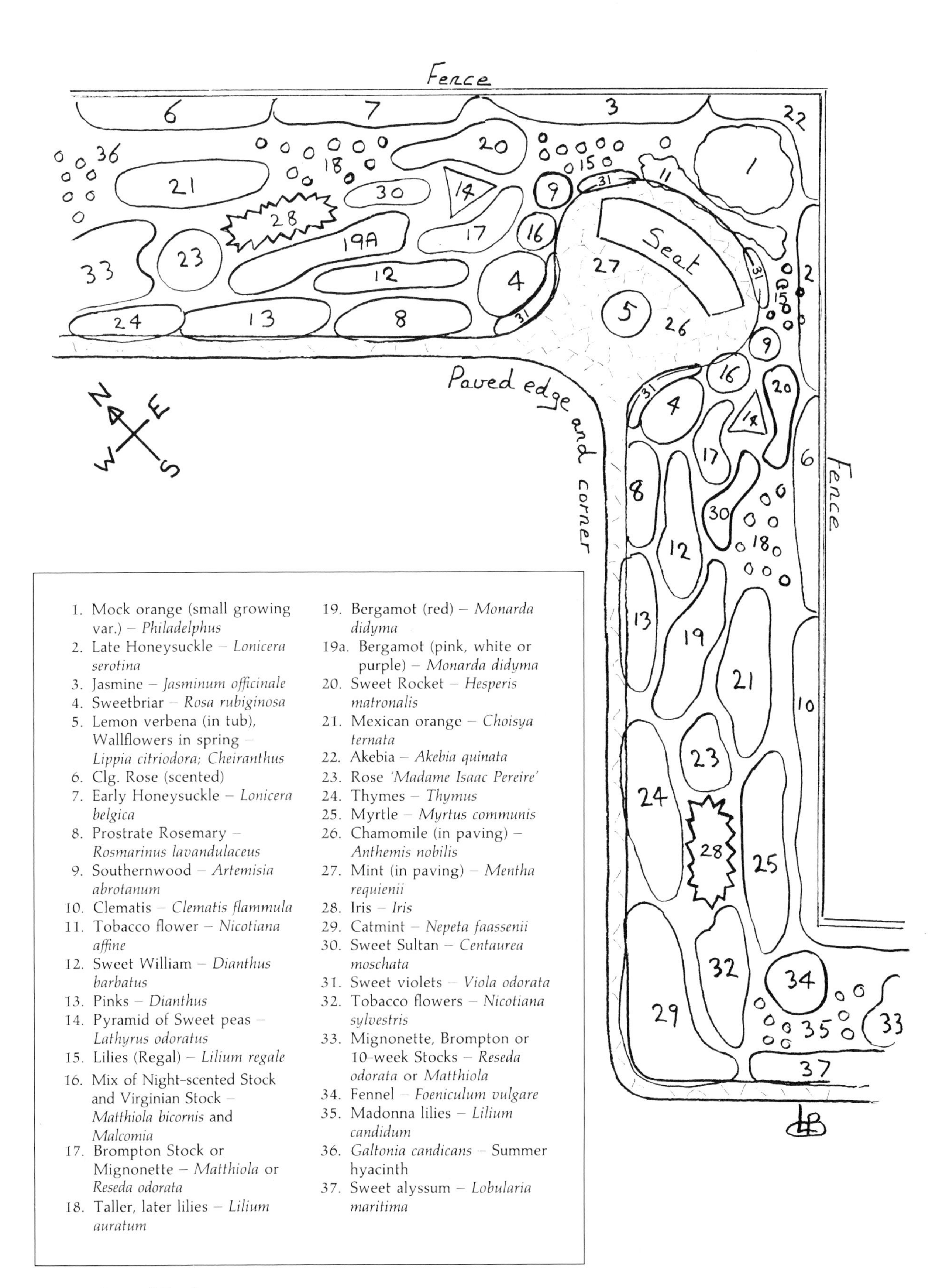

FIG. 10 Scented Border

Lathyrus odoratus (sweet pea)
Lavandula spp. (lavenders)
Lilium spp. (NS) (lily)
Limnanthes douglasii (poached egg flower)
Lippia citriodora (lemon verbena) (very tender)
Lobularia maritima (sweet alyssum)
Lonicera spp. (honeysuckles)
Lupinus arboreus (tree lupin)
Matthiola spp. (stocks, especially Brompton stock)
Matthiola bicornis (NS) (night-scented stock)
Monarda didyma (bergamot)
Muscari spp. (grape hyacinth)
Narcissus spp. and vars.
Nepeta mussinii (catmint)
Nicotiana affinis (NS) (tobacco flower)
Nicotiana sylvestris (NS) (tobacco flower)
Oenothera spp. especially *biennis* (NS) (evening primrose)
Origanum vulgare (marjoram)
Paeonia (peony)
Phlox paniculata (NS)
Reseda odorata (mignonette)
Rhododendron spp.
Rosa rubiginosa (sweetbriar)
Rosa spp. (roses) (some very much more than others)
Rosmarinus spp. (rosemary)
Smilacina racemosa (best in part shade)
Syringa spp. (lilacs)
Thymus spp. (thymes)
Verbena x *hybrida*
Viola spp. (violet, viola) (some more than others)

Plant the thymes where they can be stepped on occasionally but not walked on regularly, also *Anthemis nobilis* (now *Chamaemelum nobile*) or chamomile. Set the aromatic shrubs (lavender, southernwood, lippia, rosemary) where they can be brushed against to release their fragrance, and always have a plant of the delicious sweetbriar, *Rosa rubiginosa*, whose leaves smell of apples, especially in warm, humid weather or after rain.

SHAPES

Most border plants have individual and very characteristic outlines or silhouettes which are another important consideration, as is the texture of their leaves—shiny, ridged, matt-surfaced, hairy, prickly or furry—each catches the light in a different way. Irises have clean sword-shaped fans of leaves that make a good contrast to other more rounded shapes. Irises can, if wished, be planted for their foliage alone which is usually a pleasing pale green. Another specific shape is the substantial, rounded, leathery leaves of bergenia (again, often planted for these), the early flowers being a very welcome bonus. Dianthus (pinks) have silver-grey mats of grassy leaves that are a good contrast to other shapes, such as the excellent and ubiquitous alchemilla (lady's mantle) which has very beautiful hemispherical, pleated leaves. This plant forms a rounded hummock that is attractively neat in younger plants. Ornamental grasses have graceful, arching, curving leaves, and hemerocallis are now appreciated as much for their light green spring foliage as for their succession of flowers. Some of the geranium tribe are exceedingly useful until they grow too large and have to be replaced; the best for neatness is *G. endressii* which does not mind some shade; it forms a mound of very attractive dark green palmate (and typically geranium-like) leaves and it is excellent to set in front of less well-clothed plants or taller, wispy ones like scabiosa, some centaureas, *Allium schoenoprasum*, thalictrums and *Verbena bonariensis. Geranium macrorrhizum* has a more open and therefore slightly less tidy appearance, but its low-growing mounding habit, very lovely matt-surfaced, aromatic leaves and pink or white flowers make it invaluable in

Thick planting in early summer: iris, digitalis, nepeta, *Alchemilla mollis* (Lady's Mantle) roses, pansies and long-lasting alliums.

the garden, as it, too, does not object to partial shade.

Neat, low-growing plants with a dense habit are exceedingly useful to conceal the stalky nether parts of medium height plants and in addition to those already mentioned, the following could be used:

Anaphalis	*Sedum spectabile*
Antirrhinum	*Ruta graveolens*
Campanula glomerata	*Chrysanthemum parthenium*
Euphorbia polychroma	*Artemisia schmidtiana* 'Nana'
Origanum	*Hebe pinguifolia* 'Pagei'

Delicacy of foliage should be considered: all the thalictrums are beautiful, even when not in flower; they have maidenhair-fern-like leaves, usually in considerable quantities, and this is so lovely that for contrast these plants should be sited against something solid. Another apparently fragile-looking plant is foeniculum (fennel), which is tall-growing, with hazy, thread-like leaves of emerald-green or sombre purple-bronze which make an excellent background to stronger shapes, bright colours or white. All the dicentras have beautiful, delicate leaves of varying greens or grey and the low-growing ones, with their more dissected leaves, make very useful front-of-the-border subjects that are in flower for months. Gypsophila is one of the most useful nebulous shapes to have, forming a large, amorphous mass of tiny pink or white flowers. This cloud-like appearance is unique and can be used to hide unsightly stems, conceal gaps, soften long straight edges and as a background, contrast or separating plant.

Many medium-height herbaceous plants have a rather similar-looking appearance until they flower, which is why it is important either to separate the groups with contrasting foliage plants, grasses, small neat shrubs or to choose your border subjects for all-round harmony of shape and colour. Taller plants have visual impact because of their height but many are exceedingly handsome as well. The pale glaucous green of *Melianthus major* is almost too beautiful to hide, but as it may grow to 1.8 m (6 ft) something shorter can be set in front of it so as just to conceal its toes. The handsome pleated leaves of *Curtonus paniculatus* are a good sharp shape in the border (like assegais) while the large, shining palmate leaves of *Ricinus communis* make a very strong background to pale colours or equally powerful characters such as eremurus and kniphofia. The knowledge of what to plant next to what only comes with experience but in general try to harmonize, or contrast, the plant-shapes as well as the flowers themselves; this is easier when planting larger blocks or drifts than when using smaller quantities.

5

THE PLANTS

A = Annual
Bi = Biennial
B = Bulb
C = Corm
HHA = Half-hardy annual
P = Perennial
E = Evergreen
R = Rhizome
S = Shrub
T = Tuber

ACAENA *Rosaceae* P

There are several types of acaena and all have attractive foliage. One of the most compact semi-evergreen kinds is *A. microphylla* which has charming bronze-green leaves that quickly form compact mats of dense foliage. Interesting but rather insignificant round heads of whitish flowers appear in summer, to be followed by glistening crimson burs that shine in the sun. This plant spreads very quickly and is good as front-of-the-border ground cover, though it will have to be firmly controlled as its stolons root as they spread and can cover large areas. It has a fairly strong constitution and does not mind the occasional frost. In my garden my cats use it as a summer day-bed.

A. microphylla, New Zealand Bur, has round whitish flower heads from late spring to early summer, followed by attractive crimson, long-lasting (hookless) burs. Height to 5 cm (2 in), spread about 60 cm (2 ft).

ACANTHUS *Acanthaceae* P

A. mollis (bear's breeches) has mauve-purple and white hooded flowers interspersed with spiny green bracts. Height to 2.1 m (7 ft) with a similar spread. Midsummer. These are large, long-lived plants with handsome sculptural leaves that are shining, wavy and toothed like an enormous dandelion. The fangy roots are determined survivors; if the main plant is moved, any unexcavated portions will continue to send up leaves for many years.

A. spinosus (spiny bear's breech) has similar but even pricklier flowers. Height to 1.2 m (4 ft), spread to 1.2 m (4 ft). Midsummer. This is a more compact and usually more floriferous plant with interesting white-veined spiny leaves. Mound the crowns of both in cold areas in winter.
PROPAGATION: by seed or division when dormant.

ACHILLEA *Compositae* P

Most achilleas have flat, plate-like clusters of tiny flowers that are long-lasting in the border and when cut.

A. filipendulina 'Coronation Gold' has deep yellow-gold flowers. Height 1 m ($3\frac{1}{4}$ ft) with a spread of 60 cm (2 ft). Early to late summer.

A.f. 'Gold Plate' has similar flowers but grows from 1.2–1.5 m (4–5 ft) with a spread of 60 cm (2 ft).

A. millefolium has crimson to pink flowers. Height from 60–75 cm (2–$2\frac{1}{2}$ ft) with a spread of 38 cm (15 in). Early to mid-summer.

A. ptarmica 'The Pearl' has loose sprays of pure white button flowers. Height to 75 cm ($2\frac{1}{2}$ ft), spread to 38 cm + (15 in +). Mid-summer to early autumn. This is a delicate-looking plant whose graceful habit and pretty flowers belie its invasive nature.

Aster frikartii (Michaelmas daisy)

PROPAGATION: by division in early spring.

ACONITUM *Ranunculaceae* P

The aconites look rather like delphiniums but are much easier to grow. All parts of all aconites are very poisonous and neither flowers nor seed heads should be used for decor. These plants are quite happy in partial shade, where their tall flower spikes can be used to make a pleasingly substantial patch of colour early in the season.
A. anglicum (monkshood, wolf's bane) has spires of hooded violet-blue flowers. Height to 1.2 m (4 ft) with a spread of 45 cm (18 in). Early summer. This associates well with *Hesperis matronalis* (dame's violet).
A. napellus has indigo-blue flowers. Height to 105 cm (3½ ft), spread 38 cm (15 in). Mid- to late summer.
PROPAGATION: by seed or by division when dormant.

AGAPANTHUS *Liliaceae* P

Agapanthus can give the border an exotic appearance with their large umbels of blue or white flowers. These always lean towards the sun. They need rich soil and a sheltered position, and weekly liquid feeding from mid-spring onwards. Water well in dry spells and protect crowns in winter in colder areas.
A. campanulatus (blue African lily) has umbels of pale blue flowers; those of *A.c.* 'Isis' are lavender-blue. Height to 75 cm (2½ ft), spread to 60 cm (2 ft). Late summer. This is a deciduous species whose emerging leaves conveniently hide the fading foliage of spring bulbs.
'Headbourne Hybrids' have spherical umbels of flowers in several shades of blue, also white. Height to 75 cm (2½ ft), spread to 60 cm (2 ft). Mid- to late summer. They are, generally, hardier than the species.
PROPAGATION: by seed, or division when dormant.

AGERATUM *Compositae* A

The bushy flowers of the annual ageratum are long-lasting and solidly colourful even during periods of bad weather. They prefer a moisture-retentive soil and should be regularly dead-headed. They look better when closely planted.
A. houstonianum hybrids have blue, mauve, pink or white flowers from early summer until the frosts. Height from 13–30 cm (5–12 in). Planting distance should be from 15–30 cm (6–12 in).
PROPAGATION: from seed.

AJUGA *Labiatae* P

The burnished dark leaves of *Ajuga reptans* 'Atropurpurea' (sometimes called 'Metallica') provide patches of colour throughout the season, with the added interest of its blue flower spikes. Ajugas increase quickly by means of stoloniferous offsets which form neat and attractive rosettes, though by some they are called invasive. They must have full sun but are not particular about soil.
A. reptans 'Atropurpurea' syn. 'Purpurea' (bugle) has purple leaves and blue flowers in early to mid-summer. Height 10–30 cm (4–12 in), spread 45 cm+ (18 in+).
A.r. 'Multicolor syn. 'Rainbow' has bronze, pink and cream variegation; *A.r.* 'Burgundy Glow' has wine-red and cream leaves: *A.r.* 'Variegata' has grey, green, cream and pink leaves and is not long-lived.
PROPAGATION: detach offsets at almost any time. Evergreen.

ALCHEMILLA *Rosaceae* P

This is one of the easiest and most attractive of low-growing border plants, with soft, rounded, pleated leaves and sprays of tiny flowers. It will grow and flower in semi-shade, it softens hard, straight edges and is adept at seeding itself artistically into paving cracks and crannies.
A. mollis (lady's mantle) has sprays of long-lasting small, lime-yellow flowers

from early to late summer. Height to 45 cm (18 in), spread to 1.2 m (4 ft) in maturity.
PROPAGATION: by division in spring or by seed.

ALLIUM *Liliaceae* B

All the alliums are interesting or beautiful and many have long-lasting flower-heads that contrast well in shape or colour with other border plants. The foliage usually dies away quickly after flowering.
A. albopilosum syn. ***A. christophii*** has 15 cm (6 in) wide crowded umbels of lilac-purple star-shaped flowers in early summer. Height to 45 cm (18 in), planting distance 15–25 cm (6–10 in).
A. caeruleum has a globose head of very blue flowers in early or mid-summer. Height 60 cm (2 ft), planting distance 15 cm (6 in)).
A. giganteum has spherical heads of lilac-mauve flowers in early summer. Height 1.2 m (4 ft), planting distance 30 cm (12 in). Not for exposed positions. (Pleasing with *Euphorbia wulfenii.*)
A. moly has yellow flowers in mid-summer. Spreads quickly but leaves a gap afterwards. Height 30 cm (12 in), planting distance 10 cm (4 in).
A. karataviense is short with handsome blue-green leaves streaked with crimson and spherical metallic-looking and long-lasting heads of lilac flowers in late spring. Height 23 cm (9 in), planting distance about the same.
A. siculum has unusual nodding green, white and maroon bells in late spring to early summer which turn to turreted seed-heads by mid-summer. Foliage appears in early winter and disappears after flowering. This allium spreads quickly when established. Height 60 cm (2 ft), planting distance 10–15 cm (4–6 in).
PROPAGATION: by division of offsets and by seed.

ALSTROEMERIA *Alstroemeriaceae* P

Established clumps of alstroemerias are delicately beautiful in late summer, though they are not always easy to grow. Seeds should be sown thinly in deep peat pots, and the potful of seedlings should be planted without any disturbance at the bottom of a 23 cm (9 in) hole and earthed up as they grow, like leeks. The plants are lax-growing and may need the support of near-by shrubs, or twiggy sticks, and must be constantly protected against slugs. Alstroemerias do better in a light, rich soil and are best not moved once they are growing well.
A. auriantiaca (Peruvian lily) has red and orange flowers in mid- and late summer. Height 90 cm (3 ft), planting distance 30 cm (12 in). The variety 'Dover Orange' is taller with orange-red flowers and 'Lutea' is yellow with crimson markings.
A. ligtu has lilac, purple or pink flowers with purple markings, and is half-hardy. Height 60 cm (2 ft), planting distance 30 cm (12 in). The Ligtu hybrids are hardier and taller (to 1.2 m (4 ft)) with flowers in shades of orange, scarlet, flame, pink, yellow and white.
PROPAGATION: by seed.

ALTHAEA *Malvaceae* A/P

These are giants for the back of the border where their essential staking arrangements are not so visible. They will do better in good rich soil and are best grown as biennials or at most for three years. They appreciate extra feeding and should be watered well in dry spells. They are not for windy gardens.
A. rosea (hollyhock) has flowers in a wonderful colour-range from white through cream, pale yellow, blush, rose, pink, cerise, crimson, black-red and violet, with bicolours and single or double flowers from mid-summer to early autumn. Height to 3 m+ (10 ft+), planting distance 60 cm (2 ft).
PROPAGATION: by seed, which cannot be guaranteed to come true to colour.

ALYSSUM *Cruciferae* P

This is a good plant for border edges, where it should be cut hard back after flowering for compactness and replaced every three years or so.

A. saxatile (yellow alyssum) has brilliant yellow flowers in late spring and early summer. Height 23–30 cm (9–12 in), sprawls to 45 cm (18 in), planting distance 45 cm (18 in). Named varieties are 'Citrinum', lemon-yellow; 'Golden Queen', light yellow. *A.s.* 'Compactum', with golden yellow flowers, is smaller and neater, being 10–15 cm (4–6 in) tall and with a less voluptuous spread of about 23 cm (9 in). (For sweet alyssum, formerly *A. maritima*, see *Lobularia*.)

PROPAGATION: by seed and from cuttings. Evergrey.

AMARANTHUS *Amaranthaceae* A

Amaranthus are unusual plants with strange flowers or showy foliage. They respond well to enriched soil and regular feeding and watering in dry periods. Watch for aphids (blackfly in particular) and spray accordingly. Both these species are half-hardy.

A. caudatus (love-lies-bleeding) has long crimson or green rope-like tails of minute flowers from mid-summer until the frosts.

A. caudatus 'Viridis' has green tails, excellent in arrangements. Height 1.2 m (4 ft), planting distance 30–45 cm (12–18 in). Not for windy or exposed gardens.

A. tricolor (Joseph's coat) has exciting foliage in green, yellow, scarlet and bronze with erect brush-like crimson flowers in late summer and early autumn. Height 60–90 cm (2–3 ft), planting distance 30–45 cm (12–18 in).

PROPAGATION: by seed.

ANAPHALIS *Compositae* P

The grey leaves and white 'everlasting' flowers of anaphalis make it a reliable late-summer plant for the front of a sunny border.

A. triplinervis (pearl everlasting) has corymbs of crispy white flowers from mid-summer onwards. It is rather tender and its own stems should be left on for winter protection, and litter should be heaped over the crown in cold areas. Height 38 cm (15 in) with a similar spread.

A. yedoensis has flat heads of white flowers from mid-summer onwards. Height 60 cm (2 ft), spread 38 cm (15 in).

PROPAGATION: by division in spring or from seed.

ANCHUSA *Boraginaceae* P

Anchusas give a mass of really blue flowers which look well with pink or cream roses, gay with cosmea and lovely with campanulas. Taller kinds need staking. There are annuals or perennials to choose from, with flowers in different shades of blue.

A. azurea 'Dropmore' has deep blue flowers and is 1.5–1.8 m (5–6 ft) tall. 'Morning Glory' has rich blue flowers and is 1.2–1.5 m (4–5 ft) tall. 'Opal' is sky-blue and 1.2 m (4 ft) tall. 'Loddon Royalist' is gentian-blue and is 90 cm (3 ft) tall. 'Royal Blue' lives up to its name and is 90 cm–1.2 m (3–4 ft) tall. All should be planted 30–45 cm (12–18 in) apart and they are in flower from early to late summer.

A. capensis has forget-me-not blue flowers from mid- to late summer. Height 45 cm (18 in), planting distance 15–23 cm (6–9 in). These are biennial plants, though they will need winter protection if grown as such.

PROPAGATION: by root cuttings for perennials and seed for annuals.

ANEMONE *Ranunculaceae* R/P

This is a beautiful group of plants with flowers in every colour from late winter through to mid-autumn.

A. coronaria 'de Caen' has single flowers in red, white, blue, mauve and purple. The 'St Brigid' strain has double flowers in similar colours. Height 15–30 cm (6–12 in), planting distance 10–15 cm (4–6 in). Plant batches of rhizomes successively for continuous colour. Replace every three years or so.

Baptisia australis (False indigo)

A. blanda has blue, white, pink or mauve flowers from late winter to mid-spring. Height to 15 cm (6 in), planting distance 10 cm (4 in). Blue or white varieties can be obtained separately. The leaves disappear very quickly after flowering.
A. fulgens has brilliant scarlet white-centred flowers from early to late spring. Replace every three years.
A. x hybrida (Japanese anemone) has pink or white flowers from late summer to mid-autumn. Good varieties are 'September Charm', clear pink; 'Lorelei', rose-pink; 'Queen Charlotte', semi-double mauve-pink. All these are from 60–90 cm (2–3 ft) high, while the white-flowered 'Honorine Jobert' is taller, to 1.2 m (4 ft), planting distance 60 cm (2 ft).
PROPAGATION: by seed and division for spring and summer-flowering species and hybrids and by division in early spring for the perennial *A.* x *hybrida*, which resents all disturbance.

ANGELICA *Umbelliferae* Bi

This is a statuesque biennial that will give height and substance to a shaded border. The flowers must be cut before they are over if they are wanted for arrangements. Set out plants in groups of three or five. Seed germinates best when fresh.
A. angelica has large, spherical heads, 13 cm (5 in) in diameter, of green-yellow flowers in mid- to late summer. Height to 3 m (10 ft), spread about 90 cm (3 ft).
PROPAGATION: by seed.

ANTHEMIS *Compositae* P

The soft grey-green leaves of *A. cupaniana* will flow quickly over the edge of a border or around the stems of taller plants. The aromatic and filigree foliage topped by its white 'daisies' forms a beautiful picture when in association with Shirley poppies, tradescantia or nasturtiums. Dead-head regularly and protect in winter in cold areas.
A. cupaniana has white flowers from early to late summer. Height 30 cm (12 in) and a quick surge to 90 cm (3 ft).
A. tinctoria (ox-eye chamomile) has yellow daisies from early to late summer. Height 75 cm ($2\frac{1}{2}$ ft), planting distance 38–45 cm (15–18 in). 'E.C. Buxton' has lemon flowers and 'Wargrave Variety' has cream. All are good with *Echinops ritro* and the lustred steely-blue eryngiums.
PROPAGATION: by seed.

ANTIRRHINUM *Scrophulariaceae* A

Antirrhinums (snapdragons) are sturdy plants, making solid clumps of colour where needed. There are some very tall varieties (to 1.2 m (4 ft)) for the larger border, but in general the short to medium kinds are more often grown in a very wide range of single, double and bicoloured flowers. They are easy to grow, but they need rich soil and regular watering, feeding and dead-heading to keep them flowering from mid-summer until the frosts. There are some excellent dwarf kinds, 15 cm (6 in), which are useful at the edge of the border to fill the inevitable summer gaps or as part of a planting scheme. One-colour packets of seed can be obtained, and rust-resistant strains should be grown. Pinch out growing tips of taller kinds to encourage bushy plants.
PROPAGATION: by seed.

AQUILEGIA *Ranunculaceae* P

The more old-fashioned and easy *A. vulgaris* can be relied on to stay where it is and increase in size and floriferousness for about five years. It is a prolific seeder, and the seedlings can be transplanted to improve poor places elsewhere in the garden.
A. vulgaris (columbine, grannybonnets) has single or double flowers in lilac, pink, rose, purple, violet and white in late spring and early summer. Height to 90 cm (3 ft), planting distance or spread about 30 cm (12 in). The long-spurred but shorter-lived 'McKana Hybrids' have wonderful bi- or tri-coloured flowers in white, cream, yellow, red, crimson, purple and magenta. These grow to 90 cm (3 ft),

planting distance 30 cm (12 in). Seedlings do not come true, especially where other species or varieties of aquilegia are grown.
PROPAGATION: by seed and by division of named species, hybrids or colours in spring.

ARABIS *Cruciferae* P

Arabis is in flower for a long time and is therefore most useful at the edge of a border, particularly its pink, lilac or crimson varieties. It is, alas, often scorned for its 'ordinariness', though it should not be, as its grey-green rosettes are pleasing when the plant is not in bloom. Cut hard back after flowering. Once established it resents disturbance.
A. albida has white, pink, lilac or crimson flowers from late winter to early summer. Height 23 cm (9 in), spread to 60 cm (2 ft).
PROPAGATION: by seed and by division in autumn. Evergrey.

ARCTOTIS *Compositae* HHA

Arctotis have somewhat unreal-looking 10 cm (4 in) flowers and they need a hot position in the border where they will, nevertheless, close their petals in late afternoon and on dull days, as does that other South African daisy, dimorphotheca. Pinch out tops of young plants to promote bushiness and dead-head regularly.
A.* x *hybrida has spectacular 'daisies' with a central disk of violet, brown or purple, and long petals of yellow, orange, red, cream or white which are usually zoned in contrasting shades from mid-summer until the frosts. Height to 60 cm (2 ft), planting distance 30 cm (12 in).
PROPAGATION: by seed.

ARGEMONE *Papaveraceae* A

The pale-veined, spiny foliage of argemones is interesting on its own, though the large papery, deckle-edged poppy-flowers are an additional bonus. Grown as annuals they will flower the same year. Dead-head regularly.
A. grandiflora has clusters of large 10 cm (4 in) white flowers in early to mid-summer. Height to 90 cm (3 ft), planting distance 30 cm (12 in).
A. mexicana (prickly poppy, devil's fig) has smaller, scented yellow or orange flowers from early summer until the frosts. The spiny grey-green leaves are white-blotched. Height 60 cm (2 ft), planting distance 23 cm (9 in).
PROPAGATION: by seed.

ARMERIA *Plumbaginaceae* P

Armerias are neatly perennial 'edging' plants with round bobbles of flowers on strong but slender stems. Established plants develop long, deep roots and should not be moved. Armerias dislike damp and shade and will die in these conditions—they are plants for sunny, windy gardens. Snip off dead 'drumsticks' after flowering.
A. maritima (thrift, sea-pink) has pink, crimson or white flowers in spherical heads from late spring to mid-summer. *A.m.* 'Vindictive' is deep rosy-red, 'Alba' is white. Height 15–30 cm (6–12 in), spread to 30 cm (12 in).
PROPAGATION: by seed and basal cuttings. Evergreen.

ARTEMISIA *Compositae* P

Artemisia is grown for its silver-white, felted willow-like leaves, making it an excellent contrast plant for hot colours or as an essential part of a white and silver garden or border. It needs a well-drained site and spreads by invasive underground roots, though this is forgivable in a plant with such beautiful foliage. The flowers are dull.
A. ludoviciana (white sage) has undistinguished brown-yellow flowers in early to mid-autumn. The silvery buds are attractive but cut flowering stems off. Height 1.2 m (4 ft), spread to 90 cm+ (3 ft+).
PROPAGATION: by division in spring.

ARUNCUS *Rosaceae* P

A grand plant for shady borders and moist soil, with plumy cream panicles of tiny flowers and very beautiful fern-like leaves. Sawfly larvae will skeletonize these in a week, so watch and spray.
A. sylvester (goat's beard) has fluffy cream flower-cones in early summer. Height to 1.8 m (6 ft), spread 90 cm (3 ft). *A.s.* 'Kneiffii' is similar but only 60 cm (2 ft) tall and better for smaller gardens.
PROPAGATION: by division in spring, retaining newer outer sections and discarding exhausted central portion.

ASTER *Compositae* P

Asters or Michaelmas daisies are in flower from late summer until the frosts in a chromatic colour scale from white through pale pink, rose, crimson, purple, violet, mauve and lavender-blue, with single or double flowers and in heights varying from 15 cm (6 in) to about 1.5 m (5 ft); the latter will need some support. Most, but not all, have yellow central disks. They appreciate rich soil and an open airy position, though some kinds will need to be sprayed against mildew. Slugs will devour the young shoots unless prevented. Some good kinds are:
A. x frikartii 'Mönch', blue-mauve, 1 m (3¼ ft), late summer to mid-autumn; *A. novae-angliae* 'Harrington's Pink', pink, 1.2–1.5 m (4–5 ft), planting distance 45 cm (18 in), early autumn; *A. amellus* 'King George', violet-blue and 75 cm (2½ ft); *A.a.* 'Lye End Beauty', soft pink, 1.2 m (4 ft), late summer to early autumn; *A. novi-belgii* 'Alice Haslam', rose, cerise, 30 cm (12 in); *A.n.-b.* 'Blue Bouquet', violet-blue, 30 cm (12 in); and *A.n.-b.* 'Victor', pale lavender, 15 cm (6 in) tall, plant about 38 cm (15 in), early to mid-autumn.

There are very many more; asters are addictive, if one has the space.
PROPAGATION: by division; seed will not come true.
Note: The summer-flowering annual aster is *Callistephus* (see page 59).

ASTILBE *Saxifragaceae* P

Astilbes need moist, rich soil and do best in sun or partial shade. They have very beautiful dissected foliage that is bronze on emergence; some varieties have copper-coloured leaves that make an excellent contrast to those of near-by hostas or iris. Astilbes look like a shorter aruncus but are in no way related; some good varieties include:
A. x arendsii 'Fanal', dark red, 60 cm (2 ft); 'Federsee', rose-red, 75 cm (2½ ft); 'White Gloria', white, 60 cm (2 ft), early to late summer, planting distance 30–45 cm (12–18 in).
A. x crispa is shorter-growing; 'Gnome' is rose-pink, 15–20 cm (6–8 in); 'Peter Pan', deep pink, 15–20 cm (6–8 in) with a similar spread, early to late summer.
PROPAGATION: by division in spring.

ASTRANTIA *Umbelliferae* P

These are plants with good leaves and subtly coloured pincushion flowers, very long-lasting in the border and when cut. All need moist, humus-rich soil and they do well in partial shade. Protect from flower-arrangers.
A. major (masterwort, Hattie's pincushion, melancholy gentleman) has greenish-pink and white flowers in early and mid-summer. Height 60 cm (2 ft), spread 38 cm (15 in).
A. maxima has pink flowers in early and mid-summer. Height to 60 cm (2 ft), planting distance 38 cm (15 in).
A. minor has flowers similar to ***A. major*** but is only 23 cm (9 in) tall, and the more tender ***A. minor*** 'Variegata' has pale greenish-pink and white flowers, cream-edged leaves and needs more sun.
PROPAGATION: by division in spring.

AUBRIETA *Cruciferae* P

Aubrieta might not be called a true border plant by the purists, but it is invaluable for softening paved edges, as ground-cover and filling-in spaces. It makes a colourful

tapestried carpet in a spring border when grown with bulbs, anemones, arabis, iberis and polyanthus. It is long in bloom, but cut it hard back after flowering to make neat evergreen ground-cover; sometimes killed by extreme cold.
A. deltoides has single or double flowers in all shades of lilac to rich purple, as well as pink, white or crimson. 'Dr Mules' is purple, 'Gurgedyke' is bright purple, 'Magician' is red-purple and 'Barker's Double has rose-purple double flowers. It grows to 15 cm (4 in), spreads to 60 cm (2 ft) and does well in limy soils. Early spring to early summer.
PROPAGATION: by seed for mixtures; by cuttings or division in early autumn for special or named varieties as seeds do not come true.

BAPTISIA *Leguminosae* P

In spite of its name, *Baptisia australis* comes from North America. It has spires of elegant, lupin-like flowers followed by interesting, fat, grey-black pods.
B. australis (false indigo) has violet-blue flowers in early summer. Height 90 cm (3 ft), spread to 60 cm (2 ft).
PROPAGATION: by seed or division in early spring.

BEGONIA *Begoniaceae* Grown as A

Included here because the fibrous-rooted *B. semperflorens* is an excellent no-trouble plant, guaranteed to flower endlessly, even in bad summers. All it needs is a fortnightly liquid feed and regular watering at other times. Set plants closer together than usually recommended; they will quickly join up to form solid patches of colour that are useful for gap-filling.
Some leading seedsmen sell boxes of 'plantlets' which saves raising the heat in the greenhouse in late winter.
B. semperflorens has pink, white, crimson, red or bicoloured flowers from early summer until the frosts, with green or purple-bronze leaves. Height 15–23 cm (6–9 in) with a similar spread.
PROPAGATION: by seed.

BELLIS *Compositae* Grown as B

These very traditional flowers have a long flowering season and do better in good rich soil. The double varieties do not produce seed and therefore the pink 'Dresden China' and the red-flowered 'Rob Roy' should be increased by division in early spring. Dead-head regularly.
B. perennis (daisy, English daisy) has semi-double or very double flowers in all shades of pink, red, crimson and white from early spring to mid-autumn. Height 10–15 cm (4–6 in) according to variety, planting distance 8–13 cm (3–5 in).
PROPAGATION: by seed and division.

BERGENIA *Saxifragaceae* P

Even if bergenias never bloomed they would be among the most useful of garden plants because of their handsome leaves. They will flower in partial shade but do better in full sun, and will grace hot, dry gardens as well as shaded, damp ones. After three years or so, dig them up, revitalize the soil, remove the snails and replant all good rooted portions. There are several species and varieties which may be grown for their colourful crimson and purple winter foliage.
B.* x *schmidtii has pink flowers from late winter to early spring. Height to 30 cm (12 in), spread or planting distance 60 cm.
B. stracheyi 'Silberlicht' has white flowers from mid- to late spring and grows 30 cm (12 in) tall with a spread of 30–45 cm (12–18 in).
PROPAGATION: by division in autumn or spring, or by seed. Evergreen.

BRIZA *Gramineae* A

Quaking grass is well named because its quivering green pendants are seldom still. This very pretty grass makes a delicate contrast to other border plants and its only drawback lies in an overdeveloped determination to survive.
B. major (quaking grass) has dangling green pear-shaped spikelets from late

spring to mid-summer. Height 50 cm (20 in), planting distance to 15 cm (6 in) or closer.
PROPAGATION: by seed.

BRODIAEA *Alliaceae* C

These are delicate, grassy-leaved plants for a warm border or at the base of a south-facing wall. Their funnel-shaped flowers appear very suddenly, and associate very well with geum, heucherella, gilia and, of course, gypsophila. The leaves vanish almost immediately after flowering and at this time overcrowded clumps can be lifted and divided.
B. laxa syn. ***Triteleia laxa*** (Ithuriel's spear) has a loose umbel of violet-blue flowers in early to mid-summer. Height 50 cm (20 in), planting distance 5–8 cm (2–3 in).
PROPAGATION: seed, division of offsets.

BRUNNERA *Boraginaceae* P

Brunneras are most useful in a shaded border, with their large, rough heart-shaped leaves and sprays of forget-me-not blue flowers. They need moist, humus-rich soil to do well.
B. macrophylla has bright blue flowers from mid-spring to early summer. Height 30–45 cm (12–18 in), planting distance 45 cm (18 in). *B.m.* 'Variegata' has green and cream leaves that tend to revert: cut off any green leaves and all dead flower stems; the remaining leaves will then increase in size.
PROPAGATION: division, early spring.

CALCEOLARIA *Scrophulariaceae* P

Calceolarias have a colourful succession of fat, pouch-shaped flowers that are completely different to anything else in the border. They are usually grown as half-hardy annuals in the UK. There are many hybrids of differing degrees of hardiness and most of these should not be planted out until early summer. Those with the largest and most pinchable pouches are the most tender and have the gayest or most interesting colours. They need a warm and sheltered border and must be watered well and protected from slugs and aphids. The hardiest is:
C. integrifolia with yellow puff-ball flowers from mid-summer to early autumn and attractive wrinkled leaves. It is 60 cm (2 ft) tall, planting distance 30–38 cm (12–15 in).
PROPAGATION: by seed.

CALENDULA *Compositae* A

Marigolds are blindingly effective when planted in single-colour groups, though their characteristic bright orange may need careful placing. Any soil from average to poor suits them. Dead-head regularly and watch for blackfly.
C. officinalis (marigold, English marigold, pot marigold) has orange or yellow flowers from late spring until the frosts. Height 60 cm (2 ft), planting distance 30–38 cm (12–15 in). There are shorter varieties for the front of the border, and the newer hybrids come in lemon, cream (very beautiful), salmon, apricot or pink, with brown, toning or green central disks.
PROPAGATION: by seed.

CALLISTEPHUS *Compositae* A

These are the annual or China asters that are so attractive in the late-summer border. Traditionally, their colour-range was from pink through cerise, crimson, mauve and violet, but the newer hybrids can be chosen with single or double flowers, bicolours and in several forms such as peony, pompon, ostrich plume and chrysanthemum, with heights ranging from floriferous dwarfs of 15 cm (6 in) to substantial plants of 75 cm (30 in). Single colour flowers can be grown to complement colour schemes when the usual mixed colours might look too busy. Callistephus are in flower from mid-summer until the frosts. Dead-head regularly and do not grow in the same place in successive years as they are prone to several soil-borne diseases.
PROPAGATION: by seed.

CAMASSIA *Liliaceae* B

These tall-stemmed flowers with their heads of starry blue blooms are very striking in the border. Plant the bulbs in September or October (early to mid-autumn) and leave to form clumps. When overcrowding is evident they should be lifted and split up as the leaves die down, usually in early autumn. Camassias do well in heavy soils that do not dry out.
C. cusickii (quamash) has lavender-blue flowers in early to mid-summer. Height 1.2 m (4 ft), planting distance 23 cm (9 in).
C. leichtlinii has deep blue or white flowers at the same time and is 90 cm (3 ft) tall, planting distance 15 cm (6 in). *C.l.* 'Atrocoerulea' has dark blue-purple flowers.
PROPAGATION: by seed, or division of offsets.

CAMPANULA *Campanulaceae* P or Bi

There is a bellflower for almost every part of the garden, which makes them one of the best and most useful as well as among the most beautiful of border plants. Most will increase to form fine tall or middle-height plants, while others will spread in colourful surges all along the front edge of the border.
C. alliariifolia has ivory or cream bells in early to mid-summer. Height 45–60 cm (18–24 in), planting distance 30 cm (12 in).
C.* x *burghaltii has very unusual long lavender-grey flowers in early summer. Height 45–60 cm (18–24 in), planting distance 23–30 cm (9–12 in). Needs support.
C. carpatica has wide, upturned saucers in shades of blue, mauve, violet and white in mid- to late summer. Height 30 cm (12 in) though usually less, spread 30–38 cm (12–15 in). Protect young plants from slugs.
C. glomerata has solid heads of purple or white bells on stiff stems from late spring to mid-autumn. Height according to variety, from 10–45 cm (4–18 in), spread 30–60 cm (12–24 in). Keep dead-headed.
C. lactiflora (bellflower) has substantial rounded heads of blue, lavender, lilac or pink bell-shaped flowers from early to mid-summer. Height to 1.5 m (5 ft) according to variety, planting distance 45 cm (18 in). A fine plant when grown in groups but takes some years to attain full beauty.
C. latifolia (giant bellflower) has violet, blue or white flowers in mid-summer. Height 1.5 m (5 ft), planting distance 38–45 cm (15–18 in).
C. medium (Canterbury bell) is a biennial, with white, violet, mauve or pink flowers from late spring to mid-summer. Height according to variety, 23–90 cm (9 in–3 ft), planting distance 30–45 cm (12–18 in). *C.m. calycanthema* is the 'cup-and-saucer' variety with similarly coloured flowers.
C. portenschlagiana syn. ***C. muralis***, has purple flowers from early summer to late autumn. Height 15 cm (6 in), but spreads invasively to 60 cm+ (2 ft+).
C. poscharskyana has delicate sprays of blue-mauve flowers from early summer to late autumn. It trails or leans to 40 cm (16 in) and spreads even more quickly than the last species (to 90 cm (3 ft)). It grows prettily and usefully in semi-shade. Vigorous.
PROPAGATION: by division of established plants or by seed.

CANNA *Cannaceae* R

These handsome plants must be brought on in a warm greenhouse in northern European countries where their care and cultivation are similar to that for dahlias, except that cannas are even greedier. They should not be set out until the weather has settled to summer temperatures.
C.* x *hybrida has red, orange or yellow flowers from early summer to early autumn. Purple-brown or green foliage provides a tropical accent where this is suitable. Height to 1.2 m (4 ft), planting distance 30–45 cm (12–18 in).
PROPAGATION: by division of the rhizomes or by seed, in heated greenhouse.

CATANANCHE *Compositae* P

Catananche looks like a nicer-mannered cornflower, and its gentle colour is pleasing with soft pink herbaceous geraniums (which will swirl round its rather skimpily-clad stems) and even better with pink or white gypsophila. Seedling replacements are always useful because catananche is not long-lived. Protect from slugs.
C. caerulea (Cupid's dart, blue cupidone) has soft blue flowers from mid-summer to mid-autumn. Height to 75 cm (2½ ft), planting distance 30–45 cm (12–18 in).
PROPAGATION: by seed.

CENTAUREA *Compositae* A/P

This large and useful group includes the old-fashioned annual cornflower, as well as the more enduring perennial members of the genus.
C. cyanus (cornflower, bluebottle) has flowers in blue, white, pink, crimson, maroon, violet and all intermediate shades from early summer to early autumn. Height 30 cm (12 in) to 1.2 m (4 ft) according to variety, planting distance 23–38 cm (9–15 in). The seeds come in mixed packets, though the traditional pure blue is easily obtained separately. Cornflowers have poor foliage which needs concealment and the taller kinds need support.
C. dealbata has pink flowers in early to mid-summer. Height 90 cm (3 ft), planting distance 60 cm (2 ft). It may need a little support, such as an eryngium or some tall *Campanula glomerata* and should be dead-headed regularly. 'John Coutts' is a good, deep pink. Silver-green leaves.
C. macrocephala has shiny round brown buds and yellow flowers in early to mid-summer. Height 90 cm–1.5 m (3–5 ft), spread 60 cm (2 ft). This is a strong, stout plant with interesting knapweed-like flowers.
C. montana has deep blue flowers in late spring to early summer. Height 45–60 cm (18–24 in), planting distance 30 cm (12 in). It flops comfortably and looks well with all dianthus, especially *D. barbatus* (sweet-william).
C. moschata (sweet sultan) has pink, white, yellow or red sweet scented fluffy flowers from early summer to early autumn. Height 60 cm (2 ft), planting distance 23 cm (9 in). Annual.
PROPAGATION: by division or seed.

CENTRANTHUS (or KENTRANTHUS) *Valerianaceae* P

This is really a plant for dry walls, banks, cliffs and quarries, but it is long in flower, though it will not be as long-lived. Its tenaciously strong roots will bind an old wall together, but these roots are impossible to dislodge without major civil engineering. It produces myriads of seedlings.
C. ruber (red valerian or Padstow pride) has elongated mop-heads of crimson, pink or white flowers from late spring to early autumn. Height to 90 cm (3 ft), spread similar. It looks well with iris, nepeta, anchusa and veronica. Do not attempt to move once established; plant one of its ever-present progeny instead. It is much beloved by bees and the expatriate Cornish.
PROPAGATION: from seed.

CEPHALARIA *Dipsacaceae* P

Cephalaria is a tall, robust scabious with large flowers of a particularly pleasing gentle creamy yellow, most useful as a bridging colour between brighter yellows and pink. The plant will form a large clump and should not be grown unless there is room and to spare for it, but a well-grown group of this handsome scabious with many branching stems of pale yellow flowers is a fine sight. It is in bloom for many weeks. Dead-head and protect from blackfly.
Cephalaria gigantea, syn. ***C. tatarica*** has large cream-yellow flowers from early to mid-summer. Height 1.5–1.8 m (5–6 ft). Plant 90 cm–1.2 m (3–4 ft) apart.

Delphinium consolida (Larkspur)

CERASTIUM *Caryophyllaceae* P

This silver-leaved, mat-forming plant will cover itself with its white flowers in summer and controlled cushions of it are excellent as an edging, though it is a ground-swallower and needs to be watched. Good as a contrast to greens or the dark leaves of ajuga, *Viola labradorica* and *Lobelia fulgens*. Cerastium flowers even better when fed. Oddly enough, in cold areas it may need protection in winter. Established plants dislike disturbance. Cut back in spring.
C. tomentosum (snow-in-summer) has white flowers in late spring to early summer. Height 10–15 cm (4–6 in), spread infinite. *C.t.* 'Columnae' is smaller with similar flowers and grows to 8 cm (3 in) with a spread of 25 cm (10 in).
PROPAGATION: by division in early spring. Evergrey.

CHEIRANTHUS *Cruciferae* P grown as Bi

Two different types of cheiranthus are generally grown; the best known and most popular is *C. cheiri* (wallflower), a perennial plant usually grown as a biennial. The other is *C.* x *allionii* (more properly, *Erysimum allionii*) which has flowers of a particularly vivid orange that needs careful siting—in the right place it can be perfect but in the wrong one even bare soil is preferable.

Cheiranthus are best grown in rows in a spare part of the garden and each transplanted with a soil-ball in autumn, to avoid the check that they normally receive when purchased as bare-rooted plants. Prolonged spells of very cold weather with chilling winds can kill them if they are in exposed situations. When their (long) flowering season is over transplant *C. cheiri* carefully to a wilder part of the garden, where they will grow to bushy 1.2 m (4 ft) high plants and give abundant flowers for cutting.
C.* x *allionii (Siberian wallflower) has orange or yellow flowers from late spring to mid-summer. Height 38 cm (15 in), planting distance 30 cm (12 in).
C. cheiri (wallflower) has single or double scented flowers in red, crimson, purple, mauve, orange, apricot, pink, yellow, cream and white from mid-spring to early summer. Height 20–60 cm (8–24 in), planting distance 25–30 cm (10–12 in). Packets of single colours available.
PROPAGATION: by seed. Evergreen.

CHIONODOXA *Liliaceae* B

Chionodoxas are beautiful front-of-the-border plants with scilla-like flowers. They are easy to grow: plant them, remember not to put anything else on top of them and then forget about them until spring. Their foliage dies away quickly and tidily after flowering. Set bulbs 5–8 cm (2–3 in) deep and about 5–10 cm (2–4 in) apart, according to size.
C. gigantea syn. ***C. grandiflora*** has pale lilac-blue flowers from late winter to mid-spring. Height to 20 cm (8 in), planting distance 10 cm (4 in).
C. luciliae has light blue flowers from late winter to early spring; 'Rosea' and 'Pink Giant' are pink, 'Alba' is white. Height 15 cm (6 in), planting distance 5–10 cm (2–4 in).
C. sardensis has darker blue flowers from early to late spring. Height to 15 cm (6 in).
PROPAGATION: divide offsets, or seed.

CHRYSANTHEMUM *Compositae* A/P

This is a large genus of plants containing several favourite border plants as well as the enormous family of hybrid chrysanthemums that are grown for garden, greenhouse, show-bench or florist's shop. This vast range of plants has been divided into seven main groups: incurved, reflexed, intermediate, single, anemone-centred, pompon and other types, and these groups have been further subdivided. The simpler forms should be chosen from a reputable chrysanthemum grower; they are available in all colours except blue and in heights from 15 cm

(6 in) to 1.8 m (6 ft). They should be selected in advance for height, colour and flowering time, and on arrival, planted out shallowly in ground already prepared with a base fertilizer. Water in well and never allow to dry out in hot spells.

Specialist catalogues will recommend the months for 'stopping' or 'disbudding' so as to produce larger blooms (not always practical in the average garden with average autumnal weather). The plants will benefit from feeding every ten days until the buds have colour. After flowering, leave blackened stems until spring for winter protection in cold areas.

C. maximum (Shasta daisy, moon daisy, Marguerite) has large white flowers from early to late summer. 'Wirral Pride' has semi-double flowers and is 90 cm (3 ft) tall; the familiar 'Esther Read' is 75 cm (2½ ft) with double flowers, and 'H. Siebert' is 75 cm (2½ ft) and single with frilled petals. Plant 30–45 cm apart.

C. parthenium (feverfew) has aromatic leaves, a reputation for curing migraine and neat single or double white flowers from early summer to early autumn. Height to 45 cm (18 in) according to variety, planting distance 25 cm (10 in).

C. roseum syn. ***C. coccineum*** (pyrethrum) has single or double daisy-flowers in shades of red, pink, salmon and white in early summer. Height to 90 cm (3 ft), planting distance to 45 cm (18 in). Good single varieties are: 'Ariel', salmon; 'Kelway's Glorious', crimson-red; 'Eileen May Robinson', pink; 'Avalanche', white. Double varieties include 'Lord Rosebery', red; 'Madeleine', clear pink; 'Venus', shell-pink; 'Carl Vogt', white. These need to be propagated vegetatively.

C. uliginosum (moon daisy) has single green-centred white flowers in mid- to late autumn. Height to 1.8 m (6 ft). Good behind late asters (Michaelmas daisies), helianthus and rudbeckias. Planting distance 38 cm (15 in).

PROPAGATION: from basal cuttings or division in early to mid-spring for chrysanthemums, by division for *C. maximum* and *C. uliginosum* and by seed for *C. parthenium*.

CIMIFUGA *Ranunculaceae* P

Cimifugas need moist soil and are best in semi-shade. They form a mound of attractive fern-like foliage from which the tall flower spikes rise up in late summer. Top-dress with leaf-mould in spring, and do not move established plants except for purposes of increase.

C. foetida (bugbane) has 'pokers' of greenish-yellow flowers in mid- to late summer. Height to 1.5 m (5 ft), planting distance 45 cm (18 in). *C.f.* 'White Pearl' is a better colour and flowers from early to mid-autumn.

C. racemosa (black snake-root) has racemes of white flowers in mid- to late summer. Height to 1.5 m (5 ft), planting distance 60 cm (2 ft). *C. ramosa* is taller and flowers in early autumn.

PROPAGATION: by division.

CLARKIA *Oenotheraceae* A

Clarkias have unusual-shaped flowers and the double forms make a pleasant contrast in shape to the many 'daisies' of late summer. They all do best in a rather light acid soil and need no feeding.

C. elegans comes in mixed colours of pink, crimson, purple, mauve, salmon, orange and white from late summer to early autumn. Double forms are: 'Brilliant', carmine-pink and 'Orange King', orange-to-scarlet.

PROPAGATION: by seed.

CLEMATIS *Ranunculaceae* P

There are three forms of herbaceous clematis, and all are attractive and unusual border plants. Mulch annually with well-decayed manure or compost and water well in dry spells.

C. heracleifolia has clusters of scented, hyacinth-like blue flowers in late summer to early autumn. Height to 90 cm (3 ft), spread to 1.5 m (5 ft). The variety *C.h.* 'Wyevale' is the best. Handsome leaves.

C. integrifolia has nodding violet-blue flowers from early summer to early

autumn. Height 60 cm (2 ft), planting distance 30 cm (12 in). This makes flopping patches which need twiggy support or more rigid plants to lean against.
C. recta has clusters of scented white flowers in early to mid-summer. Height to 1.2 m (4 ft), planting distance 45 cm (18 in). *C.r. purpurea* is a more interesting plant, with similar flowers but purple-toned young foliage. Grow this up through roses or open-stemmed shrubs.
PROPAGATION: basal cuttings for *C. heracleifolia*, seed for *C. integrifolia* and *C. recta*.

CLEOME *Capparidaceae* A

Cleomes are tall, with strange, whiskery flowers that conceal spiteful thorns. Despite this, when grown in a group they make a very interesting contrast in form to other border plants. They must have full sun, and do better in good soil.
C. spinosa (spider flower) has white, pink, lilac or carmine flowers from mid-summer until the frosts. Height to 1.2 m (4 ft), planting distance 45 cm (18 in).
PROPAGATION: by seed.

COLCHICUM *Liliaceae* C

Though called autumn crocus, the colchicum is actually a member of the lily family, whereas the true spring-flowering crocus belongs to the genus Iridaceae. Colchicum flowers grow up from the bare soil and are valuable for extending the border's flowering season. Each corm has several flowers. All have large, lush leaves in spring from 25–40 cm (10–16 in) in height which need to be concealed by the foliage of other oncoming plants. Slugs adore these leaves.
C. autumnale (autumn crocus) has lilac flowers from early to late autumn. *C.a.* 'Roseum-plenum' has double rose-pink flowers like water lilies come ashore, *C.a.* 'Album' is white. Height of flowers 15 cm (6 in), of leaves to 25 cm (10 in), planting distance 23 cm (9 in).
C. speciosum has mauve flowers from early to late autumn. Height 15 cm (6 in) of leaves to 40 cm (16 in), planting distance 23–30 cm (9–12 in). There are several beautiful hybrids such as 'Atrorubens', purple-crimson: 'The Giant', large mauve, single, and 'Waterlily', large mauve, double.
PROPAGATION: by offsets or seed.

COLEUS *Labiatae* P, grown as HHA

Coleus are the most useful of plants, providing solid foliage colour for many months. They have been much debased by being used unimaginatively in municipal planting schemes, but do not let this undeserved past history prevent you from using them where summer-long colour is needed. They come in a rich range of colours that can be used with bedding plants, among other, quieter, contrasting foliage or to complement the border colour scheme. They should be planted with care, as they look sumptuous in the right place, but if dotted about at random they merely look silly.

These plants are sun-lovers and should never be planted in shade or they will get leggy. They need feeding with weak liquid manure each week, and must be lifted and brought into a warm greenhouse well before the frosts. The plants are usually too large to be used for a second year but they should be cherished in a winter temperature of not less than 13°C (55°F) so that fresh cuttings can be taken in early spring. They can be grown easily from seed but as the colours are generally labelled 'mixed', precise planting schemes cannot be planned.
C. blumei has amazing foliage in shades of scarlet, orange, pink, apricot, bronze, brown, maroon, purple, yellow and all shades of green. Height to 45 cm+ (18 in+), spread 30 cm+ (12 in+).

CONVALLARIA *Liliaceae* R

Not for sunny borders, lilies-of-the-valley should be grown in moist, humus-rich soil in the open or, best, in partial shade beneath tall trees. The scarlet berries are very poisonous.
C. majalis (lily-of-the-valley) has white

Geranium endressii

flowers in mid- to late spring. Height to 20 cm (8 in), spreading rapidly to 60 cm (2 in). *C.m.* 'Fortin's Giant' has larger flowers.
PROPAGATION: by division.

CONVOLVULUS *Convolvulaceae* A/P/S

This is a large and lovely family, though only three members of it are really suitable for the border. The tender shrubby *C. cneorum* has silver-metalled leaves that shine in the sun, but it needs cloche-protection in winter in all but the warmest areas. *C. sabatius* (*mauretanicus*) is a tender perennial, with long trails of blue-mauve flowers that twine charmingly through everything in its vicinity, though it may suffocate smaller, less vigorous neighbours.
C. cneorum has pink-throated white flowers from late spring to early autumn and beautiful foliage. Height to 60 cm (2 ft), spread 90 cm (3 ft). Very tender.
***C. sabatius* (*mauretanicus*)** has blue-mauve funnel-shaped flowers from early summer to early autumn. Height to 8 cm (3 in), spread to 90 cm (3 ft); a tender perennial.
C. tricolor has blue, pink, cerise or white flowers from mid-summer to early autumn. Height 30–38 cm (12–15 in), planting distance 15–20 cm (6–8 in). Best blue varieties are 'Royal Ensign', dark blue with a white centre, 'Deep Blue' and 'Sky Blue'.
PROPAGATION: by heel and basal cuttings and by seed.

COREOPSIS *Compositae* A/P

These are classic late-summer border flowers that are excellent for picking. Most of them are a very bright yellow.
C. tinctoria has yellow or yellow and brown or crimson flowers from mid-summer to early autumn. Height according to variety, 23–90 cm (9 in–3 ft), planting distance 13–38 cm (5–15 in). (Annual, sometimes still called 'calliopsis').
C. grandiflora (tickseed) has yellow flowers from early to late summer. Height to 45 cm (18 in), planting distance 23 cm (9 in). May need support.
C. verticillata has golden yellow flowers from early summer to early autumn and elegant dark-green ferny foliage. Height 45–60 cm (18–24 in), planting distance 30–45 cm (12–18 in). Beautiful in a group, but not near anything pink or lilac.
PROPAGATION: by seed and division.

CORYDALIS *Papaveraceae* P

The yellow corydalis grows all too easily in any garden soil or situation, though it is far greener and lusher in good soil (which it does not need) than it is in the desiccated dryness of a crumbling wall. But there are often poor places in a border where choicer plants will not thrive, and for these *C. lutea* is most effective, with its delicate maidenhair-like emerald foliage and yellow flowers. It self-sows readily.
C. lutea has tubular yellow flowers from mid-spring to mid-autumn. Height to 20 cm (8 in) and an increasing spread of 30 cm + (12 in +).
PROPAGATION: by division or seed.

COSMOS *Compositae* A

These colourful and quick-growing plants are most useful in summer with their large, single daisy flowers and finely cut dark foliage. They are good in hot summers and do well in light, poor soil.
C. bipinnatus (cosmea) has single flowers in all shades of pink, mauve, crimson, also white from mid-summer to early autumn. Height to 90 cm (3 ft), planting distance 60 cm (2 ft).
C. sulphureus has single or double flowers in yellow, orange or vermilion from mid-summer to early autumn. Height to 60 cm (2 ft), planting distance 45 cm (18 in).
PROPAGATION: from seed.

CRINUM *Amaryllidaceae* B

Crinums have handsome lily-like flowers on stiff and rigid stems, rising from

substantial strap-shaped leaves. They are best in warm areas and very sheltered gardens, being more generally grown in the greenhouse or as house plants in northern Europe. Protect well in winter if grown outside, and water well in summer.
C.* x *powellii has pink or white flowers from mid-summer to early autumn. Height to 45 cm (18 in), planting distance 30–45 cm (12–18 in) apart and 30 cm (12 in) deep.
PROPAGATION: from seeds or offsets.

CROCOSMIA *Iridaceae* C

Crocosmia and the closely related montbretia are excellent late-summer plants, with fire-coloured flowers and sheaves of light green foliage. They do well in sandy, well-drained soil and can be left to increase for several years. Water well in dry seasons.
C. masonorum has flame-red upward-facing flowers in mid- to late summer. Height 75 cm (30 in), planting distance 15–23 cm (6–9 in).
C.* x *pottsii has orange-vermilion flowers in late summer. Height 1.2 m (4 ft), planting distance 10–15 cm (4–6 in). 'Solfatare' has yellow flowers and golden-bronze leaves and is 60 cm (2 ft) tall. Not reliably hardy in cold areas.
PROPAGATION: by division in spring or after flowering.

CROCUS *Iridaceae* C

The true crocus has three stamens which helps to differentiate it from the colchicum which has six. Most crocuses are spring-flowering with narrow leaves with or after the flowers. Crocuses like to be well baked and many will set seed in the right conditions; leave undisturbed after flowering and do not plait, band, knot or cut off the corm's essential leaves with which it manufactures food. There are very many species and varieties to brighten the bare soil of the spring garden. Plant corms 5–8 cm (2–3 in) deep in average soil, deeper in light soils or where other plants are to grow over them in their dormant period.
C. tomasinianus (usually the first to bloom) has lilac, mauve, purple or white flowers from late winter to early spring. Height 8 cm (3 in), planting distance 8–10 cm (3–4 in).
C. aureus has golden-yellow flowers in early spring.
C. chrysanthus hybrids are 'Blue Pearl', pale blue outside and pearly-white within; 'Zwanenburg Bronze', golden-brown outside, yellow within; 'Ladykiller' with white-edged, purple petals and white inside. Other hybrids are: 'Pickwick', lilac and purple striped; 'Remembrance', large purple flowers; 'Cream Beauty', creamy-yellow.
PROPAGATION: by offsets or seed.

CURTONUS *Iridaceae* C

A larger 'Montbretia', curtonus has handsome pleated leaves with vivid flowers held well above them. They will do better in well-drained humus-rich soil. Remove flowered stems in autumn and leave foliage on in winter in cold areas.
C. paniculatus syn. ***Antholyza paniculata*** (Aunt Eliza) has orange-red flowers in late summer to early autumn. Height 1.2 m (4 ft), planting distance 23 cm (9 in).
PROPAGATION: by division of offsets or from seed.

CYCLAMEN *Primulaceae* T

Most cyclamen need a situation in dappled shade with well-drained humus-rich soil. They benefit from an annual mulch of leaf mould after leaves and flowers have disappeared. Their heart-shaped leaves are always attractive and those of some species are very beautiful, being zoned or patterned in green and silver.
C. coum syn. ***C. orbiculatum, C. vernum,*** has pink, carmine or white flowers from early winter to early spring. Height 8 cm (3 in), planting distance to 15 cm (6 in).
C. neapolitanum has pink or lilac flowers from late summer to late autumn though

this is variable. Height 10 cm (4 in), planting distance to 10 cm (4 in). (Marbled leaves disappear in summer.)
PROPAGATION: from seed.

DAHLIA *Compositae* T/A

Dahlias are tender plants whose tubers can only be left in the ground in warmer southern areas. They are propagated by placing the tubers in shallow boxes of moist sand and peat; leave crowns uncovered. Place these in a warm place and keep moist. The 'eyes' will be seen to swell, and the tubers can then be divided, making sure each piece has a good eye. Plant the cut tubers to 10 cm (4 in) deep in a rich compost (John Innes No. 2 or equivalent) and keep warm and moist. Plant out in warm settled weather when frosts are over, in that part of the border allocated to the dahlias, in ground that has been enriched with well-decayed manure in early spring.

Very many hybrids exist, in a wonderful range of colours and shapes. These have been divided for convenience into border dahlias (grown from tubers) and bedding dahlias which are grown as annuals from seed. The border dahlias are classified into the following groups: single-flowered, anemone-flowered, collarette, peony-flowered, formal decorative, informal decorative, show, pompon, cactus, semi-cactus and star. With this vegetable wealth to choose from it is best to decide on a shape (not too large) that is attractive and the height and colouration that suits that part of the border where the dahlias are to grow. It is, therefore, best *not* to go to a dahlia show—there will be too many to digest. The larger border dahlias almost always need strong stakes, so have these ready, and all of the same kind. Place the stakes in position before you plant the tubers, and keep the growing stems loosely tied to the stake or stakes as the plants develop. 'Stop' the main stem (to promote bushiness) a month after planting out. Border dahlias do not need feeding as this will encourage excessive leaf growth at the expense of flowers. Bedding dahlias are easier to grow, needing the same good soil but no stakes or 'stopping'. All need plenty of water, twice a day in warm seasons or areas. Dead-head regularly and watch for slugs, caterpillars, aphids and earwigs in the flowers. Lift the tubers after the first frost and store for the winter in a cool but frost-free place.
PROPAGATION: as described from tubers, or from seed for annual bedding varieties.

DELPHINIUM *Ranunculaceae* A/P

The word 'delphinium' conjures up an instant picture of tall blue spires which are hybrid descendants of the species plant that is seldom grown today. Delphiniums can be chosen to flower in every shade of blue, violet, mauve, pink, lilac and grey though there are now uncharacteristic yellow and red varieties. They are all as caviar to slugs, and the young plants must be protected from these pests by the most effective means until the stems lose some of their succulence in maturity.
D. ajacis (rocket larkspur) has blue or violet flowers from early to late summer. Height from 30–90 cm (12 in–3 ft), planting distance 15–25 cm (6–10 in).
D. consolida (larkspur) has denser spires of blue, violet, red, carmine, pink or white flowers from early to late summer. Height to 1.2 m (4 ft), planting distance 30–38 cm (12–15 in).
Delphinium hybrids derive from crosses between *D. elatum, D. grandiflorum* and others and are single or double-flowered, bicoloured and in heights from 20 cm (8 in) to 2.4 m (8 ft). These tall perennial varieties must be staked.
PROPAGATION: from seed, basal cuttings or division.

DIANTHUS *Caryophyllaceae* A/P

Pinks are almost as useful for their ever-grey foliage, though a border edged with an old variety such as 'Mrs Sinkins' in full bloom is one of the gardener's few rewards. Pinks need warm, free-draining limy soil. pH must not be below 6.5.

D. barbatus (sweet William) has sweetly scented single or double flowers in all tones of red, crimson and pink, often self- or white-zoned, in early to mid-summer. Height 30–60 cm (12–24 in), planting distance 20–25 cm (8–10 in). Grow as a biennial.
D. caryophyllus (border carnation) has perfumed flowers in every colour except blue. Height to 90 cm (3 ft), planting distance 35–45 cm (14–18 in). Tall kinds need staking, so it is best to choose shorter-growing self colours, which may need support from twiggy sticks. Short-lived.
D. chinensis (Indian pink) has bright flowers in all shades of red, crimson and pink, often zoned in white or silver, in mid-summer until the frosts. Height to 23 cm (9 in), planting distance 15 cm (6 in). Dead-head regularly. Annual.
Garden pinks are described as 'old-fashioned' or 'modern'.
Old-fashioned pinks have self, bicoloured or 'laced' single or double scented flowers in all shades of pink to crimson and white in early summer. Height to 25 cm (10 in), spread to 30 cm (12 in). These are slower-growing than the following.
Modern pinks which have similar flowers though they are more floriferous and often twice flowering in early to mid-summer and again in early autumn. These plants will need replacing every three years.
PROPAGATION: from cuttings, layers and seed.

DICENTRA *Fumariaceae* P

Dicentra spectablis is one of the most beautiful of garden plants, worthy of special care. It dies away in late summer so later flowering plants can be planned to spread into the space. It must have protection from hot sun, wind and slugs and appreciates humus-rich soil and an annual mulch of leaf-mould or compost. *D. eximia* is a pleasing plant and valuable for its long flowering season.
D. eximia has pink or white flowers from late spring to early autumn. Delicate green or grey ferny foliage. Height to 45 cm (18 in), planting distance 30 cm (12 in).
D. spectabilis (bleeding heart, Dutchman's breeches, lady-in-the-bath, lyre flower) has arching wands of pink and white 'lockets' in late spring to early summer. Height to 75 cm ($2\frac{1}{2}$ ft), planting distance 45 cm (18 in). Never move an established plant.
PROPAGATION: by seed or division.

DICTAMNUS *Rutaceae* P

An old-fashioned plant, taking some years to settle, dictamnus or the true 'burning bush' has aromatic foliage rich in volatile oils; the old flower heads have most of this and give off a nimbus which on warm still evenings can sometimes be ignited, like a Christmas pudding. Do not move established plants.
D. albus syn. ***D. fraxinella*** (burning bush) has white or, in *D.a.* 'Purpurea', pink and red flowers in early to mid-summer. Height to 60 cm (2 ft), planting distance 45 cm (18 in).
PROPAGATION: from fresh seed.

DIERAMA *Iridaceae* C

Dieramas are large plants in maturity, needing plenty of space in which to dangle their quivering, arching stems that are hung with bell-shaped flowers. The grassy leaves are saw-edged so are not always easy to site; they dislike disturbance. They do well in a well-drained soil with added humus.
D. pulcherrimum has wiry stems of pink to magenta flowers in early to mid-summer. Height to 1.8 m (6 ft), planting distance 60 cm (2 ft).
PROPAGATION: by seed or offsets.

DIGITALIS *Scrophulariaceae* Bi

Foxgloves can be chosen to complement different kinds of garden and colour schemes, having been developed from the one-sided stem of pendulous bell-shaped flowers to the almost exotic-looking modern hybrids with horizontal flowers in many colours. All like extra humus.

D. purpurea has 'foxglove-coloured' pink flowers in early to mid-summer. Height to 1.8 m (6 ft), planting distance to 60 cm (2 ft). White flower-seed is available separately. The 'Excelsior' hybrids have horizontal flowers all round the stem in white, cream, yellow, apricot, soft red, pink and maroon. Height to 1.5 m (5 ft). 'Foxy' has a branched stem of pink to purple flowers, grows 75 cm ($2\frac{1}{2}$ ft) high.
PROPAGATION: from seed.

DIMORPHOTHECA *Compositae* Tender P/A

These rather tender African daisy flowers are very beautiful, and also very vigorous in warm areas. They close up in mid-afternoon, or when the sun goes off them, and do not open on dull days. But as the backs of the petals are attractive too, all is not lost. They need very free-draining soil and protection from winter damp.

D. aurantiaca (star of the Veldt) has orange flowers with brown and blue metallic-looking central disks from early summer to early autumn. Height to 45 cm (18 in), planting distance 30 cm (12 in).

D. barberiae has white or pink petals and deep blue disks in mid- to late summer. Height to 60 cm (2 ft), planting distance to 90 cm + (3 ft +).
PROPAGATION: from seed.

DORONICUM *Compositae* P

The gay daisies of doronicum are freely borne and most attractive with late narcissus or tulips in the spring border. Protect emerging shoots from slugs and dead-head regularly. Tolerates some shade.

D. pardalianches (great leopard's bane) has bright yellow flowers from late spring to mid-summer. Height to 90 cm (3 ft), planting distance to 38 cm (15 in).

D. plantagineum (leopard's bane) has yellow flowers from mid-spring to early summer. Height to 60 cm (2 ft), planting distance to 45 cm (18 in). 'Miss Mason' is 45 cm (18 in) tall.
PROPAGATION: by division.

DRACUNCULUS *Araceae* T

This plant has a strong character, and is not to every gardener's taste. The spotted stems are sinister and the huge, evil-looking and even more evil-smelling flowers last for a maximum of three days before collapsing.

The leaves, however, are most attractive; when suited in a warm, dry border it will increase well and quickly. Lift clumps of tubers and space out every few years.

D. vulgaris (dragon arum) has large (to 60 cm (2 ft)) long maroon-purple spathes, a black spadix and a full-bodied stench in early summer. Height to 90 cm (3 ft), planting distance 23 cm (9 in), planting depth 15 cm (6 in).
PROPAGATION: by seed.

ECHINACEA *Compositae* P

This late-summer plant has magnificent and long-lasting flowers of an unusual metallic-looking mauve-pink which contrasts most agreeably with delicate thalictrums and blue-flowered veronicas and salvias. Protect emerging shoots from slugs.

E. purpurea (purple cone-flower) has large, shining dahlia-like pink flowers from mid-summer to early autumn. Height to 1.2 m (4 ft), planting distance 45–60 cm (18–24 in).
PROPAGATION: by division.

ECHINOPS *Compositae* P

Echinops has completely round and almost everlasting flower heads which make it most useful as a contrast in the border. Its stems are scratchy and unattractive, so these should be masked by other plants. Good with orange daisy flowers, magentas, purples or the soft furriness of yellow mulleins.

E. ritro (globe thistle) has spherical steely-blue flower heads from mid- to late summer. Height to 1.2 m (4 ft), planting distance 60 cm (2 ft).
PROPAGATION: by division or seed.

ENDYMION *Liliaceae* B

Bluebells for the border are most attractive, but they must be placed where oncoming plants will hide their long-lasting leaves. They will self-sow and hybridize and generally behave in a rather undisciplined manner, but as they thrive almost anywhere, in dry soil or damp, in full sun or semi-shade, they can be cajoled into beautifying awkward places in the border. As they mature they pull themselves down, so if they are to be moved do it whilst the clumps are still small and manageable. Never leave skinless bulbs uncovered for long.
E. hispanicus syn. ***E. campanulatus, Scilla hispanica*** (garden bluebell, Spanish bluebell) has almost upright stems of blue, lilac, pink or white bells from mid-spring to early summer. Height 30 cm (12 in), planting distance 15 cm (6 in), planting depth 10–15 cm (4–6 in).
PROPAGATION: from seed or division of offsets.

EPIMEDIUM *Berberidaceae* R

Often grown for their beautiful leaves, epimediums have delicate and interesting flower sprays that are best revealed by trimming away the previous season's foliage. Top-dress with leaf-mould in spring. The plants will slowly form large mats.
E. grandiflorum (bishop's hat) has white, yellow, pink or violet flowers in early summer. Height to 30 cm (12 in), planting distance 30 cm (12 in).
E. perralderianum has beautiful green and bronze foliage that changes to copper-colour in winter. Yellow flowers in early summer. Height 30 cm (12 in), planting distance 38 cm (15 in).
PROPAGATION: by division.

EREMURUS *Liliaceae* P

These plants are the monarchs of the border and worth every attempt to grow successfully. They have two drawbacks, their large starfish-like roots are very fragile and need great care in planting, and after flowering the eremurus disappears leaving a very large gap. This cannot be filled with anything else, as the roots lie just beneath the surface, so the surrounding plants should be chosen so that they grow up to hide, or fall into the space. Gypsophila will billow into it, *Rudbeckia laciniata* will grow up in front of it, many geraniums will be only too glad of the extra room, and clematis grow just as well (and more visibly) when horizontal. Mulch with well-decayed manure in autumn.
E. robustus (giant foxtail lily) has salmon-yellow 1.2 m (4 ft) columns of flowers in late spring and early summer. Height to 3 m (10 ft), planting distance 1.2 m (4 ft).
E. 'Shelford Hybrids' have pale pink, apricot and coppery-orange flower spikes in early to mid-summer. Height to 2.1 m (7 ft), planting distance 90 cm (3 ft).
E. stenophyllus bungei syn. ***E. bungei*** (foxtail lily) has golden-yellow flower spikes in early summer. Height to 90 cm (3 ft), planting distance 60 cm (2 ft).
PROPAGATION: by division or from seed.

ERIGERON *Compositae* P

These are useful and floriferous daisy flowers whose colours can be chosen to tone with or link others in the border. They do well in moisture-retentive soil. Dead-head often.
E. speciosus has lilac flowers from mid- to late summer. Height to 45 cm (18 in), planting distance 30 cm (12 in). Good varieties are: 'Darkest of All', violet-blue; 'Charity', light pink; 'Gaiety', bright pink; 'Prosperity', blue; 'Quakeress', pale mauve-pink.
PROPAGATION: by division.

ERYNGIUM *Umbelliferae* P

Eryngiums have thimble-like flowers with silvery, steely metallic-looking 'ruffs' or bracts. They are everlasting in the border and as cut flowers and are most useful as a contrast in shape.
E. alpinum has blue flower heads and

delicate feather-cut bracts from mid-summer to early autumn with greenish-blue basal leaves. Height to 60 cm (2 ft), planting distance 38 cm (15 in).
E. giganteum has silver-blue flower heads in late summer to early autumn. height to 1.2 m (4 ft), planting distance 60 cm (2 ft). Biennial.
E. variifolium has blue flower heads in mid- to late summer. Attractive dark green and white leaves. Height to 75 cm ($2\frac{1}{2}$ ft), planting distance to 30 cm (12 in). Evergreen.
PROPAGATION: by seed.

ESCHSCHOLZIA *Papaveraceae* A

These are excellent flowers to grow in a mass on poor, hot, sandy soils where they will thrive. Sow successively for continuous colour. Sow seed *in situ* and thin out; watch for slugs. The flowers close on dull or wet days.
E. californica (Californian poppy) has orange flowers from mid-summer to mid-autumn and lax pale green foliage. Height to 38 cm (15 in), planting distance 15 cm (6 in). Mixtures are obtainable with pink, red, yellow, white, crimson and carmine flowers.
PROPAGATION: by seed.

EUPHORBIA *Euphorbiaceae* P

Euphorbias make splendid border plants, though they dislike disturbance in maturity. Those mentioned here have conspicuous 'flowers' (in reality they are bracts) which remain attractive for the whole season. When cut, the stems exude a burning milky sap which can be dangerous to the eyes. They all need full sun.
E. griffithii has orange-scarlet bracts in late spring to early summer. Height to 75 cm ($2\frac{1}{2}$ ft), planting distance 60 cm (2 ft). This has wandering roots which send up new plants in a haphazard but attractive way.
E. myrsinites has lime-yellow bracts in early to mid-spring and glaucous-leaved trailing stems, much appreciated by slugs. Height to 15 cm (6 in), spread 38 cm.
E. wulfenii has lime-green inflorescences from late spring onwards. Height to 1.2 m+ (4 ft+), spread similar. *Must* have a hot and sheltered position. Best propagated from seed.
E. polychroma has bright acid-yellow bracts in mid- to late spring which later fade to green. Height to 45 cm (18 in), spread to 60 cm (2 in). Nice with white or yellow tulips.
PROPAGATION: by seed or division.

FESTUCA *Gramineae* P

Grasses make a pleasing contrast in shape and colour, especially the shorter blue-grey types which look interesting when grown with euphorbias and eryngiums. They need full sun, good drainage and no disturbance. Cut off the developing flower heads if the tufts of foliage are all that is needed.
F. glauca has purple spikelets in early to mid-summer and pleasing blue-grey foliage.
PROPAGATION: by seed or division.

FOENICULUM *Umbelliferae* P

Fennel makes a cloudy but solid mass of green or bronze hair-like foliage which is a good background for many border plants. The purple-bronze variety is the most attractive. Both are prolific seeders.
F. vulgare has umbels of yellow flowers in mid- to late summer and hazy green foliage. *F.v.* 'Purpureum' has purplish to mahogany foliage, very beautiful as a background to white flowers of distinct form. Both kinds taste the same but should not be used as flavouring if chemical sprays are employed. Height 1.5–2.4 m (5–8 ft), planting distance 30–60 cm (12–24 in).
PROPAGATION: from seed.

FRITILLARIA *Liliaceae* B

Fritillarias are not easy to establish but are worth every effort. The best way to have a good show is to replace bulbs annually, or to add more to those surviving.

Ipomoea purpurea (Morning glory)

Always try to obtain bulbs grown in the same country; imported bulbs are all right for the first year but seldom thrive thereafter. The stately *F. imperialis* likes heavy soil, and, when suited, should be left alone. Put a concealing group of uprushing, leafy plants in front of the fritillaria's yellowing foliage which will have disappeared by early summer.

F. imperialis (crown imperial) has clusters of large orange, rust-red or yellow hanging bells beneath the characteristic crown of leaves in mid-spring. Height to 90 cm (3 ft), planting distance 38 cm (15 in). Set the fragile hollow bulbs on their sides 23 cm (9 in) down on a bed of sharp sand for good drainage.

PROPAGATION: by seed and offsets from mature bulbs.

GAILLARDIA *Compositae* A/P

These bright, gay daisy flowers have a long season of bloom and associate well with other reds, yellows and oranges. To cool things down, plant grey foliage in front and tall white-flowering subjects behind or near by and keep away from pale pinks and lavenders. Taller kinds need twiggy support and all should be dead-headed regularly.

G. aristata syn. ***G.* x *grandiflora*** (blanket flower) has yellow and red flowers from early summer to mid-autumn. Height to 75 cm (2½ ft), planting distance 45 cm (18 in). Good varieties are: 'Goblin', yellow with red centre, 35 cm (14 in); 'Mandarin', flame-orange, 90 cm (3 ft); 'Burgundy', wine-red, 60 cm (2 ft).

PROPAGATION: by seed.

GALEGA *Leguminosae* P

These are tall and vigorous plants with light, attractive foliage. Needs support, but the general leafiness will hide this. Does well on poor soils.

G. officinalis (goat's rue) has pale lilac flower-sprays in early to mid-summer. Height to 1.5 m (5 ft), planting distance 75 cm (2½ ft).

PROPAGATION: by seed or division.

GALANTHUS *Amaryllidaceae* B

Snowdrops are usually the first flower in the spring garden, and are better when planted with other equally early flowers such as hellebores and violets to brighten part of a shady border. Once planted they should be left alone to increase. Buy them 'in the green' (just after flowering) as they will establish themselves more quickly than from purchased bulbs which may have dried out and died. They prefer a moisture-retentive rather heavy soil with plenty of added humus.

G. nivalis (snowdrop) has white and green flowers from mid-winter to early spring. Height 8–20 cm (3–8 in), planting distance 8–15 cm (3–6 in).

PROPAGATION: from seed and by division.

GALTONIA *Liliaceae* B

These lovely late-blooming bulbous plants have taller flowering stems rather like those of hostas. Slugs adore them also. They should be planted in groups in a good, humus-rich soil and they will then increase. Set them to flower against a dark background.

G. candicans (summer hyacinth) has white flowers from mid-summer to early autumn. Height to 1.2 m (4 ft), planting distance 18 cm (7 in), planting depth 15 cm (6 in).

PROPAGATION: by seed or division of offsets.

GAURA *Onagraceae* P

Gauras are unusual and graceful border plants with pale flowers. They are very easily grown from seed and flower in their first year, but it is best to keep one or two plants in a frame as reserves because they can be killed in bad winters.

G. lindheimeri has pink-toned white flowers from late summer until the frosts. Height to 1.2 m (4 ft), planting distance 40 cm (16 in).

PROPAGATION: from seed.

GAZANIA *Compositae* A

Gazanias are the brightest of bright flowers, usually in shades of dazzling orange, but the shapely flowers have great elegance because of the strongly contrasting dark central zone and black and white basal spots. They are very tender and survive better and longer in coastal gardens.

G.* x *hybrida has bright orange flowers from mid-summer until the frosts. Height to 23 cm (9 in), planting distance 30 cm (12 in), attractive dark green leaves with grey undersides. Mixtures include yellow, red, brown, crimson and pink flowers, all with strikingly contrasting dark zones.

G. splendens has orange flowers from mid-summer to early autumn. Height to 23 cm (9 in), planting distance 30 cm (12 in).

PROPAGATION: from seed.

GERANIUM *Geraniaceae* P

A useful and always beautiful genus which should have a place in every border. They are closely related but are not the same as the tender pelargoniums usually grown for containers or bedding out.

Geraniums have most attractive foliage, especially *G. endressii* and *G. macrorrhizum*, and this is an important asset when the flowers are gone. For even further neatness the clumps can be sheared over after flowering and they will then refurbish themselves with new leaves which will remain neat until late autumn. Most are deciduous, but *G. endressii* will remain pleasantly green in mild winters, and will grow and flower in partial shade, as will *G. phaeum*. Cut off flowering stems to encourage a second flush of flowers.

G. endressii has pink flowers from late spring to late summer. Height to 45 cm (18 in), planting distance or spread to 90 cm (3 ft). Good varieties are: 'Rose Clair', salmon-pink with purple veining; the hybrid 'Claridge Druce' has larger lilac-pink flowers.

G. ibericum has blue-purple flowers in mid- to late summer. Height to 60 cm (2 ft), planting distance or spread 45 cm (18 in).

G. macrorrhizum has pink or white flowers from late spring to mid-summer. Aromatic pale green leaves, delightful to handle. Height to 38 cm (15 in), spread to 90 cm (3 ft).

G. pratense (meadow crane's-bill) has deep blue flowers from early to late summer. Height to 75 cm ($2\frac{1}{2}$ ft), spread to 75 cm+ ($2\frac{1}{2}$ ft+). 'Mrs Kendall Clarke' has paler blue flowers. 'Johnson's Blue' has vivid blue flowers from early to late summer. Height to 38 cm (15 in), spread 75 cm ($2\frac{1}{2}$ ft).

G. psilostemon has black-centred magenta flowers in early to mid-summer. Height to 75 cm ($2\frac{1}{2}$ ft), planting distance 60 cm (2 ft).

G. sanguineum (bloody crane's-bill) has magenta flowers from early summer to early autumn. Height 23 cm (9 in), planting distance 45 cm+ (18 in+). A colourful trailer among and through taller plants. 'Album' is white.

G. phaeum (dusky crane's-bill) has small black-red flowers from late spring to mid-summer. Height to 45 cm (18 in), planting distance 60 cm (2 ft). Will grow in dryish soil in semi-shade.

PROPAGATION: by division of established plants and seed.

GEUM *Rosaceae* P

Geums are easy and attractive plants with weather-proof flowers. They should be planted in groups of five or seven for maximum effect. Divide plants in spring every third year, at the same time dig in compost or leaf-mould.

G. chiloense. Species seldom grown but varieties are 'Mrs Bradshaw', semi-double, red; 'Fire Opal', semi-double, orange-vermilion; 'Lady Stratheden', double, yellow. All grow to 60 cm (2 ft), planting distance 45 cm (18 in) and flower from early summer to early autumn).

PROPAGATION: by division of mature plants or seed.

GILIA *Polemoniaceae* P

These attractive and unusual annuals are 'different-looking' in the border and are very easy to grow. *G. capitata* has almost spherical flower-heads of a particularly pleasing misty blue that associates well with almost everything else. Good for massed planting.

G. capitata has almost round soft blue flower heads from early summer to early autumn. Height a lax 45 cm (18 in), planting distance 15 cm (6 in). Sow *in situ* and thin out.

G. tricolor has pale lilac flowers with maroon centres in early summer. Height to 60 cm (2 ft), planting distance 23 cm (9 in).

PROPAGATION: by seed.

GLADIOLUS *Iridaceae* C

Large-flowered, many-coloured gladiolus hybrids can be chosen to tone with all border colours and in addition there are attractive green-flowered varieties. That part of the border allocated to the gladiolus should be prepared by adding manure and bone-meal to the soil before setting out the corms from early to mid-spring. Plant 15 cm (6 in) deep in light soil, 10 cm (4 in) deep in heavy soil to prevent plants from falling over. When the shoots appear, add further fertilizer such as fish-meal. Do not overwater for the first eight weeks; after the flower spike has formed water well. If staking is necessary for the larger kinds, put the stake in behind the plant and secure as invisibly as possible. After flowering and when the foliage is yellowing, lift and dry off corms and store in a cool, frost-free place.

G. byzantinus has magenta or wine-red flowers in early summer. Height to 60 cm (2 ft), planting distance 10–15 cm (4–6 in). Hardy, and can be left in ground in all but the coldest areas to flower year after year.

PROPAGATION: by division of clusters of corms, or offsets.

GODETIA *Onagraceae* A

Godetias are colourful, compact 'bunches' of flowers at a useful height in the border. They are easy to grow and can be sown *in situ* and thinned out later. Best in a light moisture-retentive soil. Good with nigella or annual gypsophila.

G. grandiflora species is 30–38 cm (12–15 in) high, planting distance 15 cm (6 in). Many varieties available, with single or double flowers, and in single colours. Flowers from early to mid-summer.

PROPAGATION: by seed.

GYPSOPHILA *Caryophyllaceae* A/P

The perennial gypsophila enhances almost everything else in the border and is just as useful at the end of the season when dried for winter decor. It can be counted on to billow into spaces left by earlier plants such as eremurus and oriental poppies, and can be chosen to flower in pink or white. It is quite unique.

G. elegans has white or pink flowers from late spring to early autumn. Height to 60 cm (2 ft), planting distance 30 cm (12 in). Annual.

G. paniculata (baby's breath) has clouds of white or pink single or double flowers from early to late summer. Height to 90 cm (3 ft), spread 60–90 cm (2–3 ft). Thrives in limy soils.

PROPAGATION: by seed.

HELENIUM *Compositae* P

Useful and very attractive late-summer border plants, the red-to-mahogany shades are very good in the border, associating richly with purple, pale or dark blue. Dead-head after flowering and divide every third year.

H. autumnale varieties have flowers in all shades of yellow, orange, copper, mahogany and bronze-red from late summer to mid-autumn. Height to 1.8 m (6 ft), planting distance 45 cm (18 in). Many named varieties available.

PROPAGATION: by division or seed.

Lilium: Harlequin Hybrid

HELIANTHEMUM *Cistaceae* P

Rock roses make a sturdy and colourful edging to the border, each flower lasting for one day only. Cut back after flowering to keep neatly shaped, which will usually result in a second flush of bloom (if the weather is warm enough) in late summer and early autumn. Hard winters may kill them so it pays to have some young plants in reserve.
H. nummularium (rock rose, sun rose) flowers in early to mid-summer in a range of colours, with single or double flowers and green or grey foliage. Height 10–25 cm (4–10 in), spread to 60 cm (2 ft). The 'Ben' series are reliable: 'Ben Afflick' is orange-yellow; 'Ben Heckla' is bronze-gold; 'Ben Hope' is crimson-pink and 'Ben Nevis' is yellow with an orange centre and is smaller than the others. Other colours are white, yellow, red, crimson and pink. Grey-leaved varieties are 'Mrs Croft' with pink and orange flowers, and 'The Bride' with white flowers.
PROPAGATION: by cuttings.

HELIANTHUS *Compositae* A/P

Most sunflowers are tall and therefore best at the back of the border. *H. annuus*, with its giant flowers may be considered too large for most borders, as it needs equally solid companions to set it off and to hide the coarse foliage. This species must be strongly staked and responds to rich feeding.
H. annuus (sunflower) has huge yellow flowers with brown disks as much as 30 cm (12 in) across from mid-summer to early autumn. Height to 3 m (10 ft), planting distance 45 cm (18 in). A row of these plants never grows to an even height. Annual.
H. decapetalus has single, semi-double and double yellow flowers from mid-summer to early autumn. Height to 1.8 m (6 ft), planting distance to 60 cm (2 ft). Perennial.
PROPAGATION: by seed or division of well-established clumps.

HELICHRYSUM *Compositae* A/P

This is a useful genus, containing evergrey shrubs, and colourful annual 'everlastings' equally useful in the border or when dried for winter decor. All need free-draining soil and full sun.
H. angustifolium (curry plant) is a shrub with clusters of mustard-yellow flowers from early to late summer. Height to 45 cm (18 in), spread 60 cm (2 ft). Aromatic silver-grey foliage smelling of curry powder when bruised. Perennial.
H. bracteatum (strawflower) has everlasting flowers in yellow, red, pink, orange and white from mid-summer to early autumn. Height from 30 cm–1.2 m (12 in–4 ft) according to variety. Planting distance from 30 cm (12 in).
H. petiolatum is a tender shrub with inconspicuous flowers in late summer in warm seasons; grown for its very attractive trailing habit and silver-white felted foliage; branches can reach to 1.2 m (4 ft).
PROPAGATION: from seed or cuttings.

HELLEBORUS *Ranunculaceae* P

These are early flowering and handsome plants, long-lasting in the border. *H. orientalis* prefers semi-shade, whereas *H. corsicus* likes more sun. Both prefer good well-drained soil and benefit from an annual feeding after flowering.
H. corsicus syn. ***H. argutifolius***, has long-lasting apple-green flowers opening in early to mid-spring. Height to a lax 60 cm (2 ft), spread to 90 cm (3 ft). Evergreen leaves with prickly edges are very sculptural. It is likely to provide plenty of self-sown seedlings.
H. orientalis (Lenten rose) has greenish, pink, maroon, purple or white long-lasting flowers from late winter to early spring. Height to 60 cm (2 ft), planting distance 45 cm (18 in). Self-seeds when established, progeny does not come true. Leaves evergreen in warm districts.
PROPAGATION: by division of named clones or by seed.

HEMEROCALLIS *Liliaceae* P

The flowers of day-lilies last for one day only, but there are plenty of them when the clumps are well-cared for. They are long-lasting plants of a tough disposition which should not be abused as they sometimes are. Divide and replant clumps when they begin to flower less freely. They prefer a soil that is not too dry.
H. dumortierii has scented yellow flowers and brown buds from late spring to early summer. Height to 60 cm (2 ft), spread 60 cm (2 ft) with graceful arching pale green foliage.
Garden hybrids are 75 cm ($2\frac{1}{2}$ ft) high and should be planted 45 cm (18 in) apart, with single or double orange, yellow, maroon, pink or mahogany flowers from early to late summer.
PROPAGATION: by division.

HESPERIS *Cruciferae* P

This plant is short-lived and seed should be collected when ripe. It is scentless until about 5 pm, and then the scent becomes stronger and sweeter during the night, as it is pollinated by moths. It associates charmingly with blue aconitums. It will grow in semi-shade. Remove flower stems after flowering to prolong the life of the plant.
H. matronalis (dame's violet, sweet rocket) has white, lilac, mauve or purple night-scented flowers in early summer. Height to 105 cm ($3\frac{1}{2}$ ft), spread or planting distance 45 cm (18 in).
PROPAGATION: by seed.

HEUCHERA *Saxifragaceae* P

Heucheras are good edging plants, producing a froth of tiny flowers in various shades. The plants tend to 'heave' out of the ground after winter, so mulch them with leaf-mould or compost to provide them with a nourishing pillow on which to sit, or, every third year, lift, divide and replant firmly. Will flower in semi-shade.
H. sanguinea (coral flower) has stems of small coral-red bells from early summer to early autumn. Height to 30–45 cm (12–18 in), planting distance 45 cm (18 in). Good named varieties include 'Pearl Drops', white; 'Red Spangles', blood-red; 'Scintillation', pink; 'Sunset', bright red.
PROPAGATION: by seed or division.

HOSTA *Liliaceae* P

Hostas are plants for the shady border, with very beautiful foliage and attractive spires of white, lilac or mauve often fragrant flowers. They are best not planted in full sun where the leaves may scorch. They are exceedingly easy to grow, needing no special care apart from an annual mulch of compost or leaf-mould, though they will do better in good, humus-rich soil. The handsome deeply-veined leaves are often ruined by slugs and it is a constant struggle to prevent these pests from spoiling the plants. The foliage vanishes completely in winter. There are now very many new hybrids and introductions, best seen growing first.
H. elata has white to pale bluish-violet flowers in early to mid-summer. Height to 90 cm (3 ft), spread to 60 cm (2 ft). Dark green leaves.
F. fortunei has lilac flowers in mid-summer. Height to 90 cm (3 ft), planting distance 45 cm (18 in). Grey-green leaves. 'Albopicta' has mauve flowers and grows to 60 cm (2 ft), planting distance 45 cm (18 in) with yellow variegated green leaves, changing to green later. 'Aureomarginata' has white flowers and gold-edged green leaves.
H. lancifolia has lilac flowers from mid-summer to early autumn. Height and planting distance 60 cm (2 ft); narrow, glossy, plain green leaves.
H. sieboldiana syn. ***H. glauca,*** has whitish-mauve flowers in late summer. Height and planting distance 60 cm (2 ft). Mid-green, heart-shaped leaves. 'Elegans' has lilac flowers in mid- to late summer and blue-green leaves.
H. undulata has pale lilac flowers in late summer. Height and planting distance 60 cm (2 ft). The wavy, oblong, light

green leaves have broad white markings.
PROPAGATION: by division in spring.

HYACINTHUS *Liliaceae* B

The spring-flowering hyacinths can be planted to brighten the empty border in association with other spring bulbs, anemones, bellis, polyanthus and aubrieta. When they have flowered they should be carefully lifted and replanted where their foliage can die down naturally. (Annuals can be sown in the spaces left). The heavily scented double or single-flowered spikes can be chosen in shades of pink and blue as well as white, cream, primrose-yellow and red. Set bulbs 13–15 cm (5–6 in) deep, 15 cm (6 in) apart in full sun.
PROPAGATION: by seed.

IBERIS *Cruciferae* A/P

The lilac flowers of *I. gibraltarica* make a change from the starch-white ones of *I. semperflorens*, though, alas, the former is not reliably hardy, whereas the latter seems to be able to withstand long and very cold periods with perfect equanimity and is easily increased from cuttings. All do well on poor soils.
I. gibraltarica has lilac flowers in mid- to late spring. Height to 30 cm (12 in), spread to 45 cm (18 in). Not perfectly hardy but easily grown from seed.
I. sempervirens (perennial candytuft) has pure white flowers in late spring and early summer. Height to 23 cm (9 in), spread to 60 cm (2 ft). Dark evergreen leaves.
I. umbellata (annual candytuft) has flowers in all shades of pink, red and purple as well as white from early summer to early autumn (make successive sowings). Height to 38 cm (15 in). Planting distance 23 cm (9 in).
PROPAGATION: from seed or cuttings.

IMPATIENS *Balsaminaceae* A

Impatiens is an all-rounder of a plant, good indoors and out and brightly cheerful at the shadier end of the border, where it will flower endlessly until late autumn. All it needs is a regular liquid feed and copious watering at other times. It should not be grown in full sun. At the end of the season, select some of the better plants and bring them indoors to continue their lives as colourful house plants.
I. sultanii (busy Lizzie) has red, white, pink, purple, orange and carmine flowers from late spring until the frosts. Height to 60 cm (2 ft), spread similar. Hybrids can be grown in every colour with single or double flowers in heights from 23 cm (9 in) upwards, with a similar spread. Half-hardy perennial, grown as an annual.
PROPAGATION: from seed.

INCARVILLEA *Bignoniacea* P

These are exotic-looking plants with attractive foliage and flowers, which emerge from the soil on short stems among the unfolding leaves. All extend very quickly, with further flower stems emerging as the season goes on. There is absolutely nothing of the plant above ground in winter, so it is as well to mark the place. Best grown in groups, in rich soil. Mulch crowns with compost or peat in autumn.
I. delavayi has rich, pink trumpet flowers in late spring to early summer. Height to 60 cm (2 ft), planting distance 38 cm (15 in).
PROPAGATION: by division (difficult) or more easily from seed.

INULA *Compositae* P

Inulas grow larger and better in moist soil but will grow quite well in the average border, though they will not achieve the same height, which is perhaps just as well. They have very large leaves that can smother their neighbours and this should be taken into consideration when planning the border. Butterflies love them for their late-summer nectar.
I. hookeri has pale yellow daisies in late summer to early autumn. Height and spread to 60 cm (2 ft).
I. magnifica has brown buds opening to

golden-yellow daisies from late summer to early autumn. Height to 1.8 m (6 ft), spread 90 cm+ (3 ft+).
PROPAGATION: by division.

IRIS *Iridaceae* R/B

This is a large and always beautiful genus of which the best suited for life in a mixed border are the bearded irises (pogoniris) together with their many hybrid varieties in, literally, all the colours of the rainbow. These irises have been divided into dwarf, intermediate and tall sections and can be chosen to suit the size and aspect of the border. Some flower as early as mid-spring but their main flowering period is from late spring to late summer. Their general cultivation is similar, and the ground where they are to grow should be prepared first by digging in well-rotted manure or compost, with bone-meal added at a rate of 110 g per 0.84 sq. m (1 sq. yd). These irises do best in neutral to limy soils and are not successful in acid conditions.

The rhizomes should be only half-covered with soil, and should be set so that each gets the maximum amount of sun and is not too shielded by its neighbours (iris borders are best planned to face south, or north in the southern hemisphere). Water around, not on them, for the first three weeks if no rain falls. Trim off half the leaves of late-season plantings to minimize wind-rock. If frost lifts the rhizomes, do not press them down afterwards, build up a cushion of sand under them until the soil is right for resettling them. Try not to let other plants shade the rhizomes, and grow irises in groups for better impact and easier care. Watch for slugs, in damp weather especially, as these pests will damage rootstocks, foliage and flowers. Dead-head often. The sword-shaped leaves are an excellent contrast for other foliage and this is another reason for including them in a mixed border. These irises can be increased by dividing the rhizomes after flowering, the earlier the better to allow them to ripen before the winter. Each root-portion must have at least one and preferably two good leaf-fans. If the clumps are congested, discard central portions. Seed of these hybrids will not come true.
PROPAGATION: by division.

KNIPHOFIA *Liliaceae* P

These are plants with imposing characters, usually planted in groups as a focal point; the very tall kinds do not associate agreeably with gentle colours and smaller, softer plants. It may be better to site them at one end of a border as a dominant full-stop with appropriate foliage plants—tall grasses are good, also kochia, as buffers between these strong subjects and the rest of the border-dwellers. They have been divided for convenience into three groups according to height, and it will be found that the shorter kinds assimilate much more easily into a planting scheme. Ordinary free-draining soil suits them well and they will need plenty of water in dry summers until they are established. Cut dead flower stems off at base. In cold areas, tie up the remaining leaves over the crowns to protect them from the wet and surround the plants with a thick cover of bracken or straw during their first winter. The flowers are in all shades of red, orange, ivory, cream and greenish-cream; many have bicoloured flower spikes.

Group 1 is from 60–105 cm (2–3½ ft) tall, with a spread of 60 cm (2 ft). They flower in early to mid-summer and good varieties are: 'Alcazar', 90 cm (3 ft), orange; *K. modesta*, 60 cm (2 ft), ivory tipped with rose; 'Gold Else', 75 cm (2½ ft), yellow.

Group 2 grows to 1.5 m (5 ft), planting distance 60 cm (2 ft), flowering from early summer to early autumn. Many have pleasing broad, glaucous foliage. 'Bee's Lemon', 105 cm (3½ ft), lemon-yellow; 'Maid of Orleans', 75 cm (2½ ft), ivory-cream; 'Samuel's Sensation', 1.5 m (5 ft), scarlet.

Group 3 has shorter plants, to 75 cm (2½ ft) and flowers later from early to mid-autumn. *K. nelsonii major*, 75 cm (2½ ft), flame-red; *K. rufa*, 60 cm (2 ft), yellow,

tipped with red. These have grassy foliage.
PROPAGATION: from seed (of species only) or division.

KOCHIA *Chenopodiaceae* A

Kochia (burning bush) is exceedingly useful in the border with its fresh-coloured foliage that turns to brilliant colour in autumn. This should be taken into account when planting, and orange, red, purple or dark blue flowers will look good with both its colours. It grows into a disciplined oval-shaped plant. (Note: for the true burning bush, see *Dictamnus*.)
K. scoparia trichophylla (burning bush, summer cypress) has unnoticeable flowers in summer. Pleasing light green foliage, changing to autumnal tones. Height to 90 cm (3 ft), planting distance 60 cm (2 ft).
PROPAGATION: by seed.

LAMIUM *Labiatae* P

The lamiums do well in the shady end of the border. *L. galeobdolon* should not be allowed into a respectable border though it is very useful for poor, dry places in semi-shade. Shear over after flowering if required for ground cover.
Lamium galeobdolon 'Variegatum' syn. ***Lamiastrum galeobdolon*** (yellow archangel) has spikes of yellow flowers in early to mid-summer and silver-flashed evergreen foliage. Height to 30 cm (12 in), spread infinite. A very attractive plant but its runners are rapaciously invasive.
L. maculatum has pink flowers in late spring; *L.m.* 'Album' has white. Both have attractive variegated leaves; *L.m.* 'Aureum' has golden-yellow foliage and needs more shade and better soil.
PROPAGATION: by division.

LAMPRANTHUS *Aizoaceae* P

These brightly coloured flowers are only for the sunniest of gardens, and do even better in poor arid conditions which are not generally those of a good border. They can be grown as annuals or perennials, though are frost tender in the latter case. The flowers open only in full sun but are then shinily glorious, covering the foliage completely. All flower from early summer to early autumn.
L. aureus has flame-orange flowers 8 cm (3 in) across. Height 30 cm (12 in), spread to 45 cm (18 in).
L. spectabilis has magenta flowers, height 30 cm (12 in), spread 30 cm (12 in). Mixed species and varieties obtainable with flowers of amber, pale and darker pink, cerise, purple, red, yellow and white.
PROPAGATION: by seed and autumn cuttings.

LATHYRUS *Leguminosae* A/P

Annual sweet peas can be chosen to grow as tendril-less 38 cm (15 in) border plants or in the more traditional way on wires at the back of the border, or, to give height and interest in a large expanse, on trellis-tripods which can be shared with roses and honeysuckle. Sweet peas are greedy plants, needing well-manured soil to grow in.
L. latifolius (everlasting or perennial sweet pea) has pink to magenta flowers from early summer to early autumn. Height to 3 m + (10 ft +), planting distance 45 cm (18 in). 'White Pearl' has white flowers. Do not attempt to move established plants.
L. odoratus (sweet pea) has richly scented flowers in every colour except true yellow from early summer to early autumn. Height to 3 m (10 ft), planting distance 25 cm (10 in) for tendrilled climbers; to 38 cm (15 in), planting distance 38 cm (15 in) for new dwarf border varieties. Water daily in dry spells.
PROPAGATION: from seed.

LAVATERA *Malvaceae* A

The annual mallow is a surprisingly large and floriferous plant to come from seed in a season. It is excellent to grow whilst waiting for more permanent perennials, or in large pots, useful for later gap-filling.

L. trimestris syn. ***L. rosea*** has large, shining pink flowers from mid-summer to early autumn. 'Splendens Alba' is white. Height to 90 cm (3 ft), planting distance 60 cm (2 ft).
PROPAGATION: from seed.

LIATRIS *Compositae* P

These are unusual-looking plants whose flowers open from the top of the spike downwards. They provide an interesting contrast in shape.
L. callilepis (gayfeather) has carmine-pink flower spikes from mid-summer to early autumn. Height to 90 cm (3 ft), planting distance 45 cm (18 in). 'Kobold' is similar but smaller, 60 cm (2 ft) high; good on poor soils, though it appreciates feeding.
L. spicata has pink, purple or white flowers in early autumn. Height to 90 cm (3 ft), planting distance to 45 cm (18 in); does well in damp soils.
PROPAGATION: by division or from seed.

LIGULARIA *Compositae* P

A very striking plant, happiest in a bog-garden but tolerating a border if watered well twice daily or as soon as the leaves droop. Protect young foliage from slugs.
L. dentata syn. ***L. clivorum*** has large, shaggy orange daisies in mid- to late summer and handsome heart-shaped green leaves, with purple undersides and stems. Height to 1.5 m (5 ft) (in damp soil), planting distance 90 cm (3 ft). 'Desdemona' is an excellent variety.
L. przewalskii syn. ***Senecio przewalskii*** has tall black stems of yellow flowers in mid- to late summer. Height to 1.8 m (6 ft) (in damp soil), planting distance 75 cm (2½ ft).
PROPAGATION: by division or seed.

LILIUM *Liliaceae* B

Lilies are almost an essential in a herbaceous border, but some kinds need to be sited carefully as they dislike sun at the base of the stem, though the flowers should always be able to grow into the light. Cover is easily planned with earlier leafing perennials or low shrubs. Other species dislike lime, while a few (notably *L. candidum*) do well in full sun and a fairly alkaline soil. All appreciate annual mulching with leaf-mould, well-rotted manure or compost, in addition to peat. Water well in the growing season. Treat the scaly, fragile bulbs with care and plant about two and a half times the depth of the bulb. Lilies can be chosen to flower from early summer until the end of the season, and are obtainable in heights from 60 cm (2 ft) to 1.8 m (6 ft) or more. Colours are sumptuous, in every shade (except blue) with exotic spots and stripes or subtle satiny shadings. For specialist growers and exhibitors, lilies have been divided into nine divisions as follows: (1) Asiatic hybrids; (2) Martagon hybrids; (3) Candidum hybrids; (4) American hybrids; (5) Longiflorum hybrids; (6) Trumpet and Aurelian hybrids; (7) Oriental hybrids; (8) all hybrids not covered by these; and (9) all true species.

Slugs will damage bulbs, roots, stems, foliage and flowers. Lilies are prone to many diseases and it is better to buy good healthy bulbs (even if more expensive) from a reputable grower. Some good varieties and species are as follows.
L. auratum (golden-rayed lily of Japan) has huge scented white flowers with a gold bar and deep purple raised spots in late summer to early autumn. Height to 2.4 m (8 ft), planting distance 30 cm (12 in), planting depth 15–30 cm (6–12 in); lower stem needs shade.
L. candidum (madonna lily) has pure scented white flowers in early to mid-summer. Height to 1.5 cm (5 ft), planting distance 25 cm (10 in), planting depth 5 cm (2 in); lime tolerant, plant in sun.
L. henryi has pale apricot-yellow flowers with red spots in late summer to early autumn. Height to 2.4 m (8 ft), planting distance 30 cm (12 in), planting depth 20 cm (8 in). Ordinary soil, partial shade. May need staking.
L. regale (regal lily) has heavily scented white flowers with yellow throats and mauve-pink reverse in mid-summer.

Height to 1.8 m (6 ft), planting distance 30 cm (12 in), planting depth 15–23 cm (6–9 in). Full sun and ordinary soil. Almost the easiest to grow well.
L. tigrinum (tiger lily) has orange-red flowers, spotted black, from late summer to early autumn. Height to 1.8 m (6 ft), planting distance 23 cm (9 in), planting depth 15 cm (6 in). Lime-free soil in sun.
L. pumilum syn. ***L. tenuifolium*** has shining bright red flowers in early summer. Height to 1.2 m (4 ft), planting distance 15 cm (6 in), planting depth 10 cm (4 in). Ordinary soil in sun.
PROPAGATION: from seed (of species), bulbils or offsets.

LIMNANTHES *Limnanthaceae* A

This pretty, easy-to-grow plant has many virtues. It is bright and gay, lacks any kind of temperament, will grow in damp or dry soil so long as it has sun. It is attractive to bees and it self-sows in sufficient quantity to keep stocks going for the following season, though seedlings may need some protection in cold winters.
L. douglasii (poached egg flower) has scented white-edged yellow flowers from early to late summer. Height 15 cm (6 in), planting distance 10 cm (4 in).
PROPAGATION: by seed.

LIMONIUM *Plumbaginaceae* A/P

Limoniums can be annual or perennial but in either case the flowers are almost everlasting. *L. latifolium* is valuable in the late summer border with its hazy, gauzy cloud of tiny lilac-blue flowers; *L. suworowii* is interesting for the odd and sometimes contorted forms of the flower spikes, while *L. sinuatum* produces the well-known 'everlasting' flowers.
L. latifolium has cloudy panicles of lilac-blue flowers from mid-summer to early autumn. Height to 60 cm (2 ft), planting distance 45 cm (18 in). Perennial.
L. sinuatum (statice) has blue flowers from mid-summer to autumn. Height to 45 cm (18 in), planting distance 30 cm (12 in). Mixture seed with apricot, yellow, white, pink, carmine and mauve can be grown, or some individual colours. Annual.
L. suworowii (pink pokers) has tall and usually twisting stems of carmine flowers from mid-summer to early autumn). Height 45 cm (18 in), planting distance 30 cm (12 in). Annual.
PROPAGATION: by seed.

LINUM *Linaceae* A/P

The very blue flowers of flax on their delicate stems associate with almost everything else in the border equally pleasingly. Sow seeds of the perennial *L. narbonense* every other year to keep up stocks as cold winters can kill it.
L. flavum has yellow flowers from early to late summer. Height 45 cm (18 in), planting distance 23 cm (9 in). Perennial.
L. grandiflorum (scarlet flax) has deep rose-pink or crimson flowers from early to late summer. Height to 45 cm (18 in), planting distance 10–15 cm (4–6 in).
L. narbonense has blue flowers from late spring to early autumn in warm areas. Height 30–60 cm (12–24 in), planting distance 30 cm (12 in).
PROPAGATION: by seed.

LOBELIA *Campanulaceae* A/P

The annual lobelia is excellent for gap-filling, particularly when grown in more unusual pink or white forms. *L. fulgens* has fine purple foliage and brilliant flowers and makes a considerable impact in the border. It looks sumptuous grown with the ordinary purple-flowered tradescantia.
L. erinus (bedding lobelia) has flowers in blue, white or pink from late spring until the frosts. Height 10–23 cm (4–9 in), planting distance 10 cm (4 in). Half-hardy perennial, grown as an annual.
L. fulgens has brilliant scarlet flowers from late summer to mid-autumn and striking crimson-purple foliage. Height to 90 cm (3 ft), planting distance 38 cm (15 in). Protect from slugs. Half-hardy perennial.
PROPAGATION: by seed.

Narcissus 'King Alfred'

LOBULARIA *Cruciferae* P

This honey-scented annual can be set in some of the gaps left by lifted spring bulbs or over deeply planted, sleeping crocus whose dying foliage the plants will quickly conceal.
L. maritimum (sweet alyssum) has pink, white, lilac or purple flowers from early summer to early autumn. Height to 15 cm (6 in), spread 30 cm (12 in).
PROPAGATION: by seed.

LUNARIA *Cruciferae* Bi

Honesty is a vigorous plant that should be planted where its autumnal silver moons can be seen to advantage. It must also be sited where the jolly magenta of its flowers can harmonize with pinks, blue, purple or white, but preferably not with yellow.
L. annua syn. ***L. biennis*** (honesty) has scented magenta flowers from mid-spring to early summer. *L.a.* 'Variegata' has variegated foliage and paler, pinker flowers. Height to 90 cm (3 ft), planting distance 30 cm (12 in).
PROPAGATION: by seed.

LUPINUS *Leguminosae* P

Border lupins or lupines can be grown in a useful assortment of types—as groups of single-coloured plants, as the popular tall or dwarf Russell lupin which is always a bicolour, or as the shrubby perennial, *L. arboreus*, which has either pale yellow flowers in the type or can now be had in a mixture of colours. Lupins will last longer on light acid soils. Protect emerging foliage from slugs, and do not allow hybrids to flower in their first year.
L. arboreus (tree lupin) has scented pale yellow or white flowers from early to late summer. Height to 1.2 m (4 ft), planting distance to 90 m (3 ft). Do not count on it for more than three years. Mixture seeds can be grown for white, yellow, lilac or violet flowers.
L. polyphyllus hybrids, known as Russell lupins are bicoloured, in combinations of blue, white, cream, yellow, orange, pink, crimson, violet and lilac. They grow from 60–90 cm with a planting distance of 75 cm ($2\frac{1}{2}$ ft). Dead-head regularly. Garden-saved seed will not come true; these must be propagated vegetatively.
PROPAGATION: by seed or root cuttings.

LYCHNIS *Caryophyllaceae* P

The brightly coloured flowers of lychnis are not always easy to place in the border, though the soft grey flannel foliage of *L. coronaria* is a pleasing feature on its own. The brilliant scarlet of *L. chalcedonica* needs courage and the right companions to set it off, such as *Lobelia fulgens* and the deep violet of *Salvia superba.*
L. chalcedonica (Jerusalem cross) has very bright red flowers in mid- to late summer. Height to 90 cm (3 ft), planting distance 38 cm (15 in).
L. coronaria (rose campion) has soft silver-grey leaves and bright carmine-magenta or white flowers from mid-summer to early autumn. Height to 60 cm (2 ft), planting distance 20 cm (8 in). Short-lived; collect seed and build up replacement stocks every second year.
PROPAGATION: from division or seed.

LYSIMACHIA *Primulaceae* P

Lysimachia punctata is a brightly cheerful plant with invasive tendencies that will grow in dry or damp soil (preferring the latter), though it needs full sun. Its smaller relative, *L. nummularia* is even more obliging and is most attractive when grown to edge a path in sun or semi-shade, in dry soil or damp.
L. nummularia (creeping Jenny, moneywort) has yellow flowers in early to mid-summer. Height 4 cm ($1\frac{1}{2}$ in), spread to 60 cm (2 ft). *L.n.* 'Aurea' has yellow leaves.
L. punctata (yellow loosestrife) has similar yellow, cup-shaped flowers from early to late summer. Height to 90 cm (3 ft), according to soil, planting distance 30 cm.
PROPAGATION: by division.

LYTHRUM *Lythraceae* P

Purple loosestrife is no relation to the preceding plant, and though they both like the same sunny waterside conditions and they will both grow in ordinary soil, they look quite dreadful together.
L. salicaria (purple loosestrife) has red-purple or magenta flower spikes from early summer to early autumn. Height to 1.8 m (6 ft), planting distance 60 cm (2 ft). 'Robert' is rose-red and 'The Beacon' is deep rose-crimson.
PROPAGATION: by seed, basal cuttings for named varieties or division.

MACLEAYA *Papaveraceae* P

Macleayas are tall and stately plants, though not necessarily for the back of the border where their beautiful veined jade-green leaves might be hidden. Set them where the whole plant can be seen. Protect emerging shoots in spring.
M. cordata syn. ***Bocconia cordata*** has plumes of small white flowers from early to late summer. Height to 2.4 m (8 ft), planting distance 60 cm (2 ft).
M. microcarpa (plume poppy) has plumes of pale buff-apricot flowers earlier. Height to 2.4 m (8 ft), planting distance 60 cm (2 ft). This has invasive orange roots.
PROPAGATION: by division.

MALCOMIA *Cruciferae* A

Malcomia is for massed planting where its day-time fragrance can be appreciated. Sow successively for all-summer sweetness.
M. maritima (Virginian stock) has single but scented flowers of pink, mauve, white or crimson from early to late summer. Height to 20 cm (8 in).
PROPAGATION: from seed.

MALVA *Malvaceae* P

The easiest mallow for the border is *M. moschata* which comes into leaf early and flowers for a long period if dead-headed regularly. It is lax-growing but looks charming when its flower stems are straying among campanulas or tall blue salvia.
M. moschata (musk mallow) has satiny pink flowers from early summer to early autumn. Height to 60 cm (2 ft), spread 45 cm (18 in). *M.m.* 'Alba' is white and exceedingly pretty, with lighter green foliage.
PROPAGATION: from seed or basal cuttings.

MATTHIOLA *Cruciferae* A/Bi

The annual night-scented stock is a washy characterless flower by day. Mix the seed of the day scented and brighter-coloured Malcomia (Virginian stock) with it and sow together for a better appearance as well as round-the-clock perfume. They do well in rich, slightly limy soils; biennial plants may need some winter protection and a pinch of nitrogenous fertilizer in spring as a pick-me-up.
M. bicornis (night-scented stock) has rather weedy pink night-scented flowers in mid- to late summer. Height to 38 cm (15 in), planting distance 23 cm (9 in).
M. incana hybrids have flowers in white, cream, yellow, lilac, lavender, mauve, pink, rose, carmine, crimson, dark blue and purple.
Ten-week stocks grow from 30–75 cm (12 in–2½ ft). Half-hardy annual.
Perpetual-flowering or all-year-round stocks have double white flowers in spring. Height to 38 cm (15 in). Annual or biennial.
Brompton stocks have single or double flowers in 'stock' colours. Height to 45 cm (18 in). Biennial.
Trysomic stocks have double flowers in mixed colours seven weeks from sowing. Height 38 cm (15 in). Half-hardy annual.
PROPAGATION: from seed.

MECONOPSIS *Papaveraceae* P

The charming little *Meconopsis cambrica* (Welsh poppy) will grow anywhere and flowers for the whole summer. It self-seeds with abandon, seedlings can be

moved easily, second-year plants cannot. Does equally well in moist soils and semi-shade.
M. cambrica (Welsh poppy) has yellow or orange flowers from early summer to early autumn. Height to 30 cm (12 in), spread to 30 cm (12 in).
PROPAGATION: by seed.

MESEMBRYANTHEMUM
Aizoaceae A

This brightly coloured daisy flower makes a dazzling summer display along the dry edge of a hot border, providing the dead flowers are picked off daily. It will only open in warm or sunny weather, but the effect is like a million gaily-coloured parasols all opening simultaneously.
M. criniflorum syn. ***Dorotheanum bellidiflorus*** (Livingstone daisy) has zoned flowers in all colours except blue from early to late summer. Height 15 cm (6 in), planting distance 23 cm (9 in). The lemon-flowered variety 'Yellow Ice' is very attractive.
PROPAGATION: by seed.

MOLUCCELLA *Labiatae* A

An unusual rather euphorbia-like annual, the green flowers of moluccella provide shape and subtle colour in the border. The flowers are small and inconspicuous—it is the bell-shaped calyx that provides the main interest. The flower-stems are excellent when dried for winter arrangements.
M. laevis (bells of Ireland, shell-flower) has small white flowers in late summer and conspicuous whorls of green bracts. Height to 60 cm (2 ft), planting distance 23 cm (9 in).
PROPAGATION: by seed.

MONARDA *Labiatae* P

The mop-shaped scarlet flowers of bergamot have an interesting and distinctive shape and contrast well with all the daisies of summer. It does better in rich, moist soil and appreciates an annual feed of compost or old manure in spring. All parts of the plant are deliciously fragrant, so plant it where it can be pinched in passing. Slugs like it, too. If the scarlet flowers of the species are difficult to integrate, then choose from the other softer colours or white.
M. didyma (bergamot, Oswego tea) has scarlet flowers from early to late summer. Height to 90 cm (3 ft), planting distance 38 cm (15 in). Other varieties are 'Croftway Pink', rose-pink; 'Melissa', pale pink; 'Prairie Night', purple; 'Snow Maiden', white.
PROPAGATION: by division for named colours, or by seed.

MUSCARI *Liliaceae* B

The deep blue flowers of muscari are an essential part of the spring border, though they should be planted where their long-living foliage will be inconspicuous afterwards. Lift and divide clumps every three years.
M. botryoides (grape hyacinth) has spikes of blue, bell-flowers from early to late spring. 'Album' is white. Height to 15–20 cm (6–8 in), planting distance 8–10 cm.
PROPAGATION: by division of offsets or from seed.

MYOSOTIS *Boraginaceae* Bi

Myosotis is easily grown as an edging or to fill spaces, where it will perpetuate itself usefully for ever. Hard winters can kill the plants, so a reserve stock should be kept back in this event.
M. alpestris (forget-me-not) hybrids have distinctively blue flowers from mid-spring to early summer. Height to 20 cm (8 in), planting distance 15 cm (6 in).
PROPAGATION: by seed.

MYRRHIS *Umbelliferae* P

Myrrhis odorata, or sweet Cicely, is an excellent plant for all kinds of situations thriving in an unconcerned way in semi-shade, full sun, a sheltered site or a draughty corner. Look upon it as a substantial fill-in foliage or background plant

Nicotiana affinis (Tobacco flower)

rather than a true herbaceous border-dweller. Sweet Cicely comes very early into light green, lacy leaf and is often taken for a fern. It has pleasant though not striking heads of cow-parsley flowers that in turn form remarkable large black seeds. The leaves, pleasantly sweet smelling, are edible and are most generally used as a safe sugar-substitute by diabetics. It is an invaluable background plant in mid-summer, its leaves contrasting pleasingly with the bright colours of the herbaceous flowers.
M. odorata (sweet Cicely) has white flowers in late spring/early summer. Height to 90 cm+ (3 ft+), spread to 1.2 m (4 ft). It disappears completely in autumn.

NARCISSUS *Amaryllidaceae* B

Making a choice from the many species or varieties available is the hardest part of the narcissus cycle, and it is as well to make a list from the catalogues of names, colours and flowering times; they can beautify a barren two-to-three-month period in the border.

A fertilizer containing potash and phosphate should be dug or forked in before planting, and the bulbs should be set in holes that are three times their height. After flowering the leaves should never be knotted, plaited or cut off, but must be allowed to die away naturally (and, alas, untidily) to feed the bulb for the next season's flowers. Do not allow to dry out at this time. Narcissus have been divided into eleven groups for some sort of manageability, as follows: (1) trumpet daffodils; (2) large-cupped narcissi; (3) small-cupped narcissi; (4) double narcissi; (5) triandrus narcissi; (6) cyclamineus narcissi; (7) jonquilla narcissi; (8) tazetta narcissi; (9) poeticus narcissi; (10) species, wild forms and hybrids; (11) miscellaneous narcissi. A small selection follows listed by flowering time.
Late winter flowering: 'February Gold' (6), yellow, 30 cm (12 in); 'February Silver' (6), white petals, lemon cup, 30 cm (12 in); 'Tête-à-tête' (6), yellow, 15 cm (6 in); 'Peeping Tom' (6), golden-yellow, 40 cm (16 in).
Early spring flowering: 'March Sunshine' (6), yellow petals, orange trumpet, 30 cm (12 in); 'Pepper' (2), yellow petals, deep orange-red cup, 30 cm (12 in); 'Quince' (6), yellow, 18 cm (7 in); 'Rip van Winkle' (4), double green-yellow, 15 cm (6 in); 'Sweetness' (7), yellow, 35 cm (14 in); *Triandrus albus*, 'Angel's tears' (10), milk-white, 10 cm (4 in); 'Woodcock' (6), yellow, 30 cm (12 in).
Early to late spring flowering: Most 'garden' varieties (1) flower between early to late spring and are up to 45 cm (18 in) tall. 'Golden Harvest' is yellow; 'Mount Hood' is white; 'Fortune' has yellow petals and an orange cup; 'Ice Follies' (2) is white with a wide flattened cup; 'Yellow Cheerfulness' has one to three yellow flowers to a stem; 'Thalia' (5), exquisite pale cream petals, white cup; 'Geranium (8), pale cream petals, orange cup, two to three flowers to a stem.
Late spring flowering: 'Actaea' (9), white petals, yellow, scarlet-edged cup.
PROPAGATION: by division of offsets.

NEMESIA *Scrophulariaceae* A

Nemesias can be said to flower themselves to death and can be counted on for their bright and rather unusual blooms no matter how unpleasant the weather may be. They need light, rich soil and plenty of water; cut back after first flush and they will flower again. They benefit from fortnightly liquid feeds.
N. strumosa (poor man's orchid) has yellow, cream, white, purple, scarlet, crimson, orange and pink flowers with spotted throats from early to late summer. Height to 45 cm (18 in), planting distance 10–15 cm (4–6 in).
PROPAGATION: from seed.

NEPETA *Labiatae* P

This billowy grey-green plant with spikes of unassuming mauve flowers has always been a true border plant, long in flower, softening hard edges and associating

pleasingly with almost every other plant colour. Its only drawback is that it is an infallible magnet for cats, who will come from all points of the compass to roll in it and eat it down to the ground, so it may be impossible to grow successfully, which is infuriating, as it is an easy-tempered plant. Leave its stems on throughout the winter as cover for the roots, and do not tidy it up until mid-spring.
N.* x *faassenii syn. ***N. mussini*** (catmint) has blue-mauve flowers from late spring to early autumn. Height to 45 cm (18 in), spread 38 cm (15 in). 'Six Hills Giant' is about 60 cm (2 ft) high.
PROPAGATION: by division.

NERINE *Amaryllidaceae* B

Once established, nerines will go on flowering pinkly each year, but getting them into this state is not always easy. The long-necked bulbs need to be planted in a hot south-facing border against a wall and do best in free-draining soil. Give liquid feeds for two months or so when the leaves begin to grow; when they start to turn yellow cease feeding.
N. bowdenii (naked nannies) has brilliantly pink flowers on bare stems from early to late autumn. Height to 60 cm (2 ft), planting distance 15 cm (6 in), planting depth 15 cm (6 in).
PROPAGATION: by division of offsets or from fresh seed.

NICOTIANA *Solanaceae* P

Tobacco flowers are generally treated as annuals in the UK and provide rich night scent in the garden. The flowers hang, half-open, during the day but expand more fully during the evening and night. The leaves are sticky and so these plants are best not grown near dusty drives or roads.
N. affinis syn. ***N. alata*** (tobacco flower) has night-scented flowers from early summer to early autumn. Height to 90 cm (3 ft), planting distance 30 cm (12 in). Mixed colours of red, pink, maroon, crimson, white, lemon and cream can be obtained. The variety 'Lime Green' is an unusual colour (associating well with blue) and there are all-pink or all-red kinds from 30 cm (12 in) upwards.
PROPAGATION: by seed.

NIGELLA *Ranunculaceae* A

Soft blue flowers in hazy foliage make a charming grouping with iris, sweet-williams and pinks. When the flowers are over the expanded seed-heads are most attractive for winter arrangements. Nigella will regenerate from its self-sown seeds, if allowed, but fresh seed can be added to prolong the flowering season.
N. damascena (love-in-a-mist, devil-in-a-bush) has blue flowers from early to late summer. Height to 60 cm (2 ft), spacing 15 cm (6 in). Pink, mauve and white mixtures can be obtained. The variety 'Moody Blue' grows only to 20 cm (8 in) high.
PROPAGATION: by seed.

OENOTHERA *Onagraceae* Bi/P

Evening primrose has flowers of a pleasing, clear fresh yellow, very different to the many golden tones of late summer. Most flowers live for only half a day, and can be seen opening in the afternoon.
O. erythrosepala has dense spikes of clear yellow flowers from early summer to early autumn. Height to 1.2 m (4 ft), planting distance 38 cm (15 in). Biennial.
O. missouriensis has large clear yellow flowers from early to late summer. Height to 15 cm (6 in), spread to 45 cm (18 in). Must have space to trail into. Perennial.
O. tetragona has yellow flowers from early summer to early autumn. Height to 90 cm (3 ft), planting distance 30 cm (12 in). Foliage usually red or purple until flowering. Perennial.
PROPAGATION: by seed or division.

ONOPORDUM *Compositae* Bi

The Scotch thistle needs space in which to grow and is a sculptural plant for the white and silver garden. The leaves are at

their best in the first year. When the plant comes to flowering the leaves quite often become a dingy brown and the plants might just as well be removed at this time. It self-sows prolifically.
O. acanthium (Scotch thistle) has purple flowers in mid- to late summer. Height to 2.4 m (8 ft), planting distance 90 cm (3 ft) (best grouped closer for a more solid effect). Silver-felted, exceedingly prickly leaves are very handsome.
PROPAGATION: by seed.

ORIGANUM *Labiatae* P

The green-leaved species plant is an essential part of most Mediterranean cooking, and as such it is usually found in most herb gardens, however small. But the dwarfer, yellow-leaved form, *O. vulgare* 'Aureum' is a more ornamental plant for sunny situations, equally aromatic and just as good in soups, stews or stuffings. It thrives in hot sun and poor soil, but will not retain its golden colour in shade.
O. vulgare 'Aureum' (golden marjoram, yellow marjoram) has pink flowers from early to late summer. Height to 18 cm (7 in), spread to 60 cm (2 ft). It is deciduous.

PAEONIA *Paeoniaceae* P

These large plants need large borders to grow in, and after they have flowered there may be interesting seed-heads. The foliage is always beautiful. Peonies need gentle support or they will lie down in a huge circle like a circus tent. Proper 'peony-rings' are best and are almost invisible, stakes and string are not effective with these vast plants. In late autumn, cover the crowns with litter in cold areas, and give an annual feed of well-rotted manure or compost in mid-spring. Do not put other herbaceous plants too near peonies—they will disappear under their skirts; spring bulbs will flower timely and their leaves will be forgotten as those of the peonies grow larger. Peonies are very long-lived plants indeed, and dislike any kind of disturbance.
P. lactiflora has produced many beautiful hybrids such as 'Bowl of Beauty', semi-double, soft pink; 'La Cygne', double, pure white; 'Sarah Bernhardt', double, scented, pink; 'Solange', double, scented, creamy-buff fading to white. There are many others.
P. mlokosewitschii has exquisite pale yellow single flowers in mid- to late spring.
P. officinalis has crimson flowers in late spring to early summer. *P.o.* 'Rubra plena' is generally grown, with very double crimson flowers. Height to 75 cm (2½ ft), planting distance 90 cm (3 ft).
PROPAGATION: by division; plants may not flower for two years afterwards.

PAPAVER *Papaveraceae* A/P

Poppy petals look like creased taffeta and this is not surprising when the unopened bud is compared to the expanded flower. *P. orientalis* comes into leaf very early, often in mid-winter. These leaves grow floppily sideways afterwards, effectively preventing near-by plants from encroaching into their territory, and after flowering the whole plant vanishes, leaving a large empty whiskery gap in the border. This can be concealed by planting gypsophila on each side, rudbeckias and asters in front and encouraging large and late-flowering clematis to flow into the remaining space. These poppies have enormous and very deep roots and are difficult to move.
P. nudicaule (Iceland poppy) has single flowers in all shades or red, orange, yellow, pink, salmon, apricot and white from early to late summer. Height to 75 cm (2½ ft), spacing 30–45 cm (12–18 in). Annual, biennial or short-lived perennial.
P. somniferum (opium poppy) has either single or very double flowers in all shades of pink, mauve, crimson, red, lilac and white from mid- to late summer. Height to 90 cm (3 ft), spacing 30 cm (12 in). Biennial. Sow seeds thinly *in situ* and thin out.
Shirley poppies are the cultivated hybrids of *P. rhoeas,* with single or double flowers in all shades of red, pink, rose, crimson

and white from early to late summer. Height to 60 cm (2 ft), spacing 30 cm (12 in).
P. orientale (oriental poppy) has large single flowers of scarlet, red, orange, pink, or white in late spring to early summer. Height to 90 cm (3 ft), spread similar.
PROPAGATION: by division for *P. orientale* and by seed for the others.

PELARGONIUM *Geraniaceae* P

Zonal pelargoniums are tender plants needing warm greenhouse conditions in the winter. When hardened off, they can be planted out where their colours are appropriate; in emergencies they make excellent instant gap-fillers when planted pot and all. There are dwarf, medium- and tall-growing kinds with bright flowers in every shade of pink, red, purple, crimson, salmon and orange as well as white. Wet summers are cruel to them, especially the white-flowered kinds, causing the flower-trusses to turn brown on top.

The variegated-leaved types are particularly pleasing. Named varieties can be chosen from specialist catalogues, and these are worth preserving for another season, or cuttings can be taken in late summer, which, when rooted, will take up less bench-space in the greenhouse.
PROPAGATION: by cuttings.

PENSTEMON *Scrophulariaceae* P

Penstemons have attractive wands of foxglove-like flowers, and groups of them are a good shape in the summer border. They are not reliably hardy in cold areas and new growth can be killed by late frosts and chilling winds. Protect with litter and cloches for as long as needed.
P. barbatus syn. ***Chelone barbatus*** has pink to cerise flowers from early to late summer. Height to 90 cm (3 ft), planting distance 60 cm (2 ft).
P. hartwegii has bright scarlet flowers from early to late summer. Height 60 cm (2 ft), planting distance 30–45 cm (12–18 in). Hardier.
P. x gloxinioides hybrids have a great range of named varieties in scarlet, crimson, cerise and pink. Tender.
PROPAGATION: by cuttings of named varieties in autumn or by seed.

PEROVSKIA *Labiatae* P

This is an unusual and aromatic border shrub whose white stems enhance the violet flowers. For winter protection, leave summer stems on and cut down to within 45 cm (18 in) of the ground in spring. Good in arid conditions and coastal gardens.
P. atriplicifolia (Turkish sage) has small violet-blue flowers in late summer to early autumn. Height to 1.5 m (5 ft), planting distance 45 cm (18 in).
PROPAGATION: from cuttings.

PETUNIA *Solanaceae* P

Petunias are perennial plants in their native South America but are grown as half-hardy annuals in northern Europe. They do not like cold wet summers, and the larger, frillier ones suffer most—choose weather-resistant varieties where possible. Petunias are in flower from early summer until the frosts. Grow in ordinary, light well-drained soil; water well and do not feed. Dead-head regularly. Petunias generally come in mixed packets but it is possible to obtain F_1 varieties in single colours of white, pale pink, deep rose, scarlet, deep cream, golden-yellow and orange. Bicoloured varieties with white 'stars' are available, as are fully double kinds that look like carnations. The leaves are sticky, and light debris and dead insects will adhere to them so, as with tobacco flowers, do not grow them where there is dust. Watch for aphids and spray accordingly; dead-head often.
PROPAGATION: by seed.

PHACELIA *Hydrophyllaceae* A

These very blue flowers look almost like gentians, but only because of their wonderful colouration. They are attractive to bees and are good when grown with

purple violas and the silver-leaved *Convolvulus cneorum*. Protect from slugs.
P. campanularia has brilliant blue flowers from early summer to early autumn. Height to a lax 23 cm (9 in), planting distance 15 cm (6 in).
PROPAGATION: by seed.

PHALARIS *Graminiae* P

This grass makes an excellent contrast both in foliage colour and shape, but it is rampantly invasive and is best planted in an old bottomless bucket, like mint, otherwise it will engulf everything else in the border and creep out into the lawn.
***P. arundinaceae* 'Picta'** (gardener's garters) has purplish flower panicles in early to mid-summer and smartly striped leaves in cream and green. Excellent in association with bergenias and alchemilla. Height to 60 cm (2 ft), spread infinite. Confine rhizomatous roots in concrete.
PROPAGATION: by division.

PHLOMIS *Labiatae* P

This is an unusual and handsome plant to grow in a hot border, with dull evergreen leaves and tall flower-spikes that remain stiffly interesting after the actual flowers have faded. They are excellent for winter decoration. Cold, wet winters may kill newly divided plants, so do this in spring.
P. samia syn. ***P. russelliana*** has tall stems of whorled creamy-yellow flowers in early and mid-summer. Height to 90 cm (3 ft), spread to 60 cm (2 ft).
PROPAGATION: by division.

PHLOX *Polemoniaceae* A/P

The late summer flowers of *P. paniculata* are another border stand-by, and can be kept going by feeding and mulching annually in spring with well-rotted compost or old manure. Water well during dry periods, and divide old but healthy clumps in spring. Eelworm is a pest with these plants so propagation should be from root cuttings only. Burn infected plants and do not grow other phloxes in that place. The variety 'Norah Leigh' is very beautiful but being variegated it is weak-growing and easily lost.
P. drummondii has dense flower-heads in shades of pink, purple, mauve, crimson and white from mid-summer to early autumn. Height to 38 cm (15 in), planting distance 23 cm (9 in). Annual.
P. paniculata has dome-shaped flower-heads in pink, rose, mauve, scarlet, salmon, crimson, purple and white, often centrally zoned with lighter or darker tones, from mid-summer to early autumn. 'Norah Leigh' has variegated foliage and lilac-pink flowers. Height from 45 cm–1.2 m ($1\frac{1}{2}$–4 ft), planting distance 45–60 cm (18–24 in).
PROPAGATION: by seed, division or root cuttings.

PHUOPSIS *Rubiaceae* P

Phuopsis is a low-growing plant with attractive light green foliage. It is vigorous and looks well at the front of the border where it associates well with and scrambles among violet or blue flowers to great effect.
P. stylosa has pink 'pincushion' flower-heads in early to mid-summer. Height to 23 cm (9 in), spread to 60 cm (2 ft).
PROPAGATION: by division.

PHYGELIUS *Scrophulariaceae* P

These are beautiful plants whose rust or coral-red flowers have great distinction and delicacy. They are doubtfully hardy, and may succumb in bad winters but are always worth replacing and are quite easily grown from seed. They can be grown as wall shrubs but are more easily kept going by treating them as herbaceous plants; cut them back to ground-level in mid-spring. They do best in light soils.
P. aequalis has coral-orange tubular flowers from mid-summer to mid-autumn. Height to 75 cm ($2\frac{1}{2}$ ft), planting distance 60 cm (2 ft). This is more bushy than *P. capensis*.
P. capensis (Cape fuchsia) which has rust

or red flowers from mid-summer to mid-autumn. Height to 1.8 m (6 ft) (only against a wall). *P.c.* 'Coccineus' has bright scarlet flowers.
PROPAGATION: by seed or division.

PHYSALIS *Solanaceae* P

Chinese lanterns are wonderful in late summer, but until that stage they are like poor relations and best kept as hidden as possible, because their leafy growth and rather dull white flowers are not attractive. They do need their share of sun, so must be sited where something more exciting will distract the eye, but also where, in early autumn, the orange calyxes can harmonize with chrysanthemums and asters. Be ruthless with the running roots and chop them out with a sharp spade in autumn.
P. alkekengii (Chinese lantern) has undistinguished white flowers in mid- to late summer followed in early autumn by more rounded orange 'lanterns'. Height to 38 cm (15 in), spread to 60 cm + (2 ft +).
P. franchetii is similar, growing to 60 cm (2 ft) with a similar spread. *P.f.* 'Gigantea' is taller, to 90 cm (3 ft) with longer lantern-wands.
PROPAGATION: by seed or division of well developed clumps.

PHYSOSTEGIA *Labiatae* P

The 'obedient plant' is so called because when the flowers are gently pushed to one side they will stay there (their stalks are hinged). These are angular and rather rigid plants whose form and late flowering is most useful in the border. They are very easy to grow in moisture-retentive soil; they benefit from an annual spring mulch.
P. virginiana (obedient plant) has interesting pink, mauve or white flowers in mid- to late summer. Height from 75 cm–1.2 m ($2\frac{1}{2}$–4 ft), spread 60 cm (2 ft). 'Vivid' is deep pink; 'Summer Snow' is white; 'Summer Spire' is lilac-purple.
PROPAGATION: by division of well-established plants.

PLATYCODON *Campanulaceae* P

These are very beautiful flowers with fascinatingly inflated buds. The new season's growth resembles purple asparagus stems and should be protected from slugs. They dislike disturbance.
P. grandiflorum (balloon flower) has wide flat blue-mauve flowers from early to late summer. Height to 60 cm (2 ft), planting distance 38 cm (15 in). *P.g.* 'Album' is white. *P.g. mariesii* is less tall, to 38 cm (15 in), planting distance 30 cm (12 in). All are beautiful grown in association with thalictrums.
PROPAGATION: by seed.

POLEMONIUM *Polemoneaceae* P

Jacob's ladder is an easy plant which will grow in any soil, though in richer soils it will perform even better. Both species grown together are pleasing and even more so with pink *Malva moschata*.
P. coeruleum (Jacob's ladder) has blue or white flowers from mid-spring to mid-summer. Height to 60 cm (2 ft), spread 30 cm (12 in). Self-seeds prolifically.
P. foliosissimum has mauve-blue flowers from early summer to early autumn. Height to 90 cm (3 ft), planting distance 45 cm (18 in).
PROPAGATION: by seed or division of established clumps.

POLYGONATUM *Liliaceae* R

Solomon's seal is a graceful plant for the partially shady border, preferring humus-rich soil, though it will survive almost any conditions as long as the rhizomes are shaded from the sun. Watch for the larvae of sawflies which will skeletonize the leaves.
P.* x *hybridum (Solomon's seal) has arching stems with dangling white and green flowers in early summer. Height to 1.2 m (4 ft), planting distance 30–45 cm (12–18 in).
PROPAGATION: by division.

POLYGONUM *Polygonaceae* P

Most of this family are very vigorous, long in flower and often very handsome, especially when grown in large numbers.
P. amplexicaule has red flower-spikes from early summer until late autumn. Height to 1.2 m (4 ft), spread to 90 cm+ (3 ft+). *P.a. atrosanguineum* is the form most generally obtainable.
P. bistorta 'Superbum' (bistort) has pink pokers in late spring to early summer with a second crop sometimes following if stems are cut down. Height to 90 cm (3 ft), spread 90 cm (3 ft).
PROPAGATION: by division.

POTENTILLA *Rosaceae* P

These are bright, easy, long-lived border plants with attractive leaves. They benefit from an annual mulch of well-decayed manure or compost. Garden hybrids are the lax-growing 'Gibson's Scarlet', bright red, height 30 cm (12 in), planting distance 45 cm (18 in). Allow space for the stems to lie down in. 'Glory of Nancy' has semi-double, crimson to maroon flowers, height to 45 cm (18 in), planting distance 45 cm (18 in). 'Yellow Queen' has semi-double flowers, height and spread 38 cm (15 in). All flower from early summer to early autumn.
PROPAGATION: by division.

PRIMULA *Primulaceae* P

The best primula for the spring border is, of course, the polyanthus, a much-hybridized descendant of the wild primrose, *P. vulgaris.* Polyanthus always do better in moisture-retentive soil that has been organically enriched (preferably with old manure), with peat incorporated to preserve moisture and a further peat-mulch after planting. Named varieties or good colours should be divided immediately after flowering (or during, if you can be strong-minded enough) and replanted elsewhere to grow on; do not allow to dry out during the summer. The fine seed should be sown in a moist, peat compost and covered with sheets of glass or polythene to keep up the humidity level. One-colour seed-packets can be obtained, as well as the more usual mixtures, and flower heights can be chosen from stemless to a tall-stemmed, 23 cm+ (9 in+). The species *P. juliae* is a parent of the early-flowering and popular *P.* 'Wanda', which has intense violet-cerise flowers often from Christmas onwards. Height to 8 cm (3 in), planting distance 15 cm (6 in). This variety looks richly colourful with the blue of scillas and muscari.
PROPAGATION: by seed or division.

PRUNELLA *Labiatae* P

These appear to be rather 'quiet' plants with attractive heads of pink or purple flowers. They are low and mat-forming and do not mind being shaded by taller plants, but they are strong-growing and are unlikely to be smothered; when suited, in moisture-retentive soil, they can become invasive. Cold wet winters can kill them.
P. grandiflora (self-heal) has purple flowers from late spring to mid-autumn. Height 15 cm (6 in), spread to 45 cm (18 in).
P. webbiana has pink flowers from late spring to mid-autumn. Height 23–30 cm (9–12 in), spread 38 cm (15 in). 'Pink Loveliness' is pink; 'Loveliness' is lilac; 'Rosea' is rose-pink and 'Alba' is white.
PROPAGATION: by division.

PULMONARIA *Boraginaceae* P

Pulmonarias are best in good, moisture-retentive soil and partial shade, where their silver-spotted leaves show up more clearly and do not get scorched by the sun. The flowers are quietly attractive and in some species they change from pink to blue as they age. These plants associate very naturally with pink and blue endymion (bluebells).
P. officinalis (lungwort, spotted dog) has pink, purple and blue flowers on the same plant in mid- to late spring. White-

Polyanthus

spotted leaves. Height and spread to 30 cm (12 in).
P. saccharata has pink, changing to blue flowers in early to mid-spring and very handsome silver-spotted and blotched leaves.
PROPAGATION: by division.

PULSATILLA *Ranunculaceae* P

The silky-furred pulsatillas should be planted near the edge of the border so that they can be easily examined. They need good drainage and good soil, and, given these conditions, the clumps will increase in size and beauty.
P. vulgaris (Pasque flower) has amethyst flowers at Easter time—mid- to late spring, hence its name. Height and spread to 15 cm (6 in), but hybrids are much taller. 'Budapest' is reddish-purple; 'Rubra' is red.
PROPAGATION: by division or by seed.

PUSCHKINIA *Liliaceae* B

These early-flowering bulbs are a pleasing and distinctive pale blue, quite different to most other colours in spring. They are eyecatching when planted with the lime-yellow *Euphorbia myrsinites*.
P. scilloides syn. ***P. libanotica*** has pale blue flowers with a darker blue stripe on each petal from early to late spring. Height from 10–20 cm (4–8 in), planting distance 5–8 cm (2–3 in).
PROPAGATION: by ripe seeds or offsets.

PYRETHRUM *Compositae* P

See under *Chrysanthemum*.

RANUNCULUS *Ranunculaceae* T

The unreally-perfect poppy blooms of *Ranunculus asiaticus* look as though they are made of silk tissue. These are demanding plants needing rich soil and plenty of watering. The tubers should be lifted when the leaves begin to yellow, dried in the sun, then cleaned; store in a frost-free, airy place until planting time.
R. asiaticus has beautifully semi-double and double flowers in red, orange, yellow, pink and white from late spring to early summer or early to mid-summer, according to the mildness of the area. Height to 38 cm (15 in), planting distance 15 cm (6 in).
PROPAGATION: by separating tubers.

RESEDA *Resedaceae* A

Mignonette could not be called a pretty flower but its fragrance is sweet to both man and bee; it is best planted in the mass where space permits. It does better in rich, limy soil and is pleasing when planted with blue, orange or red flowers.
R. odorata (mignonette) has very sweet-scented greenish-yellow flowers with prominent orange stamens from early summer to mid-autumn. Height to 30 cm (12 in), planting distance 15–23 cm (6–9 in). 'Goliath' has larger, redder flower-spikes.
PROPAGATION: by seed.

RICINUS *Euphorbiaceae* A

Ricinus is a magnificent and quick-growing foliage plant, though not for picking as all its parts are poisonous. Grow in groups where the bronze or wine-coloured foliage will act as a focal point, or as a fine background to yellow, red and white late-summer daisy flowers, solidago or pink asters.
R. communis (castor-oil plant) has insignificant greenish flowers in mid-summer followed by spiky seed-pods. Height to 1.5 m (5 ft), planting distance 90 cm (3 ft). 'Gibsonii' has sheeny crimson foliage; 'Impala' has more prominent creamy flowers and seeds, bronze foliage and red stems.

Note: the large seeds are exceedingly poisonous; handle with gloves.
PROPAGATION: by seed.

RUDBECKIA *Compositae* P

Rudbeckias flower on and on until summer has gone, with a variety of gold-

yellow or red and yellow flowers. All the dark-centred types are called black-eyed Susans and all are easy to grow in good soil.
R. fulgida var. ***deamii*** has dark-centred yellow flowers from mid-summer to early autumn. Height to 60 cm (2 ft), planting distance 30 cm (12 in). Variety 'Goldsturm' has large, up to 13 cm (5 in), golden-yellow flowers with dark brown central cones from late summer to mid-autumn. Height to 60 cm (2 ft), planting distance to 60 cm (2 ft).
R. nitida (coneflower) has golden-yellow flowers with prominent green central cones from late summer to mid-autumn. Height to 2.1 m (7 ft), planting distance 60 cm (2 ft). Dead-head to prolong flowering, protect emerging foliage from slugs. 'Herbstonne' is the most popular variety.
PROPAGATION: by division.

RUTA *Rutaceae* P

The blue-leaved 'Jackman's Blue' is an excellent foliage plant for partially shaded (best) or sunny borders. Its unique coloration harmonizes with every colour of the spectrum and in every garden aspect; it is very easy to have too much of it. Prune this sub-shrub hard in mid-spring.
R. graveolens var. 'Jackman's Blue' has small yellow flowers in mid-summer and striking blue-grey foliage. Height to 60 cm (2 ft), planting distance 40 cm (16 in). Evergreen.
PROPAGATION: by cuttings.

SALPIGLOSSIS *Solanaceae* A

These delicate and exotic-looking flowers are set off better against quiet-toned foliage, where there is less to distract the eye from their pencilled petals. They need good soil to do well, a little discreet support and spraying against aphids.
S. sinuata (painted tongue) has scarlet, orange, yellow, lavender, pink and crimson flowers, yellow-zoned, and veined in self or constrasting colours from mid-summer to early autumn. Height to 60 cm (2 ft), planting distance 30 cm (12 in). 'Splash' is an F_1 hybrid that does better on poorer soil. 'Grandiflora' grows to 90 cm (3 ft).
PROPAGATION: by seed.

SALVIA *Labiatae* A/P

There are salvias to suit all tastes and all need full sun.
S. horminum is grown for its blue, pink or white-coloured bracts, which last throughout the season. Height to 45 cm (18 in), planting distance 20 cm (8 in). The flowers are insignificant. Single-colour or mixed seed is available. Annual.
S. splendens 'Salvia' has brilliant scarlet flowers from mid-summer until the frosts. Height to 38 cm (15 in), planting distance 25 cm (10 in). Also uncharacteristically but interestingly available in purple, pink, salmon and white. Annual.
S. virgata nemorosa syn. ***S.* x *superba*** has purple-blue flower-spikes from mid-summer to early autumn. Height and spread to 60 cm (2 ft). Rather tender; beautiful with pale pinks, pale yellow and cream or mahogany-red.
PROPAGATION: by seeds or division.

SAPONARIA *Caryophyllaceae* P

Saponaria officinalis is a flopping plant which is useful for covering gaps, though it will also indiscriminately cover other border plants. In late autumn (while its whereabouts can still be seen) ruthlessly chop round the main plant with a sharp spade and dispose of the surplus runners or it will pop up, rudely, from the middle of a much choicer plant.
S. ocymoides has rose-pink flowers from mid-summer to early autumn. Height 8 cm (3 in), spread 30 cm (12 in). Excellent for front edge of a border or to trail over a low wall.
S. officinalis (soapwort, bouncing Bet) has pale pink single or double flowers from mid-summer to early autumn. Height, a lax 90 cm (3 ft), spread considerable due to its loose growth.
PROPAGATION: by division.

SAXIFRAGA *Saxifragaceae* P

Most of this beautiful family can be classed as 'alpine' but varieties of *S. moschata*, the 'mossy' Saxifrage, make good evergreen border-edging, especially with spring bulbs, aubrieta and arabis.
S. moschata (mossy saxifrage) has cream or white flowers in mid- to late spring. Height to 8 cm (3 in), spread 45 cm (18 in). 'Atropurpurea' has red flowers; *S.* x 'Peter Pan' is clear pink; *S.* x 'Pixie' is 5 cm (2 in) high and spreads to 30 cm (12 in) with red flowers.
S. umbrosa syn. ***S.* x *urbicum*** (London pride) has delicate pale pink flowers in late spring. Height to 30 cm (12 in), spread to 45 cm (18 in). Best in partial shade in humus-rich soil. Leaf rosettes neat, attractive and evergreen.
PROPAGATION: by division.

SCABIOSA *Dipsaceae* A/P

Scabious are slender-stemmed, graceful flowers that truly belong in a herbaceous border, if only as a perch for butterflies. Good on limy soils (lime can be added in neutral areas). Dead-head regularly down to a joint to encourage continued flowering.
S. atropurpurea (sweet scabious) has long-stemmed crimson flowers from midsummer to early autumn. Height to 90 cm (3 ft), planting distance 23 cm (9 in). Mixture seeds of purple, cherry-red, salmon, pink, lavender, blue and white are available. Annual.
S. caucasica has blue-mauve flowers from early summer to early autumn. Height to 60 cm (2 ft), planting distance 45 cm (18 in). 'Clive Greaves' is deep mauve; 'Moonstone' is light blue; 'Moorheim Blue' is dark violet-blue.
PROPAGATION: by seed, basal cuttings or division.

SCHIZANTHUS *Solanaceae* A

This is another annual with exotic-looking flowers in wonderful colours. These are often grown in greenhouses though this type of seed is more expensive than that for outdoor plants, so check the wording on the packet. Grow in light, rich soil with added humus. Support taller kinds with twiggy sticks, and water well in dry periods, though do not over-do things.
S. pinnatus syn. ***S. grandiflorus*** (butterfly flower) has orchid-like flowers in rose, pink, crimson, purple, lilac, violet, salmon and amber from early summer to mid-autumn. Height from 15 cm–1.2 m (6 in–4 ft) according to type, planting distance 23–45 cm (9–18 in).
PROPAGATION: by seed.

SCHIZOSTYLIS *Iridaceae* R

Schizostylis are 'travelling' plants, and will move along a border to where they think the grass is greener. They are excellent for late-season colour and form, enduring the first frosts with fortitude and continuing to open their starry flowers in spite of the low temperatures. Water well in summer, divide and replant every three years. Protect as well as possible in winter in cold areas.
S. coccinea (kaffir lily) has scarlet flowers in mid- to late autumn. Height to 90 cm (3 ft), spread considerable. 'Major' is darker red; 'Mrs Hegerty' is pink and flowers earlier; 'Viscountess Byng' has pale pink flowers.
PROPAGATION: by division.

SCILLA *Liliaceae* B

The blue flowers of scillas follow closely behind the snowdrops and associate pleasingly with early dwarf narcissi, bellis and white anemone blanda. Do not plant the bulbs near or among the blue variety of this as the blues do not go well together.
S. siberica has intensely blue flowers in early spring. Height to 15 cm (6 in), planting distance 8–10 cm (3–4 in). 'Spring Beauty' flowers earlier and is an even better blue.
PROPAGATION: seeds or offsets.

Schizostylis coccinea 'Viscountess Byng'
(Kaffir lily)

SEDUM *Crassulaceae* P

Sedum spectabile is an attractive plant throughout the season, with pale jade-green leaves and matching flat flower heads that do not turn colour until early autumn. This plant should be grown in small groups and it looks particularly attractive near stonework. Both kinds are beloved by late butterflies.
S. spectabile (ice-plant) has pink-to-mauve flowers from early to mid-autumn. Height to 45 cm (18 in), planting distance 45 cm (18 in).
***S.* x** 'Autumn Joy' is taller, to 60 cm (2 ft), with pink flowers at first in early autumn, later turning to crimson and red-brown; these are good for winter arrangements.
PROPAGATION: by division.

SENECIO *Compositae* A/P

These silver-leaved plants are excellent as foliage among hot-coloured border flowers or elegant with blue, purple and white.
S. maritima syn. ***Cineraria maritima*** hybrids have undistinguished yellow flowers (best removed) and silver-white felted foliage. Both are surprisingly hardy, and though grown as annuals they will last for several seasons. 'Diamond' has deeply divided silver-white leaves; 'Silver Dust' has more dissected and even whiter leaves. Height to 60 cm (2 ft), planting distance 30 cm (12 in).
PROPAGATION: by seed.

SIDALCEA *Malvaceae* P

Sidalceas should be left alone to form fine clumps of delicate hollyhock-like flowers. They need a warm (but not too hot) position and good soil. They may perish in very cold winters, and will need discreet staking. Cut down after flowering to encourage secondary blooms.
S. malvaeflora has pink flowers from early summer to early autumn. Height to 1.3 m ($4\frac{1}{2}$ ft), planting distance to 60 cm (2 ft). 'Croftway Red' is a rich shining red 90 cm (3 ft) tall; 'Rose Queen' is 75 cm ($2\frac{1}{2}$ ft) tall and is rose-pink.
PROPAGATION: by division in spring.

SISYRINCHIUM *Iridaceae* P

This plant needs exceptionally sharp drainage, doing better in the gravel path beside the border than in the border itself. Simulate these conditions and it will thrive. The flowering stems are unusual in appearance and colour.
S. striatum has stems of creamy-yellow flowers in early to mid-summer. Height to 45 cm (18 in), planting distance 15–30 cm (6–12 in) and sculptural flat fans of leaves. One form has variegated leaves.
PROPAGATION: by seed or division.

SMILACINA *Liliaceae* R

An imposing plant for semi-shade, bearing fluffy flower panicles atop handsome leafy stems. It needs rich moisture-retentive soil to do well. The leaves turn to butter-yellow in autumn.
S. racemosa (false spikenard) has scented cream 10 cm (4 in) flower sprays in late spring to early summer. Height to 90 cm (3 ft), planting distance 60 cm (2 ft). Watch for sawfly larvae.
PROPAGATION: by division or seed.

SOLIDAGO *Compositae* P

Solidago is an essential part of the late-summer garden and the newer varieties are less prone to mildew. Given plenty of space, a group of the taller kinds looks like a fountain of golden rain. Good in poor soil.
S. canadensis (golden-rod) has sprays of golden-yellow flowers from late summer to mid-autumn. Height to 1.8 m (6 ft), spread to 90 cm+ (3 ft+). 'Golden Wings' is a good named variety.
Other hybrids are 'Goldenmosa', height to 90 cm (3 ft) with yellow terminal foliage and flowers; 'Golden Thumb' is 30 cm (12 in) high with softly rounded golden flower sprays.
PROPAGATION: by division.

STACHYS *Labiatae* P

The species of this genus most often grown is the flannel-leaved *S. lanata*, with or without flowers. The flowerless variety is not as constitutionally strong as the flowering kind, and a series of wet winters can deplete stocks almost to extinction, therefore regular propagation of this delightfully cosy plant is essential. It is subject to mildew.

S. lanata (lamb's ears) has tall spikes of mauve flowers in mid-summer which can be removed if they make the plant too tall. Height to 45 cm (18 in), planting distance 30 cm (12 in) or closer. Silver-white woolly foliage throughout the year makes it an excellent contrast or foliage plant. The variety 'Silver Carpet' has no flowers. Evergrey.

S. macrantha has spikes of rose-purple flowers from late spring to mid-summer. Height to 75 cm ($2\frac{1}{2}$ ft), spread to 38 cm (15 in).

PROPAGATION: by division.

TAGETES *Compositae* A

These bright marigolds provide reliable and unendingly cheerful colour throughout the season whatever the weather. All they ask for is a place in the sun and protection from slugs. Dead-head regularly.

***T. erecta* hybrids** (African marigold) has lemon, golden or orange flowers from mid-summer until the frosts. Height from 30–90 cm (12 in–3 ft), planting distance 20–45 cm (8–18 in).

T. patula (French marigold) has single or double flowers in lemon, golden yellow, orange, red, mahogany, brown, maroon and crimson from mid-summer until the frosts. Height from 15–36 cm (6–14 in), planting distance 20–30 cm (8–12 in).

PROPAGATION: by seed.

TELLIMA *Saxifragaceae* P

This quiet but beautiful-leaved foliage plant does better in semi-shade, though it will grow in an open border if the soil is moisture-retentive.

T. grandiflora has tall wands of tiny green bell-shaped flowers from mid-spring to early summer. Height from 45–60 cm (18–24 in), planting distance 45 cm (18 in). *T.g.* 'Purpurea' has bronze-purple leaves in winter.

PROPAGATION: by division or seed.

THALICTRUM *Ranunculaceae* P

These are very graceful, delicate plants, with masses of small-leaved foliage and tall stems of gauzy flowers. In autumn the ferny foliage turns to a pleasing yellow. They are best grown from seed as they resent disturbance of any kind. Tall kinds should be discreetly staked, taking care not to damage roots.

T. aquilegifolium has fluffy panicles of mauve flowers in early summer and blue-grey foliage. Height to 90 cm (3 ft), planting distance 45 cm (18 in). 'Album' is white.

T. dipterocarpum has sprays of tiny mauve flowers with cream anthers from early to late summer. 'Album' is white and very beautiful; 'Hewitt's Double' has mauve double flowers.

PROPAGATION: species by seed.

THYMUS *Labiatae* S

Excellent as border-edging, and strong enough, with its woody stems, to withstand the occasional foot, thymes can also be used as ground-cover for low-growing borders. They are not totally hardy and can be killed by cold, wet winters. Cut off dead flower heads to keep plants neat.

T.* x *citriodorus (lemon-scented thyme) has lilac flowers from early to late summer. Height to 30 cm (12 in), spread to 38 cm (15 in). 'Aureus' has yellow leaves; 'Silver Queen' is variegated: both may revert to green.

T. drucei syn. ***T. serpyllum*** has pink, white or mauve flowers from early to late summer; 'Coccineus' is crimson.

PROPAGATION: by division or cuttings.

TIARELLA *Saxifragaceae* P

These plants will carpet the shaded end of the border, with attractive foliage and spires of soft flowers. There are several species but of these *T. trifoliata* and *T. polyphylla* adapt to border life better than the others which need moister soil.
T. polyphylla has pink-tinged white flowers from early to late summer. Height to 60 cm (2 ft), planting distance 30 cm (12 in).
T. trifoliata has slender panicles of white flowers from early to late summer. Height to 50 cm (20 in), planting distance 30 cm (12 in).
PROPAGATION: by seed or division.

TIGRIDIA *Iridaceae* C

These astonishing and exotic-looking flowers should be planted where their neighbours do not conflict in interest in any way. They need a warm and sunny border with rich, well-drained soil but should not be allowed to dry out; water well in hot weather. Tigridias are tender and should not be set out before the end of April and they should be lifted and brought in before the frosts. The flowers last for one day only but there are usually about six or more to a stem.
T. pavonia (tiger flower, peacock flower) has crimson, scarlet, orange, yellow or white flowers consisting of three large unmarked petals and three smaller brown, crimson or red-spotted petals spreading from a spotted, saucer-shaped central base. They are in bloom from mid-summer to early autumn. Height to 60 cm (2 ft), planting distance 10 cm (4 in). 'Alba' is white; 'Red Giant' is very red and 'Rubra' is orange-red.
PROPAGATION: by division of offsets.

TOLMIEA *Saxifragaceae* R

This is a very useful plant for almost any situation, though it prefers semi-shade. It has attractive and interesting foliage, with young plantlets being produced on the leaves, hence its common name. The flowers are undistinguished.
T. menziesii (pick-a-back plant) has greenish-rust whiskery flower-spikes in early summer. Height to 60 cm (2 ft), planting distance 40 cm (16 in). *T.m.* 'Variegata' has most attractive dappled cream and yellow-green foliage which lights up shaded corners (not for sunny borders).
PROPAGATION: by pegging down stem with leaf and plantlet, or by detaching these and setting in seed compost.

TRADESCANTIA *Commelinaceae* P

Tradescantias do well and flower longer in moisture-retentive soil, but can be grown in ordinary conditions with extra watering. They have interesting three-petalled flowers, and the ordinary purple kind looks particularly rich when associated with the many colours of Shirley poppies. Protect young foliage from slugs.
T. virginiana syn. ***T.*** x ***andersoniana*** (spider flower, Trinity flower) has purple, blue or white flowers from early summer to early autumn. 'Blue Stone' has blue flowers; 'Isis' is royal blue (good near agapanthus and red and purple fuchsias) and 'Osprey' is white with a blue centre. Height 60 cm (2 ft), planting distance 45 cm (18 in).
PROPAGATION: by division.

TROPAEOLUM *Tropaeolaceae* A

Nasturtiums are excellent plants for quick gap-filling, where they will bush out well and remain in flower until the first frosts. The trailing kinds are not to be recommended as their heavy skeins of leaves and flowers will suffocate smaller plants. Choose the modern hybrids with blooms held well above the foliage. They will flower better in poor, hot soil. Watch for aphids and the larvae of the cabbage white butterfly.
T. majus (nasturtium) has red, yellow or orange flowers from early summer to early autumn. Height from 25–38 cm (10–15 in), spread or planting distance

38 cm (15 in). 'Alaska' has striking green and white marbled foliage and is only 20 cm (8 in) high. Half-hardy annual.
PROPAGATION: by seed.

TULIPA *Liliaceae* B

Tulips prefer warm, free-draining alkaline soil, and in these ideal conditions will remain floriferous for many years. In reality, they usually flower well in the first year and then come up 'blind' or flowerless in successive seasons. Try planting the next batch more deeply, to 23–30 cm (9–12 in), except on heavy soil where depth should not exceed 15 cm (6 in). In acid soil, add lime at a rate of 85–115 g (3–4 oz) per 0.84 sq. m. (1 sq. yd). Set out bulbs in late autumn and leave foliage and stems unmolested to feed the bulbs until the leaves yellow, then lift and dry. Clean off and store until planting time in an airy place, with regular checks against mice and mould; always destroy mouldy bulbs as these can infect healthy stock.

Tulips can be had to flower from early to late spring and are excellent to give colour among the emerging herbaceous plants. Cut off heads when the petals fall and protect early-flowering kinds from slugs.

Tulips have been divided into 15 sections and some good varieties to grow are as follows.

Group 1, single, early: flowering mid-spring, 15–38 cm (6–15 in) high, planting distance 15 cm (6 in). 'Pink Beauty', pink; 'Bellona', yellow; 'Keizerskroon', red and yellow; 'Diana', white.

Group 2, double early: flowering mid-spring, 30–38 cm (12–15 in) high, planting distance 15 cm (6 in). 'Marachal Niel', yellow; 'Schoonoord', white; 'Electra' cherry-red.

Group 3, Mendel: flowering mid- to late spring, 38–50 cm (15–20 in) high, planting distance 15 cm (6 in). 'Athleet', white; 'Van der Eerden', red.

Group 4, Triumph: flowering mid-spring, 50 cm (20 in) high, planting distance 20 cm (8 in). 'Garden Party', pink-edged white; 'Pax', white; 'Dreaming Maid', white-edged pink; 'Orange Wonder', brilliant orange.

Group 5, Darwin hybrids: flowering mid- to late spring, 60–75 cm (2–2½ ft) high, planting distance 20 cm (8 in). 'Apeldoorn', red; 'Gudoschnik', yellow, spotted and lightly flamed red.

Group 6, Darwin: flowering late spring, 60–75 cm (2–2½ ft) high, planting distance 20 cm (8 in). 'Clara Butt', salmon-pink; 'La Tulipe Noire', maroon-black; 'The Bishop', violet-mauve; 'Niphetos', pale yellow.

Group 7, lily-flowered: flowering mid-spring, 45–60 cm (18–24 in) high, planting distance 15 cm (6 in). 'Arkadia', yellow; 'Queen of Sheba', red with yellow edges; 'White Triumphator', white.

Group 8, cottage: flowering mid- to late spring, 90 cm (3 ft) high, planting distance 15–20 cm (6–8 in). 'Artist', green-edged pink; 'Dillenburg', orange; 'Mrs John T. Scheepers', yellow; 'Viridiflora', green.

Group 9, Rembrandt: same height, size and flowering time as Group 6. 'Absalon', yellow, brown and crimson; 'May Blossom', cream and purple.

Group 10, parrot: flowering mid- to late spring, 45–60 cm (18–24 in) high, planting distance 20 cm (8 in). 'Black Parrot', dark purple; 'Blue Parrot', blue-mauve; also 'Orange Parrot', 'White Parrot' and 'Red Parrot'.

Group 11, double late: long-lasting flowers in mid-spring, 45–60 cm (18–24 in) high, planting distance 15 cm. 'Brilliant Fire', scented, red; 'Eros', scented, white; 'Gold Medal', deep yellow.

Group 12, *T. kaufmanniana* hybrids: flowering early to mid-spring, 10–25 cm (4–10 in) high, planting distance 8–15 cm (3–6 in). 'Johann Strauss', cream, white and red: 'Shakespeare', yellow, salmon and red; 'The First', pale yellow, blood-red throat, flushed red exterior.

Group 13, *T. fosteriana* hybrids: flowering mid-spring, 30–45 cm (12–18 in) high, planting distance 15 cm (6 in). 'Easter Parade', yellow; 'Cantata', red; 'Princeps' syn. 'Red Emperor', red; 'Purissima', cream.

Group 14, *T. greigii* hybrids: maroon-veined foliage. Flowering time, mid-

spring. 'Red Riding Hood' scarlet, 'Pandour' red-white. Height 23–30 cm (9–12 in), plant 15 cm (6 in) apart.
Group 15, species including *T. kaufmanniana* (water-lily tulip) flowering from early to mid-spring, white, flushed red and yellow; *T. tarda,* flat star-shaped yellow and white flowers, five to a stem in early spring. Height 15 cm (6 in), planting distance 8 cm (3 in). *T. turkestanica* has cream, white and green flowers, sometimes nine to a stem, in early to mid-spring. Height to 25 cm (10 in), planting distance 10 cm (4 in).
PROPAGATION: from offsets.

VERATRUM *Liliaceae* P

It is rare to see a well-grown clump of these stately plants with their broad, ribbed leaves, because slugs are as partial to these as they are to those of hostas. *Note:* The roots are very poisonous.
V. album has long, dense sprays of small greenish-white flowers in mid-summer. Height to 1.2 m (4 ft), planting distance 38 cm (15 in). Beautiful foliage.
V. nigrum has spikes of tiny blackish-red flowers in late summer. Height to 1.2 m (4 ft), planting distance 45 cm (18 in).
V. viride has sprays of green-yellow flowers in mid-summer. Height to 2.1 m (7 ft), planting distance 60 cm (2 ft).
PROPAGATION: from seed or division.

VERBASCUM *Scrophulariaceae* Bi/P

Verbascums have a very characteristic shape and their tall and tapering flower stems, with striking crimson-maroon stamens—good with *Ricinus communis*—make an interesting silhouette in the border. Many of them have white-felted or silvery foliage. Cut off finished flower-spikes to encourage secondary flowering.
V. bombyciferum has yellow flower-spikes in early to mid-summer with silver stems and leaves. Height from 1.2–1.8 m (4–6 ft), planting distance 45–60 cm (18–24 in). This softness is good with blue-toned spiky plants such as eryngium.
V. chaixii has soft yellow flowers in mid- to late summer and woolly white foliage. Height from 90 cm–1.5 m (3–5 ft), planting distance 45 cm (18 in). *V.c.* 'Album' is white. Good against dark backgrounds.
V.* x *hybridum varieties are generally tall and flower from early to mid-summer. 'C. L. Adams' is deep yellow, height 1.8 m (6 ft). The 'Cotswold' collection are about 1.2 m (4 ft) high with flowers in purple, orange, pink and maroon. The pink-to-red shades can look rather like sidalcea, so grow other colours if this is already in the border. 'Gainsborough', has lemon-yellow flowers and grey leaves.
PROPAGATION: by root cuttings from named varieties and seed for species.

VERBENA *Verbenaceae* A/P

Verbenas have neat and attractive flowers in many colours at various levels, and there is one for every part of a sunny garden. They are best in their first year from seed when this is sown early enough. Dead-head regularly, water well in dry periods and give weak liquid feeds.
V. bonariensis has tall, rather bare stems of rosy-lavender flowers from early summer to mid-autumn. Height 1.2–1.5 m (4–5 ft), planting distance 60 cm (2 ft). Plant to come up through loose-growing leafier plants or shrubs. Perennial.
V.* x *hybrida syn. ***V. hortensis*** are the jolly bedding verbenas that flower from early summer until the frosts. Height to 45 cm (18 in), planting distance 30 cm (12 in). (Peg the outside stems down to make denser ground cover.) Many very bright forms exist which need care in placing. It may be better to plant the more dazzling shades elsewhere in the garden.
PROPAGATION: from seed and division.

VERONICA *Scrophulariaceae* P

Veronicas are generally rather a quiet genus with flowers in all shades of blue, which blend with or form good backgrounds to other plants. No border should be without a group of at least one of them. They appreciate enriched, well-drained soil.

V. exaltata has 23 cm (9 in) spikes of pale blue flowers in mid- to late summer. Height to 1.5 m (5 ft), planting distance 60 cm 2 ft). Beautiful with rose-pink, soft orange or pale yellow.
V. gentianoides has pale blue flower-spikes in late spring to early summer. Height to 40 cm (16 in), planting distance 23 cm (9 in). *V.g.* 'Variegata' has cream and green leaves with similar flowers.
V. incana has 15 cm (6 in) blue flower-spikes from early to late summer. Height to 40 cm (16 in), planting distance 25 cm (10 in).
V. spicata has pale, medium or dark blue flowers from early to late summer. Height from 15–45 cm (6–18 in), planting distance 15–30 cm (6–12 in). 'Crater Lake Blue' is ultramarine, 'Pavane' is pink and 'Alba' is white.
PROPAGATION: by division.

VINCA *Apocynaceae* P(S)

Though many vincas crawl about at ground level they are botanically classed as shrubs. The more vigorous kinds are best not planted anywhere near the border, but the many forms of *V. minor* are early and long flowering, evergreen, and very colourful in semi-shaded areas.
V. minor (lesser periwinkle) has amethyst-blue flowers from early spring to mid-summer. Height to 10 cm (4 in), spread to 1.2 m (4 ft). 'Alba' is white; 'Albo-plena' has double white flowers; 'Aurea-variegata' has yellow-variegated leaves with blue flowers; 'Burgundy' is wine-red; 'La Grave', deep blue-purple.
PROPAGATION: by division or layering.

VIOLA *Violaceae* A/P

Violas, pansies, violets—all are closely related and all are regarded with deep affection even by non-gardeners. At least one, if not more, will make a charming addition to the front of the border. *V. labradorica* establishes easily and self-seeds; it makes an interesting foliage contrast with its year-round purple leaves. *V. odorata*, the sweet violet, is better in semi-shade, as is *V. cornuta*. The many hybrid descendants of *V.* x *wittrockiana*, the garden pansy, merely ask for good, well-drained soil with some shade. Dead-head constantly to encourage continuous flowering. When sowing seed do not allow compost to dry out; named varieties need vegetative propagation.
V. cornuta has angular-petalled lavender-blue flowers in early to mid-summer. Height from 10–30 cm (4–12 in), spread to 40 cm (16 in). 'Alba' is white. Short-lived perennial.
V. labradorica has small blue-mauve flowers in mid- or late spring. Height to 13 cm (5 in), spread to 40 cm (16 in); chiefly remarkable for its purple-toned foliage. Quite unfussy as to conditions though the leaves lose colour in shade. Perennial.
V. odorata (sweet violet) has scented purple, mauve or white flowers from late winter to early spring. Height to 15 cm (6 in), spread to 30 cm (12 in). Perennial.
V. tricolor (heartsease) has bicoloured yellow or cream and purple-to-blue flowers from late spring to early autumn. Height from 5–15 cm (2–6 in), spread to 23 cm (9 in). Self-seeds. Annual.
V.* x *wittrockiana (garden pansy) has larger, up to 10 cm (4 in), flowers in every colour. Most grow to 15 cm (6 in) and spread to 30 cm (12 in). They are in flower from late spring to early autumn. Single-colour packets can be obtained and one of the most exciting is 'King of the Blacks' which is a velvety black shot with purple. Grow it next to an all-white variety for maximum impact.
PROPAGATION: from seed or basal non-flowering cuttings.

ZANTEDESCHIA *Araceae* R

When grown in a warm border, arum lilies should not be planted deeper than 10 cm (4 in) when young. The plants must be very well protected in winter by mounding the crowns with peat or ashes and finally with bracken. Though evergreen in their native South Africa, they will lose their leaves in UK gardens. Given a series

of mild winters they will put down deep roots. Water and feed copiously during the growing season.
Z. aethiopica syn. ***Richardia aethiopica*** (arum lily) has waxy white spathes in late spring or early summer. Height to 90 cm (3 ft), planting distance 90 cm (3 ft). *Z.a.* 'Crowborough' is the hardiest form.
PROPAGATION: by division.

ZINNIA *Compositae* A

There are many types of zinnia for the border, from neat, bushy little plants only 18 cm (7 in) high to stately plants of 75 cm ($2\frac{1}{2}$ ft). Such rigid plants as these need careful placing in the border and their neighbours need to have enough character to harmonize with them. Choose the colour, shape and height first; zinnias can look like marigolds, dahlias, chrysanthemums, gaillardias or scabious but of these it is better to grow zinnias that look like zinnias.

They need a rich, well-drained sunny patch of soil and as they cannot abide root disturbance, they must be pricked off into small pots to grow on and then planted out most carefully in early summer. Pinch out tops to promote bushy plants and dead-head regularly.
Z. elegans has a very large colour range—everything except blue—and many forms. Flowering is from early summer until the frosts. An unusual colour is the lime-green dahlia-flowered 'Envy'.
PROPAGATION: by seed.

6

Shrubs, Roses and Climbers

Shrubs

The shrubs that often form part of the background and some of the backbone of the border should, on the whole, be rather unobtrusive as it is, after all, mainly a border for herbaceous plants: the shrubs are there for extra support. It may be desired to have low-growing evergreen shrubs at intervals throughout the border, especially in a formal one. One of the easiest and hardiest is *Buxus sempervirens* (box) which can be easily clipped into appropriate neatness; this is best done in late summer to early autumn. There are several forms to choose from, including blue-toned or variegated according to the requirements of the situation, and all are slow-growing.

The evergreen species of elaeagnus are handsome background shrubs to set against fences; they grow fairly quickly, are wind-resistant and provide solid green (or variegated) backgrounds. *Elaeagnus pungens* is the plainer sister, effective where green only is required. *E.p. maculata* has leaves that are centrally splashed with daffodil-yellow, which when seen in the mass is very cheering especially in late winter, but this may be too 'busy' for a background plant except in a green and gold border. Both achieve a height and spread of 1.8–3.6 m (8–12 ft), though *E.p. maculata* is slower-growing and more tender.

The distinctive pale apple-green leaves of *Griselinia littoralis* make a very attractive background shrub, though it may be found to be tender in colder areas. It is much used for hedging and screening in coastal gardens, and flower-arranging friends will only be too glad of your prunings because the leaves are an attractive texture, shape and colour. There is a variegated type, *G.l.* 'Variegata', which is less hardy.

The hebes (formerly known as veronicas) are another large group of pleasant evergreens for mild or coastal districts. They are also very floriferous in their season, and the flowers can form part of a colour scheme. There are many types and forms

Late summer flowers give essential vitality to the garden: pentstemons, *Phlox paniculata,* oenothera and campanulas.

A wall is a perfect background for sun-lovers, with the raised bed adding another valuable dimension. Dianthus, (pinks) sedums, iris and verbena enjoy warmth and good drainage.

such as the well-known variety *Hebe speciosa* 'Autumn Glory', with purple flowers and a height and spread of about 90 cm (3 ft) and 'Alicia Amhurst' with fine purple flowers. The latter grows to 1.2 m (4 ft) or so with a similar spread, according to the area. *H. speciosa* 'Simon Deleaux' has rich crimson flowers and is smaller, with a neat, rounded habit of growth. The variegated hebes are even more tender, though very suitable for certain positions because of their attractively coloured foliage.

Choisya ternata (Mexican orange) has attractive, glossy evergreen foliage arranged in trifoliate sprays which is aromatic when crushed. This is a good-looking shrub in its own right, growing to a rounded shape some 1.8 m (6 ft) high and wide eventually, with orange-blossom scented flowers in mid- to late spring or early summer.

Viburnum davidii is another handsome evergreen, with large, dark green deeply veined leaves. It grows to a convenient 90 cm (3 ft) but may spread to some 1.5 m (5 ft). It has neat clusters of pink-white flowers in early summer and sometimes a plant will be almost continuous-flowering. It is dioecious and if certified male and female plants are grown together the most beautiful sapphire-blue berries will be produced in late autumn which will last on the bush all winter. They are amiable shrubs and will stand being pruned back if they grow over-large but it is better to recognize that they will grow to a good 1.5 m (5 ft) in width and to plant them (or not) accordingly.

The olearias (daisy-bush) are a group of attractively leaved evergreen shrubs that cover themselves with scented white daisy flowers in early to mid-summer or late summer according to the type of ground. They are somewhat tender in cold areas and the variety *Olearia macrodonta* is almost hardy, with glossy, silver-green holly-like leathery leaves. It grows to 3.6 m (12 ft) with a spread of 2.4 m (8 ft) in time and flowers in early to mid-summer. *O. haastii* is lower but wider growing, to 2.4 m (8 ft) with a spread of 3 m (10 ft). It has glossy, ovate, mid-green leaves, and flowers in mid- to late summer. It is useful in town gardens, because it accepts urban pollution and carries on flowering despite it.

For gardens on acid soil there are many dwarf or slow-growing rhododendrons that will start the season off well with their colourful blooms, often very large for the size of the plant.

Potentilla fruticosa is a compact shrub, growing to an eventual height of 1.2 m (4 ft) with a spread of about 1.5 m (5 ft), though it can be kept smaller by shortening the flowered growths at the end of the summer and by cutting harder back in spring (it flowers better and longer when left unpruned). The small, neat leaves are a pleasing pale green and the shrub would be valuable for these alone without the unceasing ebullience of flowers produced from early summer to mid-autumn. The single yellow-flowered forms are more vigorous and generally more floriferous; there are tangerine-, red-, pink-, white- and cream-flowered varieties to fit in obligingly with colour schemes. It is deciduous.

The spiraeas are another group of shrubs that can be planted to bloom in summer with the border plants, or varieties can be chosen that flower on bare branches in early spring, thus producing cut flowers and blossom at that time. Such a one is *Spiraea thunbergii* with clusters of white flowers in early spring. It grows to some 1.8 m (6 ft) with a spread of about 2.4 m (8 ft). After the flowers the leaves are quietly attractive, forming a good solid green background to the border plants. *S.* x *bumalda* (the variety 'Anthony Waterer' is most generally grown) has neat, mid-green leaves and corymbs of long-lasting rose-coloured flowers in late summer. Its branches should be left on during the winter and cut hard back in March; this will keep it to an annually similar size and shape of about 90 cm–1.2 m (3–4 ft) by 1.2–1.5 m (4–5 ft).

Berberis make usefully solid (but prickly) background shrubs though they are all deciduous. Most have decidedly yellow to orange-red flowers in spring and this should be remembered when planning spring colour schemes (good with bluebells, which will grow up through the base of the shrub). *B. darwinii* grows to 3 m (10 ft) with a similar spread, and is very good as hedging, standing moderate clipping well. It will have bloomy-blue berries in summer. *B. thunbergii* is not as tall, growing to 1.2 m (4 ft) with a spread of about 1.8 m (6 ft). This has a rounded outline with pale yellow flowers in spring; followed by small, jewel-like scarlet berries and brilliant autumn coloration. This species has several usefully dwarf varieties, such as *B.t. atropurpurea* (already mentioned), *B.t.* 'Minor' growing to 13 cm (5 in) only, and *B.t.* 'Rose Glow' with purple leaves that are mottled with silver-pink and rose-pink. *B.t.* 'Aurea' has yellow leaves, gradually changing to pale green in late summer and is more tender.

Lavandula (lavender) is a traditional border shrub, often being used as a neatly clipped corner-piece or 'full stop'. Flowers can be had in pink and white as well as very pale or very dark 'lavender' colours, and for small gardens several low-growing types exist such as *L.* 'Nana Alba' growing to 38 cm (15 in), *L. nana atropurpurea* growing to 60 cm (2 ft) with a similar spread. *L. vera* (Dutch lavender) grows to 45 cm (18 in) with an eventual spread of 90 cm (3 ft), and *L.* 'Folgate' grows to 45 cm (18 in) and the same across. Lavenders should be clipped to shape in spring, and the dead flower stems removed in late summer, at the same time lightly trimming the plant. If they have grown large and sprawling, never cut them down into the old wood, they will not regenerate; instead discard the plants and start again. The pleasing grey-green of the bushes is a gentle foil to the soft colours of old roses, with blue and white iris and catmint to complete the harmony.

Rosmarinus (rosemary) is not an elegant shrub, nor can it ever be tamed to tidiness. But it is so much a part of older gardens in times gone by that it, too, should have a place in the border. The flowers come at odd times in the year (for no particular reason), though most plants flower mainly in the spring. Others that I know of, with a determined contrariness, begin to bloom in October and continue on and off through the winter. There are several tall-growing kinds: *R. officinalis* grows to 2.1 m (7 ft) with a spread to 1.8 m (6 ft); there are also very useful dwarf or really prostrate varieties such as the blue-flowered *R.o. prostratus* 'Severn Sea' which is no more than 15 cm (6 in) tall but spreads to some 90 cm or 1.2 m—very useful for the front of a border or near a seat. The taller sorts have flowers in light mauve, pale blue, dark blue and white.

Most of the grey- and silver-leaved shrubs were dealt with

The delicate pale colours in this border look even more beautiful against old stone walls and elegant ironwork. Phlox, lavateria, *Chrysanthemum maximum* (Shasta Daisy) and tradescantia.

Contrasting silver foliage heightens colour interest: *Artemisia ludoviciana* (Turkish sage) with alliums and alstroemerias.

more appropriately in Chapter 4, pages 32–38, though I did not mention *Ballota pseudo-dictamnus* which has heart-shaped, felty-furry grey-green leaves that are delightful to touch. In addition, the plant produces whorls of perfect miniature dolls' hat-flowers that look as though cut out of pale green suede. Ballota is quite weatherproof during the summer months, but may succumb in cold wet winters. If it does, get another (unless you have taken sensible 'insurance' cuttings during the previous year) because there is nothing quite like it for textural and visual charm. It grows to about 60 cm (2 ft) with a similar spread. One last grey shrub is *Phlomis fruticosa* (Jerusalem sage) which has light grey-green, rather woolly leaves and striking soft yellow flowers in whorls in early and mid-summer. It grows to a flopping 1.2 m (4 ft) or so in height with a similar spread and needs a hot and sheltered position in the border, where it looks like a herbaceous plant, until you see the woody stems.

Variegated-leaved shrubs can play a part in the border (though not too large a part as a little goes a long way when it comes to variegation). *Euonymus fortunei* 'Gracilis' is a small-leaved 'evergreen' shrub to add sparkle in the right place; set it against a wall and it will send up long sprays with sucker-feet which will attach themselves to the wall and so climb it, though this plant is not generally sold as a climber. It is variegated in grey, green and cream and tinges to pink or even crimson in cold weather. *E.f.* 'Emerald 'n Gold' is its green and yellow counterpart which has the same useful climbing propensities. Both are good as ground-cover plants and to keep them within bounds their branches can be picked straight into vases at any time—flower-arranging friends will quickly oblige.

Fuchsia magellanica 'Variegata' is an exquisite (though a touch tender) shrub with grey, green, cream and rose-coloured foliage; in late summer it has delicate fuchsia flowers of crimson and purple. This is a lovely plant for a good site, and should have complementary white or rose-to-purple toned flowers as neighbours. It grows to about 1.2 m (4 ft) high by as much through. The tender *Hypericum* x *moserianum* 'Tricolor' has green, white and crimson leaves and is brightly colourful, and even more so when it produces its small yellow flowers as well, which can be too much of a good thing in some planting schemes. Best as a foliage plant only, it is deciduous as is *Cornus alba* 'Elegantissima' which is a superb, large-growing 3 m (10 ft) high and wide shrub with green and cream leaves. This looks well in front of a tall evergreen hedge and then itself provides a good background for *Chrysanthemum maximum* (Shasta daisy) and the brilliant orange-red flowers of curtonus or crocosmia. The variegated-leaved ligustrums (privet) can have a place in the border as they are not (quite) as greedy as their plain-leaved relatives. *Ligustrum ovalifolium* 'Argenteum' is cream and green while *Ligustrum ovalifolium* 'Aureum' is rich yellow and green.

Two shrubby salvias make softly interesting colour harmonies all on their own. *S. officinalis* 'Icterina' is green and gold, while *S.o.* 'Tricolor' is purple, green and cream, with touches of crimson. Both can be used to stuff the turkey as well. *Vinca major* 'Variegata' has evergreen cream and green foliage. It is not as rampant as the plain-leaved vinca, and should be cossetted a little in hard winters as it is more tender. *Weigela florida* 'Variegata' is a slower-growing elegantly coloured shrub, attaining an eventual height of 3 m (10 ft). Its pale green leaves are cream-edged and complement the pale pink flowers in their season. There are several small-leaved variegated hederas (ivy) such as 'Glacier', 'Silver Queen' and 'Goldheart' which can be used as ground, wall or fence cover. Watch them, or they will outgrow their allotted space while your back is turned.

I have described suitable larger-growing shrubs because, though they have no place in a small border, many people move to a new home with an arid waste of left-over builders' detritus instead of a garden and it is some comfort to plan and plant large-growing and beautiful shrubs as part of a hedge or against inadequate fencing. These shrubs will then form an excellent background to a mixed border. Or one may move to a different house with a neglected garden and the same principle applies—start anew, but with the largest-growing things first. Even though they will recede into the background when the border is in flower, their presence is very important and an extra growing season in your garden will make a great deal of difference—in addition, you will be getting to know the shrubs, always a good thing, and, being fairly small initially, it will be possible to move them (at the correct season) if they are not quite in the right place to start with.

ROSES

Roses are a different story—they can range in height from a few inches (these are mainly for rockeries and raised beds) to fifty feet or so if one takes in the Himalayan giants. But as in most things there is a median position and so it is with roses. They have a wonderful colour range and can be chosen to blend with any colour scheme. The tremendous flowering capacity of the so-called 'old-fashioned' roses may appeal to some gardeners and their colours, from white and cream through pale pink, rose-pink, carmine, magenta and purple are very suitable to a border where these softer colours predominate. These 'old' roses can grow to very large specimens in some cases, so it is best to do some homework among the catalogues before ordering. If space is not a problem these roses will last for most of your gardening life, requiring less general maintenance than the more unusually coloured or vibrant-toned modern kinds which need more feeding, mulching, correct pruning and appropriate spraying against pests and disease. However, the newer roses are smaller-growing and some flower for long periods, and in addition, their colours are quite astonishing, which is where they score. There are copper-coloured ones, brown ones, mahogany ones, red-black ones, grey ones, lilac ones, red-and-yellow striped ones, bicoloured ones (also to be found among the 'old' roses, but in more subdued tones), and with brilliant, almost fluorescent scarlets and oranges if these are the colours that you favour. Modern roses flower well for their (relatively) short lives and may be just what you need and there are a great number of standard roses with blooms of varying sizes and colours, very suitable for the formal border.

There are some excellent climbing roses with varying degrees of vigour which should be considered before buying, as some hardly merit the title of climber—'languid leaner' would be more truthful because these cannot really achieve more than

Flower shapes are important: flat achilleas sort well with all the mallow tribe and the silver-furred stems of the verbascums (mulleins).

2.1 or 2.4 m (7 or 8 ft) at the most, though this is generally quite sufficient as a wall plant for the border; it is nice to know that the rose has no aspirations to climb up and over the shed or fence to give of its best to your (possibly) undeserving neighbours next door.

It should be remembered that with old roses, all the flowers come in one glorious flush of bloom, except in a few cases where (in good years) a second flowering occurs in late summer. A border is the best place for these lovely plants, because when they have established themselves, which they certainly will, they grow to substantial specimens and in a large, mixed border it is to be hoped that there will be space for one or two at least; near-by plants, suffocating under the flower-decked flounces of the roses, can be rescued at a later date. Left unpruned, these roses will reward the gardener with a foaming cascade of pale and perfumed blossom, luminous in the dusk, or a sumptuous richness of soft pinks and purples quite unparalleled by their modern counterparts which unfortunately in many cases have no scent.

Since this is just a part of a chapter in a book about border flowers, I will list only the more outstanding (though obtainable) roses.

Albas: 'Celestial' grows to 1.8 m (6 ft) and as much through with beautifully shaped clear pink scented flowers set off by grey-green foliage. 'Great Maiden's Blush' grows to 1.8 m (6 ft) and as much through with flowers that open to soft pink and age to blush. Grey-green foliage.

Bourbons: 'Zigeuner Knabe' ('Gipsy Boy') grows to 2.4 m (8 ft) and spreads to 2.1 m (7 ft) with dark violet-crimson, smallish double flowers on *very* thorny branches. 'Madame Isaac Pereire' grows to 1.8 m (6 ft) and as much through, in time. Huge, rich, raspberry-scented flowers in early summer and again in early autumn. 'Zephirine Drouhin', the famous thornless rose, grows to 1.8 m (6 ft) and is sometimes listed as a climber, which it is not. Vivid double pink flowers flowering on and off all summer.

Centifolias: 'Fantin Latour' grows to 1.5 m (5 ft) high and as much through, with very double pale pink scented flowers. 'Tour de Malakoff' grows to 1.5 m (5 ft) and as much wide, with pendulous branches of large, double pink-to-violet flowers that age to lavender-grey. Not good in wet summers, wonderful in dry ones.

China roses: 'Cecile Brunner' grows to 60 cm (2 ft) by 60 cm (2 ft) (though my own is 1.5 m (5 ft) high) with quantities of perfectly formed miniature peach-to-pink tea-rose scented flowers. (There is an equally lovely climbing variety called 'Climbing Cecile Brunner' or 'Bloomfield Abundance'.) 'Mutabilis' grows to 1.5 m (5 ft) and as much wide, with dark leaves and single flame-coloured buds opening to cream and apricot, changing finally to deep rose-pink. A dainty, dark-leaved shrub, needing a sunny situation. Prone to defoliation by black spot.

Damask roses: 'Ispahan' grows to 1.8 m (6 ft) by about 1.2 m (4 ft) with very scented double pink flowers. Long in bloom. 'Leda' grows to 1.2 m (4 ft) by 90 cm (3 ft), with scented crimson-edged white petals. Reflexed.

Gallica roses: 'Camaieux' grows to a neat 90 cm (3 ft) by 90 cm (3 ft) with double white flowers whose petals are striped with purple and crimson, ageing to lilac and grey. 'Tuscany' grows to 1.2 m (4 ft) by 90 cm (3 ft), with almost black crimson-purple flowers and gold anthers. 'Rosa Mundi' grows to 90 cm (3 ft) by 90 cm (3 ft), with palest pink petals striped and spotted with cerise and golden anthers. A very weatherproof rose which has a strong constitution.

Moss roses: 'Capitaine John Ingram' grows to 1.8 m (6 ft) by about 1.8 m (6 ft), with scented double flowers of claret-purple and brown 'moss'. 'White Bath' grows to 1.5 m (5 ft) by 1.5 m (5 ft) with double white flowers and dark 'moss'. 'William Lobb' grows to a tall, gaunt 2.4 m (8 ft) by 2.4 m (8 ft) with very double rich mauve-purple flowers ageing to lavender and green 'moss'.

Climbing roses (perpetual flowering): 'Danse du Feu' grows to 3 m (10 ft) with vivid vermilion-orange flowers on and off all summer. 'Dreaming Spires' grows to 2.4 m (8 ft) with apricot buds opening to creamy-buff flowers. 'Golden Showers' grows to 2.4 m (8 ft) with double golden-yellow flowers on and off all summer. May be grown as a tall bush. 'Handel' grows to 2.4 m (8 ft) with scented cream-white petals flushed at the edges with pink. 'Morning Jewel' grows to 2.1 m (7 ft) with bright rose-pink scented flowers all summer. Free-flowering, with good dark foliage.

Rambler roses (with clusters of smaller flowers): 'Alberic Barbier' grows to 6 m (20 ft) with scented cream-buff buds opening to rather untidy cream flowers in early and mid-summer. Good, shiny dark foliage. An old favourite. 'Albertine' grows to 6 m (20 ft) with clusters of copper-pink buds opening to short-lived scented pink flowers in early summer. Very vigorous, with one gorgeous flush of bloom. 'Dr Van Fleet' grows to 6 m (20 ft) with clusters of large, pale silvery-pink flowers and dark foliage.

Other climbing roses: 'Crimson Glory' grows to 5.4 m (18 ft) with very dark crimson flowers. 'Cupid' grows to 3.6 m (12 ft) with large, single pale peach-pink flowers in early summer. 'Gloire de Dijon' grows to 4.5 m (15 ft) with scented, creamy, buff-yellow flowers all summer. 'Lady Hillingdon' grows to 3 m (10 ft) with soft orange-to-apricot tea-scented flowers. Crimson foliage. One of the most beautiful of roses, best on a south wall. 'Mrs Sam McGredy' grows to 4.5 m (15 ft) with orange to vermilion buds opening to salmon-pink. Good copper-coloured foliage.

Modern shrub roses: There are so many colours available among the vast numbers of modern roses that I have only included the more unusual ones, most of which I have grown. Wonderful colour schemes can be planned with them.
'Amberlight' grows to 75 cm ($2\frac{1}{2}$ ft) with pale brown-buff flowers. 'Butterfly Wings' grows to 1.2 m (4 ft) with cream-

white petals edged with rose-crimson. Long-stemmed flowers. 'Cafe' grows to 90 cm (3 ft) with coffee-brown flowers and light green foliage. 'Copper Pot' grows to 90 cm (3 ft) with apricot-to orange buds opening to pale creamy-pink. Copper foliage. 'Eye Paint' grows to 105 cm ($3\frac{1}{2}$ ft) with clusters of white-centred, single scarlet flowers. 'Fan Tan' grows to 75 cm ($2\frac{1}{2}$ ft) with brownish-pink flowers ageing to cream-white. 'Harry Edland' grows to 90 cm (3 ft) with strongly scented lavender-mauve flowers. 'Joseph's Coat' grows to an upright 1.2 m (4 ft) with astonishing flowers in yellow, gold and orange, tinted pink and with crimson edges. Much better than 'Masquerade'. 'Korbleu' grows to 90 cm (3 ft), with purple buds opening to scented dark mauve flowers. 'Lavender Lassie' grows to 1.2 m (4 ft) with sprays of double pale lilac-pink flowers. 'News' grows to 60 cm (2 ft) with startling, royal-purple semi-double flowers. Slightly scented. Dark foliage. 'Playboy' grows to 75 cm ($2\frac{1}{2}$ ft) with scarlet buds opening to orange-crimson and yellow. 'Purple Splendour' grows to 75 cm ($2\frac{1}{2}$ ft) with strongly perfumed large double flowers of violet-purple. 'Vespers' grows to 75 cm ($2\frac{1}{2}$ ft) with brown-to-apricot flowers opening to beige-yellow.

Hybrid tea roses: (Again, there is space only for the most unusual, not necessarily the best.)
'Brandy Butter' grows to 75 cm ($2\frac{1}{2}$ ft), with scented pale amber-gold buds opening to creamy-white. 'Black Velvet' grows to 60 cm (2 ft) with black-red flowers. 'Harry Wheatcroft' grows to 90 cm (3 ft) with bright yellow-striped red petals (like a Punch-and-Judy show). 'Julias Rose' grows to 75 cm ($2\frac{1}{2}$ ft) with subtle grey-brown flowers and purple-toned leaves. 'Memoriam' grows to 75 cm ($2\frac{1}{2}$ ft) with large, palest pink flowers. 'Message' grows to 90 cm (3 ft) with scented greenish-white flowers ageing to pure white. Pale foliage and good buds. 'Whisky Mac' grows to 75 cm ($2\frac{1}{2}$ ft) with amber-orange buds opening to soft apricot-cream scented flowers. Crimson-purple young foliage.

For other modern roses to complement planting schemes, consult several comprehensive catalogues rather than one only. It is best to order your roses early direct from a grower as there will be a much better chance of getting exactly what you want; the roses will come direct to you in autumn and will be in better condition. Garden-centre roses will, in any case, have been purchased in bulk from rose growers.

CLIMBERS

Climbers are another dimension in a mixed border, and in addition to the roses already described, there are many other plants to clothe the walls or fences, or add height in the border on posts or trellis pyramids. Here one can use Loniceras such as *L. periclymemum* 'Belgica' or 'Serotina'; the first blooms earlier than the second, so a succession of scented bloom can be had by planting each, though perhaps not on the same post or pyramid as each can achieve a height of 6 m (20 ft). The strong-growing *L.* x *tellmanniana* has large yellow and orange flower clusters but absolutely no scent at all. It does not grow quite as tall, usually achieving about 4.5 m (15 ft) in maturity. Loniceras are woodland plants and prefer to have their roots cool and to grow towards the sun. They appreciate regular watering, feeding and spraying against aphids if these pests are a problem. Examine the spiral-growing stems and their supports periodically—if the supports are of other shrubs, then the lonicera might be partway towards killing its host with a slowly tightening stranglehold and you may have to release the host-shrub with a hatchet. The scars will remain, of course, to remind you never to turn your back on anything in the garden for too long.

Clematis

Clematis are another group of plants that will bring glorious colour to a tall wall, fence or post. They should be chosen to associate with the planned colour scheme, and can be had to flower from late spring until autumn. Certain kinds such as *C. montana* and its varieties and the glossily evergreen *C. armandii* are exceedingly strong-growing and vigorous, and it may not be possible to use them because of the lack of space, though *C. montana* will quickly clothe a chain-link fence into invisibility. It is deciduous but will make such a tangle of stems that the wire fencing will almost disappear even in winter, until more solid hedging plants have had a chance to grow up. *C. armandii* needs to have cool roots and to grow towards the sun, and should be given an annual feed of compost or well-rotted manure in spring and needs to be regularly watered, even in winter. Clematis have now been divided into three groups—Group 1 (or A) flowers from mid-winter to early spring on the previous season's growth. These should be lightly pruned immediately after flowering (yet another reason for the essential 'service path' behind the border). Group 2 (or B) flowers from late spring to mid-summer on lateral shoots from the previous season's growths. These are pruned in early spring by cutting all growth down to within 23 cm (9 in) of the ground. Thereafter, cut down growth by one-third each spring to keep leaves and flowers low down; clematis is always trying to escape. Group 3 (or C) are the later-flowering (mid-summer onwards) hybrids and species which produce their flowers on the current season's axilliary growths. Again, cut all growth down to within 30 cm (12 in) of the ground in the second year and train subsequent new growth sideways as much as space permits. Clematis dislike growing sideways and care must be taken with the delicate shoots until the leaf-petioles take hold (which they do very quickly), but these shoots will in time become firm and woody. Subsequent pruning consists of cutting away all vertical growth above each pair of plump buds nearest to the horizontal 'branches'. Clematis are subject to the mysterious disease known as 'wilt'. It causes new growth to wilt, collapse and blacken. There is nothing to be done about this, as no cure is as yet known. The only preventative is to set the new plants 15 cm (6 in) below the existing soil surface, in the hope that, if and when wilt strikes, new and healthy growth will appear eventually. *Never* plant a newly purchased replacement clematis in the site previously occupied by a plant that has been overcome by clematis wilt, or it, too, will be affected. If this is the only place possible for your clematis, then remove the soil and replace it to a depth of 45 cm (18 in) with new topsoil from the vegetable garden and then wait a year, or two.

As the area at the back of the border is likely to be well shaded, this position, at the foot of a tall wall or fence, is very

A wall makes a perfect background for the pale colours of althaea, (hollyhock) and white chrysanthemums.

suitable for clematis as long as they are kept regularly watered. Some gloriously large-flowered kinds are obtainable which can be grown up and through other wall shrubs, to flower at the same time as these, or before, or after, to bring colour to the other surrounding leaves. Again, when choosing clematis, get a catalogue from a nursery that specializes in these lovely plants. They do very well on chalk.

For wire fence-covers: *C. montana rubra* or *C.m.* 'Elizabeth', soft pink; *C.m. grandiflora alba* with large white flowers, in late spring to early summer.

Small-flowered varieties: *C. macropetala* 'Blue Lagoon' has nodding blue and violet flowers in late spring. *C. viticella* 'Etoile Violette' has larger flat violet flowers, *C.v.* 'Rubra' is wine-red and *C.v.* 'Abundance' has rosy-red flowers; all bloom from mid-summer to early autumn and all grow to about 3.5 cm (11½ ft). The very similar *C. orientalis* and *C. tangutica* have nodding yellow flowers from mid-summer to early autumn; both will grow to 5 m (16½ ft) and both are excellent on a wall as part of a yellow colour scheme.

Large-flowered varieties: Can be chosen in almost every colour except true yellow. Most grow to between 2.5–3 m (8¼–10 ft) and can be made fairly happy on a post, or, better, wound spirally round a trellis pyramid, or allowed to climb into a tall near-by shrub. Good whites are *C.* 'Edith' and 'Marie Boisselot'; *C.* 'Perle d'Azur' is azure, while *C.* 'Laserstern' is blue. *C.* 'Ernest Markham' is red, while the flowers of *C.* 'Ville de Lyon' are carmine with darker carmine-red edges. *C.* 'Hagley Hybrid' is a lilac-toned pink, exactly right with many of the old roses. *C.* 'Jackmanii Superba' is a rich, dark purple as is *C.* 'Gipsy Queen' while *C.* 'The President' is mauve. That old favourite 'Nellie (or Nelly) Moser' is pale lilac with a carmine bar and keeps its colour better when grown in partial shade. It is quite possible to grow these and other large-flowered clematis horizontally where their flowers will often be better seen; they can be allowed to trail their way through low but rigid-growing herbaceous plants, and it may be found very convenient indeed to have such large and colourful flowers in the border in late summer.

Other climbers

Other climbers are many, and can be chosen according to the type of support available. For very large areas, and where the fearless gardener can get at it to manage it, then there is nothing to equal the gigantic covering capacity of *Polygonum baldschuanicum* (Russian vine). This will produce long strands of delicate-looking pinkish-white flowers which is the only delicate thing about it. The plant will drape an ugly fence by the end of its first season and cover it completely in its second. In its third it will look round for fresh territory and will gobble up the garage, a bicycle shed where the children's rabbit lives in winter, and the oil tank for the central heating. It is very beautiful, and I have always called it 'Ivan the Terrible' because it is; but it can be controlled (or almost) and it most certainly has its uses in many garden designs, providing the gardener is sound in wind and limb. It is, fortunately, deciduous and can be attacked in winter.

Hedera (ivy) is excellent, again for fences and not-such good walls, which it will permanently beautify. The most popular is the variegated *H. canariensis* 'Variegata' syn. 'Gloire de Marengo', which has cream, grey and green leaves. It is a mite tender in very cold winters, so take a few cuttings. In good years it grows lustily, liking a sunny, sheltered situation as befits its origins. *Vitis* (grape vine) has beautiful leaves, quite sufficient to earn it a place on a warm wall. The variety *V. vinifera* 'Brandt', has wonderful autumn coloration, while the leaves of *V.v.* 'Purpurea' are an appropriate wine-red all the summer, turning to purple and crimson in autumn.

Jasminum officinale is not really a climber, being a bushy-growing tall 'leaner' but as it can lean up a wall to about 9 m (30 ft) it is included here. It has sprays of heavily perfumed small white flowers from early summer to mid-autumn. It 'climbs' by means of its flexible, twining shoots and is deciduous.

Humulus lupulus (common hop) is very attractive when it produces its dangling clusters of green hop-bells. If space can be found for it (it is deciduous but grows quickly each year to 6 m (20 ft) then it might be better to grow *H.l.* 'Aureus' which has very attractive yellow leaves. This plant is best in sun.

Lathyrus latifolia (everlasting pea) is an excellent perennial to grow, either up (and over) a wall or fence or up and through wire mesh or trellis. It dies down completely in winter but grows quickly once the soil warms up, producing 3 m (10 ft) long tendrilled sprays of leaves with pink, cerise or magenta flowers; there is a very beautiful but more tender white variety. The pink-flowered kinds look delightful when allowed to scramble over and through a lavender hedge. Once established it is impossible to move the huge root and it is better to start again from seed, which will grow very rapidly.

The annual *Ipomoea caerulea* (now more properly called *Pharbitis purpurea-rubra*) (morning glory) grows quickly once the weather is warm. It must be germinated in gentle heat in a greenhouse or, even better, in a propagator, and grown on in a frost-free greenhouse or conservatory until such time as it can be hardened off and planted out. All this trouble is well worth it when the wonderful blue moons begin to flower. Set the young plants out in close groups (they like each other's company) with their supporting canes, which they will have twiddled round: do not attempt to remove these canes, but put other taller ones beside the groups of seedlings or provide trellis, wires or strings. It is the nature of the plant for each of its open flowers to die in the afternoon, but their life and beauty can be a little prolonged by growing them in a position that receives the hottest afternoon sun. Protect the young plants from slugs.

Tropaeolum majus (annual nasturtium) has a lusty climbing variety which needs assistance, as it is heavy when in full leaf and flower. Tie in the stems as it grows and do not feed it at all. It would rather crawl along the border, suffocating all lesser plants in its path, so this propensity has to be watched for and checked. Another species of this family is *T. peregrinum* (Canary creeper). This is a delightful annual, growing to about 3.6 m (12 ft), with attractive pale green, palmate leaves and small, flat, whiskered flowers, like faces; it blooms luxuriantly until the frosts. Water well in dry weather, but it needs no feeding. It is a daintier plant and (in limited numbers) may be allowed to play hide-and-seek among the other border flowers.

This is only a small selection of the climbing plants that can give another dimension to the border. They will need a certain amount of attention at times and for this see Chapters 7 and 8 as appropriate.

7

Before the Summer Comes

It is not as if summer arrives on the first Monday in May, though this would certainly be an excellent arrangement all round. As things are, all the jobs in the various kinds of borders described will now be shouting for attention.

If the summer border has been tidied up in autumn then now is the time to give it a good spring-clean. If recent weather has been wet but time is getting on, then get out some boards to work on so that the soil does not become compacted with treading. Begin at one end and work gradually through, weeding, generally tidying and examining each plant or group of plants to see how they have fared during the winter. Where

A warm border for grey and silver foliage plants. Eryngiums remain interesting all summer long, white flowers are cool by day and luminous at night.

you were hoping for seedlings to appear leave the whole area around the plant—it is perhaps too early for them. Where you have protected the crowns with ashes, mounded peat, litter or bracken, leave well alone, for the moment. If more frosts are likely it may be as well to add extra protective litter if it has been blown away by the winter gales. Peg it down with diagonally placed canes, or wire it in place for the time being. Go around and lift up all the leaves of the bergenias and exterminate the snails that will be sheltering there, and look under the mats of edging plants at the same time—another favourite place of concealment. When the border is tidy, review last year's successes and face up to the failures. The successes can be repeated and this is the time to do something about the failures (unfortunate colour clashes, short plants sited behind things that got too tall too quickly, other plants being smothered by the exuberance of their neighbours and so on). In early spring most plants can be moved without any check. Divide over-large clumps of phlox, aruncus, *Chrysanthemum maximum* (Shasta daisy), campanulas, asters (Michaelmas daisy), helianthemum (sunflowers) and geraniums and all other too-large clumps: discard the exhausted central portions and replant good rooted pieces in groups. Some of these may not flower too well this season but they will have regenerated by next year. If you are a plant-labeller, then re-do them all—they may soon have faded irrevocably. The labels should be wired (not tied with string, it will rot) to short sticks which can then be pushed into the ground somewhere in the middle of the plant-groups. They need not show but they are there if you should need them to prove a point to a visitor.

Feed the dianthus with dried blood, and sweep out the winter-blown detritus that may have collected around them: give the lilies some compost. Leave the dead stems on the nepeta until the new growth is well up. Thin out the montbretia and crocosmia corms at this time if they are overcrowded and are pushing up out of the ground, but be sure to plant them 5–8 cm (2–3 in) deep. If the weather is cold, cover the ground with some litter or a mound of ashes until all danger of frosts are gone—even the ordinary old-fashioned montbretia is more tender (when disturbed) than supposed. If the peonies are beginning to shoot, prepare their rings or supports if you are intending to use them; and though they would look forlorn in the empty garden, it will soon be time to install them among the uprushing spring growth.

If you have narcissus, tulips and other spring bulbs in bloom then make sure that the annual seeds are ready to sow *in situ* as soon as the bulbs are lifted—everything will begin to happen quickly from now on. If the bulbs have been planted where they are to remain, now is the time to discover whether or not their foliage is likely to be concealed by the clever planting that you planned last autumn.

Light some all-coal fires in the house and keep the clinkers—still the best protection, with added pellets, from slugs—for the previous delphiniums (and spare some of these clinkers for the lupins as well—the gastropods might well have *their* emerging shoots as a starter).

Give the roses in the bed some manure, making quite sure that none of it touches the rose-stems or anything else near by, and keep a little back to make tea for the greedy agapanthus a little later on. Decide whether or not you are going to have some sweet peas on the post or the trellis pyramid and dig in some of your oldest manure deeply here if you did not do this in the autumn.

Review all the plants at this time and decide whether to give those that are not living up to expectations just one more season—and tell them so (you may be surprised at the results). Or, and more practically, move them to another place in the garden, space is always at a premium in a good border. The oriental poppies will be pushing up their bristly leaves—give them a little support if they needed it last year. Prepare something to fall into or hide their space in mid-summer when they have finished flowering.

Each group of plants in the border may need a little attention of some kind, whether it be removing last season's stems, feeding, dividing, labelling or just getting stakes or twiggy sticks ready. If there is a narrow bed against a wall behind the border in which climbing plants live, then these may need pruning, feeding and, for the roses, the first spraying of the year against black spot and aphids. Now is the time to do it, before the summer comes.

8

Autumn

Fortunately, autumn comes slowly, and with it come many compensations — there is less of a rush to do the jobs, though those that are seasonal must be attended to now. Many shrubs produce unexpected colouration in some years and this propensity can be planned into an 'autumn colour' grouping for the future. The seed heads of many herbaceous plants are quite fascinating in their variety of shape and subtle colouration, and many gardener–flower arrangers will have left these to ripen on the plant for winter decor. Late colour in the border can be gorgeous, and it is quite hurtful to the gardener's soul to have to begin the autumn tidy-up. This can, of course, be left until spring but a herbaceous border becomes such a mass of leaning, lying stems and decaying foliage that it is better to sort it out gradually through the winter months so that there is less to do when everything starts to grow again.

The first clear-up is rather superficial, merely a question of cutting off the more untidy flowering stems of mid-summer plants, unless this has already been done routinely. This is the time to mark the resting places of plants that disappear completely such as incarvillea, some alliums, alstroemeria, smilacina, platycodon and so on, also such summer-flowering bulbs as camassia, galtonia and lilies. This can be done either with bamboo canes, stakes (sometimes dangerous to the dormant bulb if it is already resting) or (safer) circles of peat or silver-sand. These are a good indication of a resting plant, and though the patches will get disturbed and dissipated by birds and cats, the main part of the marker-substance will remain. Annuals should be taken out now to make way for the bulbs, and a good general-purpose fertilizer can be spread over the border either now or in spring, unless you have sufficient quantity of your own compost.

If narcissus and tulips are to be a spring-flowering part of the summer border then plant the narcissus as early as possible (this means the whole daffodil/narcissus tribe). Tulips can go in much later (from mid- to late autumn). Be objective about the choice

(Opposite)
A traditional border, full of interest and colour. In the foreground, poppies are bright and gay for months.

of all these, remembering that the leaves will remain visible as they feed the bulbs until early summer. If the bulbs are to be lifted after flowering to finish off their growing and feeding cycle elsewhere in the garden, then there is less of a space problem, though it is as well to remember that both narcissus and tulips take up a certain amount of sideways room when in full leaf, about 35 cm+ (14 in+) for large narcissus and about 23 cm+ (9 in+) for big tulips. Though you may have grouped the bulbs quite closely for effect, their peripheral leaves when in flower will have an inhibiting effect (for about a month) on oncoming herbaceous plants, and may distort the shapes of those plants near the narcissus or tulips. This should be taken into consideration while planting. It is as well, perhaps, in a summer border to choose early-flowering bulbs that will have had their month of glory before the new herbaceous growth really begins.

If the border is to be completely tidied for winter now, then in mild areas seeds of some annuals can be sown thinly (with silver sand to mark the place); this is best done in early to mid-autumn. The seedlings will suddenly appear by the thousand when the soil warms up, and are stronger and, of course, much further forward than spring-sown seeds. Mark these patches either with labelled canes at each end or a layer of silver sand (or peat, if the soil is naturally a light colour) to remind you not to tread there, or, more important, not to plant anything else in an apparently empty space.

If wallflowers are to be part of the border, as they may be in a formal one and certainly in that for a cottage garden, then these should be planted, though this *can* be left until later if you are growing them yourself. When they have recovered from the move and are growing again then nip out the tops (even though there may well already be flower buds) to make bushy and floriferous plants. Forget-me-nots can be moved in mild, damp weather and the various spring-flowering bedding plants such as pansies, bellis and polyanthus set in place. Crocuses should be planted, with other small bulbs and corms such as muscari, *Anemone blanda*, chionodoxa and scilla, remembering that the foliage of muscari remains for most of the summer. A band of ajuga is an excellent spring-flowering edging, but remember that it is all too easy to set crocuses too close to its rear edge where, after flowering, the slowly withering crocus leaves will spoil the shining beauty of the ajuga's foliage.

Prune the roses according to type and spray for the last time to kill off overwintering pests and the spores of disease. Spray the stems and ground well at this time and thereafter do not disturb the surface until the spring. Decide where to put any herbaceous plants that may be disappearing under the skirts of the roses; it may be that this part of the border will need complete readjustment to accommodate the large-growing roses. (I *did* give sizes in Chapter 7 but your soil and treatment may suit them so well that they are exceeding these approximations.) So plan these changes, and make a start on them; though in colder areas some plants should not be moved until the spring. Plant narcissus (best) or tulips deeply near the roses or deciduous shrubs; the bulbs can be left there permanently. Tulips are stiffer in habit and need good clearance above their heads, or the wind-blown moving branches will decapitate them.

Collect such seeds as you will need by cutting off the upper part of the stems and laying them in labelled batches in an airy room to finish drying. Some seeds may need to be sown as soon as ripe, others can be sown in the spring, while some are viable for many years: poppies, acanthium, oenothera, ipomoea, lathyrus, *Aquilegia vulgaris*, endymion are a few of the long-lived ones.

Some really noxious weeds such as bindweed, ground elder and enchanter's nightshade may still be visible enough to attack more thoroughly—inevitably the running roots of ground elder will have threaded themselves through clumps of the herbaceous plants. These can be lifted entirely and the roots removed at this time—it is one job less to do in the onward-rushing days of spring growth when all the weeds will reappear once more. Those plants which may have moved forwards too far, such as some asters, geraniums, alchemilla, phlomis, schizostylis, polygonum and so on, can also be sorted out and replanted.

In cold areas (and even in some warm ones) many plants need some kind of winter protection. A mound of ash and clinkers is an old-fashioned method but still good. For fireplace-less houses then a mixture of peat and sand or grit will do; this can be gathered up and re-used in the spring (peat is inert). Best are home-made birds' nests of border-tidyings (usually and unfortunately called 'litter') or bracken, or straw; with these one covers the crowns of cherished peonies, eremurus, macleaya and all the other plants that emerge too soon for their own good. Peg the birds' nests in place with several diagonally slanted canes to prevent the litter blowing away. Some larger plants do not disappear but remain above ground where they can be badly damaged by alternate spells of wet, cold and, even worse, freezing, desiccating wind. For these one can make a tube of chicken wire or wire trellis, whatever is to hand, and weave straw or bracken (the latter is longer-lasting) through the holes.

Clipped yew enhances the flower colours, arranged in structured layers: phlox, delphiniums, tradescantia, campanulas, lychnis, onopordum and many, many more.

Unusual plants feature in this border, set against a protective brick wall. Eremurus, (fox-tail lily) onopordums, and *Cephalaria gigantea* (Giant yellow scabious).

This border is planted for a succession of colour, with delphiniums, verbascums, campanulas, kniphofia and poppies in flower: later will come *Echinops ritro*, solidago (golden-rod), phlox asnd many more for late-summer interest.

(This task will keep the children occupied usefully for some time depending on the number of tubes you will need.) The tube can then be pegged firmly in place with canes, with a little more litter threaded loosely among the remaining stems of the plant to be protected. Hessian or thin sacking can be used on wire or cane supports but this has a way of coming undone when your back is turned, though you can tie or (better) 'sew' it in place with wire. Never use plastic sheeting—it prevents the air getting to the plants and presents too much surface area to the wind, which will worry away at it until the flapping and banging of the loosening plastic will fetch you out of bed on a cold and frosty morning at 1 am.

For really precious plants there is nothing like a cloche, so have them ready to install as soon as the weather begins to turn cold. Cloches keep the soil just that little bit warmer, prevent the treasure from getting cold rain in its hair and protect it from icy winds.

9

WINTER

A large garden diary (perhaps an advance Christmas present to yourself from the garden) is an excellent thing to have in which to jot down, then and there with muddied hands, all the brilliant planting ideas that occur to you throughout the year. It is never humanly possible to remember them all, but if noted down in the appropriate months as jobs to attend to then your garden will always be better next season.

Such a diary will have yielded a number of what seem to be minor jobs and are not. Seeds and plants to order, with a few roses for spring delivery (not good, but better in your garden than put off for yet another season).

Certain areas of the border soil might need a little help— more well-rotted manure dug in where the sweet peas are to go, for instance, and a little lime for the lime-lovers, though this is best done after Christmas. Heavy soils are unworkable in winter, and should not be trodden on. The tiresomeness of this may provoke you to begin the task of lightening the soil with home-made compost and leafmould, silver sand or the finest grit, wood ash from the incinerator (*never* a mix of coal and wood from the indoor fireplace) and chopped straw and bracken (buy one of those invaluable compost-mincers for this). Improving the soil is a long job and can take many years.

The formal border may need attention: if standard roses are grown, their ties or stakes may need replacement. Some of the shrubs may have grown too large and will need extra-hard pruning in spring if they are to remain for another season; if not then have them out, now, and refresh the soil ready for their replacements, which should be ordered for spring delivery.

The informal border has its problems which you will have lived with for a season or so. Now is the time to remove shrubs or roses that are past their best, or that are not doing as well as they should. Try these last elsewhere in the garden for two more seasons (one to get over the shock of being moved and the next and maybe last to prove their worth, or not, as the case may be).

Continue with the ceaseless garden task of improving poor

soil in problem areas. If shade and greedy tree roots are one of the difficulties here, then consider having the tree removed altogether by a professional tree-surgeon who will take it down piece by piece so that little damage is done to the garden, except when the roots have to come out. There is a time when young trees, initially things of grace and beauty, suddenly begin to be a worry because of their increasing size. It may be that they were rather carelessly planted too near the house, in which case they really must be removed, or a bird-sown yew grew so quickly up, and looked so attractive as an evergreen (especially in winter) that it was permitted to stay, but now its increasing height and girth is cutting out all the morning sun and the borders near by are suffering. Or that matching pair of leylandii (x *Chamaecyparis leylandii*) once so handsome by the gate when planted (was it only a few years ago?) have now grown so huge that their roots have cracked the garden wall (and the drive) and it is an unending struggle to keep them clipped back. So have them out while the garden is dormant and any resulting damage can be tidied up well before next summer.

Have a look at all the vines and creepers and cut them back while you can see what you are doing. You may, in some cases, lose a season's flowers but somehow there is never time to tame the montana in late spring when everything else is happening, and all at once.

In mild areas and in fine frost-free weather, paths can be repaired or replanned, and stone or brick edging can be laid round the edges of lawns. The damage to the lawn itself from these operations will disappear quite soon in spring. Turf can be laid at this time, so do any work in near-by beds and borders before the new grass is laid, so that you do not have to walk on it.

Check that the trellis-work and fencing are in good condition, and restore missing fixings, ties and wire supports for strong-growing climbers.

Resist the temptation to sow seeds too early—the day-length is not yet right for them. Wait just a little longer, and make the most of this cold, quiet time for those final careful plans or improvements which will make all the difference to the appearance of your borders.

Unusual plants are a fine feature in this border, with veratrums rising proudly from a froth of the ubiquitous but always useful alchemilla.

Many tones of green are featured here with the flower-shapes playing an important part in the general border-plan. Astrantia (masterwort), hostas, *Polygonum amplexicaule atrosanguineum* and *Aruncus sylvester* (Goat's-beard).

10

Timing it All

The following chart will save a great deal of time when planning the border. From it can be seen at a glance the average height both in metric and imperial measurements, the spread or suggested planting distance apart, the colour of the flowers and, most importantly, when the plant is in bloom. This can vary according to geographical locality and weather conditions but is a good guide in general, and there are brief 'character' notes or reminders which may be found helpful. A sunny open position is best for most plants except for a minority that do better in partial shade; for this situation, see the 'reminders' column. It will be seen that many favourite and familiar border plants flower from the end of late spring until some time in late summer and therefore appropriately coloured groupings flowering at the same time can be chosen from the chart initially, afterwards referring to the main descriptive text in Chapter 5. The code letters after the bar-chart are abbreviations for the following:

A	= Annual	F/A	= Of interest to flower-arrangers
B	= Bulb	HHA	= Half-hardy annual
Bi	= Biennial	HHP	= Half-hardy perennial
C	= Corm	P	= Perennial
E	= Evergreen or evergrey	R	= Rhizome
		S	= Shrub

Latin	Common or varietal name	Colour	Height	Spread or p.d.	Spring			Summer			Aut		Reminders
					E	M	L	E	M	L	E	M	
Acaena microphylla	New Zealand Burr	Whitish	5 cm (2 in)	30 cm (12 in)			■	■					P, Invasive
Acanthus mollis	Bear's breeches	Mauve & white	2.1 m (7 ft)	2.1 m (7 ft)				■					P, Fine foliage
A. spinosus	Spiny Bear's breeches	Mauve & white	1.2 m (4 ft)	1.2 m (4 ft)				■					P, More floriferous
Achillea filipendulina	'Coronation Gold'	Yellow/gold	1 m (3¼ ft)	60 cm (2 ft)				■	■	■			P, F/A
A. filipendulina	'Gold Plate'	Yellow/gold	1.2–1.5 m (4–5 ft)	60 cm (2 ft)				■	■	■			P, F/A
A. millefolium		Crimson to pink	60–75 cm (2–2½ ft)	38 cm (15 in)				■	■				P
A. ptarmica	'The Pearl'	White	75 cm (2½ ft)	38 cm (15 in)					■	■	■		P, Invasive
Aconitum anglicum	Monkshood	Violet blue	1.2 cm (4 ft)	45 cm (18 in)				■					P, Poisonous
A. napellus	Monkshood	Indigo blue	105 cm (3½ ft)	38 cm (15 in)					■	■			P, Poisonous
Agapanthus campanulatum	Blue African lily	Pale blue	75 cm (2½ ft)	60 cm (2 ft)						■			P, Protect in winter
A. campanulatum	'Isis'	Lavender blue	75 cm (2½ ft)	60 cm (2 ft)						■			P, Protect in winter
A. campanulatum	'Headbourne Hybrids'	Shades of blue; white	75 cm (2½ ft)	60 cm (2 ft)					■	■			P, Hardier
Ageratum houstonianum		Blue, mauve pink or white	13–30 cm (5–12 in)	15–30 cm (6–12 in)				■	■	■	■	■	A
Ajuga reptans	'Atropurpurea', Bugle	Blue or white	10–30 cm (4–12 in)	45 cm (18 in)				■	■				P, E
A. reptans	'Multicolor', 'Burgundy Glow' and 'Variegata'	Blue	10–30 cm (4–12 in)	45 cm (18 in)				■	■				P, Somewhat tender
Alchemilla mollis	Lady's mantle	Lime yellow	45 cm (18 in)	1.2 m (4 ft)					■	■			P, Self-seeds well
Allium albopilosum		Lilac purple	45 cm (18 in)	15–25 cm (6–10 in)				■					B, F/A
A. caeruleum		Blue	60 cm (2 ft)	15 cm (6 in)				■	■				B
Allium giganteum		Lilac-mauve	1.2 m (4 ft)	30 cm (12 in)				■					B, F/A
A. moly		Yellow	30 cm (12 in)	10 cm (4 in)					■				B, increases quickly
A. karataviense		Lilac	23 cm (9 in)	23 cm (9 in)			■						B, F/A
A. siculum		Green, white, maroon	60 cm (2 ft)	10–15 cm (4–6 in)			■	■					B, F/A
Alstroemeria auriantica	Peruvian lily	Red and orange	90 cm (3 ft)	30 cm (12 in)				■	■				P, Not easy to establish
A. auriantica	'Dover Orange'	Orange	1.2 m (4 ft)	45 cm (18 in)				■	■				P, Not easy to establish

Latin	Common or varietal name	Colour	Height	Spread or p.d.	Spring			Summer			Aut		Reminders
					E	M	L	E	M	L	E	M	
A. auriantica	'Lutea'	Yellow and crimson	90 cm (3 ft)	30 cm (12 in)				■	■				P, Not easy to establish
Althea rosea	Hollyhock	All except blue	3 m + (10 ft +)	60 cm (2 ft)							■		B, Needs support
Alyssum saxatile	Yellow alyssum	Yellow	23–30 cm (9–12 in)	45 cm (18 in)		■	■						E, Cut back after flowering and replace after three years
A. compactum		Golden yellow	10–15 cm (4–6 in)	23 cm (9 in)		■	■						E
Amaranthus caudatus	Love-lies-bleeding	Crimson	1.2 m (4 ft)	30–45 cm (12–18 in)				■	■	■	■		A, F/A, Not for windy gardens
Amaranthus caudatus	'Viridis'	Green	1.2 m (4 ft)	30–45 cm (12–18 in)				■	■	■	■	■	A, F/A
A. tricolor	Joseph's coat	Crimson	60–90 cm (2–3 ft)	30–45 cm (12–18 in)					■	■	■	■	A, F/A, Good foliage
Anaphalis triplinervis	Pearl everlasting	White	38 cm (15 in)	38 cm (15 in)					■	■	■	■	P, F/A, Slightly tender
A. yedoensis		White	60 cm (2 ft)	38 cm (15 in)					■	■	■	■	P, F/A
Anchusa azurea	'Dropmore'	Deep blue	1.5–1.8 m (5–6 ft)	30–45 cm (12–18 in)				■	■	■			P
A. azurea	'Opal'	Sky-blue	1.2 m (4 ft)	30–45 cm (12–18 in)				■	■	■			P
A. azurea	'Loddon Royalist'	Gentian blue	90 cm (3 ft)	30–35 cm (12–18 in)				■	■	■			P
A. azurea	'Royal Blue'	Royal blue	90 cm (3 ft)	30–45 cm (12–18 in)				■	■	■			P
A. capensis		Forget-me-not blue	45 cm (18 in)	15–23 cm (6–9 in)					■	■			Bi
Anemone coronaria	'de Caen'	Red, white, blue, purple	15–30 cm (6–12 in)	10–15 cm (4–6 in)			■	■	■	■	■		R
A. coronaria	'St Brigid'	Red, white, blue, purple	15–30 cm (6–12 in)	10–15 cm (4–6 in)			■	■	■	■	■		R, double
A. blanda		Blue, white, pink	15 cm (6 in)	10 cm (4 in)		■	■						R
A. × hybrida	Japanese anemone	Pink, white	60–90 cm (2–3 ft)	60 cm (2 ft)						■	■	■	P
A. × hybrida	'September Charm'	Clear pink	60–90 cm (2–3 ft)	60 cm (2 ft)						■	■	■	P
A. × hybrida	'Lorelei'	Rose pink	60–90 cm (2–3 ft)	60 cm (2 ft)						■	■	■	P
A. × hybrida	'Queen Charlotte'	Mauve pink	60–90 cm (2–3 ft)	60 cm (2 ft)						■	■	■	P, Semi-double
A. × hybrida	'Honorine Jobert'	White	1.2 m (4 ft)	60 cm (2 ft)						■	■	■	P
Angelica archangelica		Green-yellow	3 m (10 ft)	90 cm (3 ft)					■	■			Bi, F/A
Anthemis cupaniana		White	30 cm (12 in)	90 cm (3 ft)				■	■	■			P, grows quickly, good foliage

Latin	Common or varietal name	Colour	Height	Spread or p.d.	Spring			Summer			Aut		Reminders
					E	M	L	E	M	L	E	M	
A. tinctoria	Ox-eye chamomile	Yellow	75 cm (2½ ft)	38–45 cm (15–18 in)				■	■	■			P
A. tinctoria	'E.C. Buxton'	Lemon	75 cm (2½ ft)	38–45 cm (15–18 in)				■	■	■			P
A. tinctoria	'Wargrave Variety'	Cream	75 cm (2½ ft)	38–45 cm (15–18 in)				■	■	■			P
Antirrhinum (hybrids)	Snapdragon	All except blue	15 cm–1.2 m (6 in–4 ft)	15–60 cm (6 in–2 ft)					■	■	■	■	A, Single or double
Aquilegia vulgaris	Columbine, grannybonnets	Lilac, purple, pink	90 cm (3 ft)	30 cm (12 in)		■	■						P
Aquilegia	'McKana Hybrids'	Many bi-colours	90 cm (3 ft)	30 cm (12 in)			■	■					P
Arabis albida		White, pink, crimson	23 cm (9 in)	60 cm (2 ft)	■	■	■	■					P, E Vigorous
Arctotis × hybrida		Many, zoned	60 cm (2 ft)	30 cm (12 in)					■	■	■	■	A
Argemone grandiflora		White	90 cm (3 ft)	30 cm (12 in)				■	■				A
A. mexicana	Prickly poppy, devil's fig	Yellow or orange	60 cm (2 ft)	30 cm (12 in)				■	■	■	■	■	A, Scented
Armeria maritima	Thrift, sea-pink	Pink, white, crimson	15–30 cm (6–12 in)	30 cm (12 in)			■	■	■				P, E
A. maritima	'Vindictive'	Deep red	15–30 cm (6–12 in)	30 cm (12 in)			■	■	■				P, E
A. maritima	'Alba'	White	15–30 cm (6–12 in)	30 cm (12 in)			■	■	■				P, E
Artemisia ludoviciana	White sage	Yellowish	1.2 m (4 ft)	90 cm + (3 ft +)						■	■		P, Vigorous, silver foliage
Aruncus sylvester	Goat's beard	Cream	1.8 m (6 ft)	90 cm + (3 ft +)				■					P
A. sylvester	'Knieffii'	Cream	60 cm (2 ft)	45 cm (18 in)				■					P
Aster (hybrids)	Michaelmas daisy	Very many	15 cm–1.5 m (6 in–5 ft)	acc. to size						■	■	■	P
A. × frikartii	'Mönch'	Blue-mauve	1 m (3¼ ft)	35 cm (14 in)						■	■	■	P
A. novae-angliae	'Harrington's Pink'	Pink	1.2–1.5 m (4–5 ft)	45 cm (18 in)							■		P
A. amellus	'King George'	Violet-blue	45–60 cm (18–24 in)	38 cm (15 in)						■	■		P
A. amellus	'Lye End Beauty'	Soft pink	1.2 m (4 ft)	60 cm (2 ft)						■	■		P
A. novi-belgii	'Alice Haslam'	Rose-cerise	30 cm (12 in)	20 cm (8 in)						■	■		P
A. novi-belgii	'Blue Bouquet'	Violet-blue	30 cm (12 in)	20 cm (8 in)							■	■	P
A. novi-belgii	'Victor'	Pale lavender	15 cm (6 in)	38 cm (15 in)							■	■	P

Latin	Common or varietal name	Colour	Height	Spread or p.d.	Spring			Summer			Aut		Reminders
					E	M	L	E	M	L	E	M	
Astilbe × arendsii	'Fanal'	Dark red	60 cm (2 ft)	30–45 cm (12–18 in)					■	■			P, Moist soil, good foliage
A. × arendsii	'Federsee'	Rose-red	75 cm (2½ ft)	30–45 cm (12–18 in)					■	■			P, Moist soil, good foliage
A. × arendsii	'White Gloria'	White	60 cm (2 ft)	30–45 cm (12–18 in)					■	■			P, Moist soil, good foliage
A. × crispa	'Gnome'	Rose-pink	15–20 cm (6–8 in)	15–20 cm (6–8 in)					■	■			P, Moist soil, good foliage
A. × crispa	'Peter Pan'	Deep pink	15–20 cm (6–8 in)	15–20 cm (6–8 in)						■	■		P, Moist soil, good foliage
Astrantia major	Masterwort, Hattie's pincushion	Greenish pink & white	60 cm (2 ft)	38 cm (15 in)				■	■				P, F/A, Semi-shade
A. maxima		Pink	60 cm (2 ft)	38 cm (15 in)				■	■				P, F/A, Semi-shade
A. minor		Greenish pink & white	23 cm (9 in)	38 cm (15 in)				■	■				P, F/A, Semi-shade
A. minor	'Variegata'	Greenish pink & white	23 cm (9 in)	38 cm (15 in)				■	■				P, Needs more sun
Aubrieta deltoides		Lilac, pink, purple, crimson, white	15 cm (6 in)	60 cm (2 ft)	■	■	■	■					P, E, Likes limey soils
A. deltoides	'Dr Mules'	Purple	15 cm (6 in)	60 cm (2 ft)	■	■	■	■					P
A. deltoides	'Gurgedyke'	Bright purple	15 cm (6 in)	60 cm (2 ft)	■	■	■	■					P
A. deltoides	'Magician'	Red purple	15 cm (6 in)	60 cm (2 ft)	■	■	■	■					P
A. deltoides	'Barker's Double'	Rose purple	15 cm (6 in)	60 cm (2 ft)	■	■	■	■					P
Baptisia australis	False indigo	Violet blue	90 cm (3 ft)	60 cm (2 ft)			■	■					P
Begonia semperflorens		Pink, red, white, crimson	15–23 cm (6–9 in)	15–23 cm (6–9 in)				■	■	■	■	■	A
Bellis perennis	Daisy	Pink, white crimson	10–15 cm (4–6 in)	8–13 cm (3–5 in)	■	■	■	■	■	■	■	■	B
Bergenia × Schmidtii	Elephant's ears	Pink	30 cm (12 in)	60 cm (2 ft)	■								P, E
B. stracheyi	'Silberlicht'	White	30 cm (12 in)	30–45 cm (12–18 in)		■	■						P, E
Briza major	Quaking grass	Green	50 cm (20 in)	15 cm (6 in)			■	■	■				A, F/A, Prolific seeder
Brodiaea laxa	Ithuriel's Spear	Blue	50 cm (20 in)	5–8 cm (2–3 in)				■	■				B, Needs a warm site
Brunnera macrophylla		Blue	30–45 cm (12–18 in)	45 cm (18 in)		■	■	■					P
B. macrophylla	'Variegata'	Blue	30–45 cm (12–18 in)	45 cm (18 in)		■	■	■					P, Handsome leaves

Latin	Common or varietal name	Colour	Height	Spread or p.d.	Spring			Summer			Aut		Reminders
					E	M	L	E	M	L	E	M	
Calceolaria integrifolia		Yellow	60 cm (2 ft)	30–38 cm (12–15 in)					■	■	■		P, Tender
Calendula officinalis	Marigold	Orange or yellow	60 cm (2 ft)	30–38 cm (12–15 in)			■	■	■	■	■	■	A, Prolific seeder
Callistephus (hybrids)	China asters	All except yellow	15–75 cm (6–30 in)	acc. to type				■	■	■	■	■	A
Camassia cusickii	Quamash	Lavender-blue	1.2 m (4 ft)	23 cm (9 in)				■	■				B. Best in heavy soils
C. cusickii	'Leichtlinii'	Deep blue, white	90 cm (3 ft)	15 cm (6 in)				■	■				B
C. cusickii	'Atrocoerulea'	Dark blue-purple	90 cm (3 ft)	15 cm (6 in)				■	■				B
Campanula alliariifolia		Ivory	45–60 cm (18–24 in)	30 cm (12 in)				■	■				P
C. burghaltii		Lavender-grey	45–60 cm (18–24 in)	23–30 cm (9–12 in)				■					P, Needs support
C. carpatica		Blue, mauve, violet, white	up to 30 cm (up to 12 in)	30–38 cm (12–15 in)					■	■			P, Protect from slugs
C. glomerata	Clustered bellflower	Purple or white	10–45 cm (4–18 in)	30–60 cm (12–24 in)			■	■	■	■	■	■	P, Dead-head regularly
C. lactiflora		Blue, pink, lavender, lilac	90–150 cm (3–5 ft)	38–45 cm (15–18 in)				■	■				P
C. latifolia	Giant bellflower	Violet, blue or white	1.5 m (5 ft)	38–45 cm (15–18 in)					■				P
C. medium	Canterbury bell	Violet, pink, mauve, white	23–90 cm (9 in–3 ft)	30–45 cm (12–18 in)			■	■	■				Bi
C. medium	'Cup and Saucer' var. 'Calycanthema'	Violet, pink, mauve, white	23–90 cm (9 in–3 ft)	30–45 cm (12–18 in)			■	■	■				Bi
C. portenschlagiana		Purple	15 cm (6 in)	60 cm + (2 ft +)				■	■	■	■	■	P, Invasive
C. poscharskyana		Blue-mauve	40 cm (16 in)	90 cm + (3ft +)				■	■	■	■	■	P, Invasive
Canna × hybrida		Red, orange or yellow	1.2 m (4 ft)	30–45 cm (12–18 in)				■	■	■	■		R, Lift in autumn
Catananche caerulea	Cupid's dart	Soft blue	75 cm (2½ ft)	30–45 cm (12–18 in)					■	■			P, Not long-lived
Centaurea cyanus	Cornflower	Blue and mixed colours	30 cm–1.2 m (12 in–4 ft)	23–38 cm (9–15 in)				■	■	■	■		A, or B, Tall vars. need support
C. dealbata		Pink	90 cm (3 ft)	60 cm (2 ft)					■	■			P
C. dealbata	'John Coutts'	Deep pink	90 cm (3 ft)	60 cm (2 ft)					■	■			P
C. macrocephala		Yellow	90 cm–1.5 m (3–5 ft)	60 cm (2 ft)				■	■				P, F/A
C. montana		Deep blue	45–60 cm (18–24 in)	30 cm (12 in)			■	■					P
C. moschata	Sweet sultan	Mixed	60 cm (2 ft)	23 cm (9 in)				■	■	■	■		A, Scented flowers

Latin	Common or varietal name	Colour	Height	Spread or p.d.	Spring			Summer			Aut		Reminders
					E	M	L	E	M	L	E	M	
Centranthus ruber	Red valerian	Pink, white or crimson	90 cm (3 ft)	90 cm (3 ft)			■	■	■	■	■		P, Needs very good drainage, invasive and strong growing
Cephalaria gigantea		Creamy-yellow	1·5–1·8 m (5–6 ft)	90 cm (3 ft)				■	■	■			P
Cerastium tomentosum	Snow-in-summmer	White	10–15 cm (4–6 in)	infinite			■	■					P, E, Invasive
C. tomentosum	'Columnae'	White	8 cm (3 in)	25 cm (10 in)			■	■					P, E
Cheiranthus × *allionii*	Siberian wallflower	Orange or yellow	38 cm (15 in)	30 cm (12 in)			■	■	■				Bi
C. cheiri	Wallflower	All colours except blue	20–60 cm (8–24 in)	25–30 cm (10–12 in)		■	■	■					Bi
Chionodoxa gigantea		Blue	20 cm (8 in)	5–10 cm (2–4 in)	■	■							B
C. luciliae		Light blue	15 cm (6 in)	5–10 cm (2–4 in)	■								B
C. sardensis		Dark blue	15 cm (6 in)	5–10 cm (2–4 in)		■	■						B
Chrysanthemum (hybrids)		All except blue	15 cm–1.8 m (6 in–6 ft)	acc. to type					■	■	■	■	P or A
C. maximum	Shasta daisy	White	75–90 cm ($2\frac{1}{2}$–3 ft)	30–45 cm (12–18 in)				■	■	■			P
C. maximum	'Wirral Pride'	White	90 cm (3 ft)	30–45 cm (12–18 in)				■	■	■			P
C. maximum	'Esther Read'	White	75 cm ($2\frac{1}{2}$ ft)	30–45 cm (12–18 in)				■	■	■			P
C. maximum	'H Siebert'	White	75 cm ($2\frac{1}{2}$ ft)	30–45 cm (12–18 in)				■	■	■			P
C. parthenium	Feverfew	White	45 cm (18 in)	25 cm (10 in)				■	■	■	■		P
C. roseum	Pyrethrum	Pink, red, white	90 cm (3 ft)	45 cm (18 in)				■					P
C. roseum	Pyrethrum 'Ariel'	Salmon	90 cm (3 ft)	45 cm (18 in)				■					P All named varieties must be propagated vegetatively
C. roseum	Pyrethrum 'Kelway's Glorious'	Crimson red	90 cm (3 ft)	45 cm (18 in)				■					P
C. roseum	Pyrethrum 'Eileen May Robinson'	Pink	90 cm (3 ft)	45 cm (18 in)				■					P
C. roseum	Pyrethrum 'Avalanche'	White	90 cm (3 ft)	45 cm (18 in)				■					P
C. roseum	Pyrethrum 'Lord Roseberry'	Red	90 cm (3 ft)	45 cm (18 in)				■					P
C. roseum	Pyrethrum 'Madeleine'	Clear pink	90 cm (3 ft)	45 cm (18 in)				■					P
C. roseum	Pyrethrum 'Venus'	Shell pink	90 cm (3 ft)	45 cm (18 in)				■					P
C. roseum	Pyrethrum 'Carl Vogt'	White	90 cm (3 ft)	45 cm (18 in)				■					P

Latin	Common or varietal name	Colour	Height	Spread or p.d.	Spring			Summer			Aut		Reminders
					E	M	L	E	M	L	E	M	
C. uliginosum	Moon daisy	White	1.8 m (6 ft)	38 cm (15 in)								■	P
Cimicifuga foetida	Bugbane	Greenish yellow	1.5 m (5 ft)	45 cm (18 in)					■	■			P, These prefer moist soil and semi-shade
C. foetida	'White Pearl'	White	1.5 m (5 ft)	45 cm (18 in)							■	■	P
C. racemosa	Black snake-root	White	1.5 m (5 ft)	60 cm (2 ft)					■	■			P
Clarkia elegans		All except blue	up to 60 cm (2 ft)	30 cm (12 in)						■	■		A, Prefers a light acid soil
Clematis heracleifolia	'Wyevale'	Blue	90 cm (3 ft)	1.5 m (5 ft)						■	■		P
C. integrifolia		Violet-blue	60 cm (2 ft)	30 cm (12 in)					■	■	■		P, May need support
C. recta		White	1.2 m (4 ft)	45 cm (18 in)				■	■				P, Scented
C. recta	'Purpurea'	White	1.2 m (4 ft)	45 cm (18 in)				■	■				P, Purple foliage
Cleome spinosa	Spider flower	White. pink, lilac, carmine	1.2 m (4 ft)	45 cm (18 in)					■	■	■	■	A, Thorny
Colchicum autumnale	Autumn crocus	Lilac	15–25 cm (6–10 in)	23 cm (9 in)							■	■	B Dying foliage is untidy. Plant taller growing
C. autumnale	'Roseum-plenum'	Rose-pink	15–25 cm (6–10 in)	23 cm (9 in)							■	■	B subjects so as to conceal this
C. autumnale	'Album'	White	15–25 cm (6–10 in)	23 cm (9 in)							■	■	B
C. speciosum		Mauve	15–40 cm (6–16 in)	23–30 cm (9–12 in)							■	■	B
C. speciosum	'Atrorubens'	Purple-crimson	15–40 cm (6–16 in)	23–30 cm (9–12 in)							■	■	B
C. speciosum	'The Giant'	Purple-crimson	15–40 cm (6–16 in)	23–30 cm (9–12 in)							■	■	B
C. speciosum	'Waterlily'	Mauve	15–40 cm (6–16 in)	23–30 cm (9–12 in)							■	■	B
Coleus blumei	Coleus		to 45 cm (to 18 in)	to 30 cm (to 12 in)									A, Grown for brilliantly coloured foliage
Convallaria majalis	Lily-of-the-valley	White	20 cm (8 in)	60 cm (2 ft)		■	■						R, Needs moist rich soil and semi-shade
C. majalis	'Fortin's Giant'	White	20 cm (8 in)	60 cm (2 ft)		■	■						R, Has larger flowers
Convolvulus cneorum		White	60 cm (2 ft)	90 cm (3 ft)			■	■	■	■	■		S, Silver foliage, very tender
C. mauretanicus		Blue-mauve	8 cm (3 in)	90 cm (3 ft)				■	■	■	■		P, Trailing, very tender
C. tricolor		Blue, white, cerise, pink	30–38 cm (12–15 in)	15–20 cm (6–8 in)					■	■	■		A
C. tricolor	'Royal Ensign'	Dark blue and white	30–38 cm (12–15 cm)	15–20 cm (6–8 in)					■	■	■		A

(*Opposite*) A border with mid-season colour and shape; kniphofias (red-hot pokers) macleayas (plume poppies) verbascums (mullein) and campanulas.

Latin	Common or varietal name	Colour	Height	Spread or p.d.	Spring			Summer			Aut		Reminders
					E	M	L	E	M	L	E	M	
C. tricolor	'Deep Blue'	Blue	30–38 cm (12–15 cm)	15–20 cm (6–8 in)					■	■	■		A
C. tricolor	'Sky Blue'	Blue	30–38 cm (12–15 in)	15–20 cm (6–8 in)						■	■	■	A
Coreopsis tinctoria		Yellow, brown, crimson	23–90 cm (9 in–3 ft)	13–38 cm (5–15 in)					■	■	■		P
C. grandiflora	Tickseed	Yellow	45 cm (18 in)	23 cm (9 in)				■	■	■			P, May need support
C. verticillata		Golden yellow	45–60 cm (18–24 in)	30–45 cm (12–18 in)				■	■	■	■		P, Attractive dark green foliage
Corydalis lutea	Yellow corydalis	Yellow	20 cm (8 in)	30 cm + (12 in +)			■	■	■	■	■	■	P, Good in poor soil
Cosmos bipinnatus	Cosmea	Pink, mauve crimson	90 cm (3 ft)	60 cm (2 ft)					■	■	■		A
C. sulphureus		Yellow to vermilion	60 cm (2 ft)	45 cm (18 in)					■	■	■		A
Crinum × powellii		Pink or white	45 cm (18 in)	30–45 cm (12–18 in)					■	■	■		B, plant 30 cm (12 in) deep
Crocosmia masonorum		Flame-red	75 cm (2½ ft)	15–23 cm (6–9 in)					■	■			C
C. × pottsii		Orange-vermilion	1.2 m (4 ft)	10–15 cm (4–6 in)						■			C
C. × pottsii	'Solfatare'	Yellow	60 cm (2 ft)	10–15 cm (4–6 in)						■			C, Bronze foliage, not reliably hardy
Crocus tomasinianus		Lilac, mauve, purple, white	8 cm (3 in)	8–10 cm (3–4 in)	■								C Plant 5–8 cm (2–3 in) deep, or deeper where other plants are to grow over them
C. aureus		Golden yellow	10 cm (4 in)	8–10 cm (3–4 in)	■	■							C
C. chrysanthus	'Blue Pearl'	Pale blue and white	10 cm (4 in)	8–10 cm (3–4 in)	■								C
C. chrysanthus	'Zwanenburg Bronze'	Golden brown and yellow	10 cm (4 in)	8–10 cm (3–4 in)	■								C
C. chrysanthus	'Ladykiller'	White and purple	10 cm (4 in)	8–10 cm (3–4 in)	■								C
C. chrysanthus	'Cream Beauty'	Cream	10 cm (4 in)	8–10 cm (3–4 in)	■								C
C. hybrid	'Pickwick'	Lilac and purple	10 cm (4 in)	8–10 cm (3–4 in)	■								C
C. hybrid	'Remembrance'	Purple	10 cm (4 in)	8–10 cm (3–4 in)	■								C
Cyclamen coum		Pink or white	8 cm (3 in)	15 cm (6 in)	■								T, Mulch with leafmould after flowering
C. neapolitanum		Pink or lilac	10 cm (4 in)	10 cm (4 in)						■	■	■	T, Leaves vanish in summer
Dahlia (hybrids)		All except blue	30 cm–1.8 m (12 in–6 ft)	acc. to type						■	■	■	T or A

Latin	Common or varietal name	Colour	Height	Spread or p.d.	Spring			Summer			Aut		Reminders
					E	M	L	E	M	L	E	M	
Delphinium ajacis	Rocket larkspur	Blue or violet	30–90 cm (12 in–3 ft)	15–25 cm (6–10 in)				■	■	■			A
D. consolida	Larkspur	Blue thro' cerise to white	1.2 m (4 ft)	30–38 cm (12–15 in)				■	■	■			A
D. (hybrid)	Delphineum	Blue, mauve, pink, white	20 cm–2.4 m (8 in–8 ft)	acc. to type				■	■				P, Tall vars. need staking
Dianthus barbatus	Sweet William	Pink, white, crimson	30–60 cm (12–24 in)	20–25 cm (8–10 in)				■	■				Bi, Sweetly scented
D. caryophyllus	Border carnation	All except blue	to 90 cm (to 3 ft)	35–45 cm (14–18 in)					■				P, May need staking, short-lived, usually perfumed
D. chinensis	Indian pink	Red, pink white	to 23 cm (to 9 in)	15 cm (6 in)					■	■	■	■	A, Dead-head often
D. chinensis	Garden pink, 'old fashioned'	Red, pink, white	to 25 cm (to 10 in)	to 30 cm (to 12 in)				■					P
D. chinensis	Garden pink, 'modern'	Red, pink, white	25–38 cm (10–15 in)	23–30 cm (9–12 in)				■	■		■		P, Shorter-lived
Dicentra eximia		Pink or white	45 cm (18 in)	30 cm (12 in)			■	■	■	■	■		P
D. spectabilis	Bleeding heart	Pink or white	75 cm (2½ ft)	45 cm (18 in)			■	■					P, Needs shelter, protect in winter
Dictamnus albus	Burning bush	White	60 cm (2 ft)	45 cm (18 in)				■	■				P, Do not move established plants
D. albus	'Purpurea'	Pink and red	60 cm (2 ft)	45 cm (18 in)				■	■				P, Do not move established plants
Dierama pulcherrimum	Angel's fishing rods	Pink to magenta	1.8 m (6 ft)	60 cm (2 ft)				■	■				C, Needs space
Digitalis purpurea	Foxglove	Pink, mauve, white	1.8 m (6 ft)	60 cm (2 ft)				■	■				Bi
D. purpurea	'Excelsior' hybrids	White, pink, mauve, yellow, maroon	1.5 m (5 ft)	60 cm (2 ft)				■	■				Bi
D. purpurea	'Foxy'	Pink to purple	75 cm (2½ ft)	30–40 cm (12–16 in)				■	■				Bi
Dimorphotheca aurantiaca	Star of the veldt	Orange	45 cm (18 in)	30 cm (12 in)				■	■	■	■		P, Tender
D. barberiae		White or pink	60 cm (2 ft)	90 cm + (3 ft +)					■	■			P, Tender
Doronicum pardalianches	Great leopard's bane	Yellow	90 cm (3 ft)	38 cm (15 in)			■	■	■				P
D. plantagineum	Leopard's bane	Yellow	60 cm (2 ft)	45 cm (18 in)		■	■	■					P
D. plantagineum	'Miss Mason'	Yellow	60 cm (2 ft)	45 cm (18 in)		■	■	■					P
Dracunculus vulgaris	Dragon arum	Maroon	90 cm (3 ft)	23 cm (9 in)				■					T, Plant 15 cm (6 in) deep
Echinacea purpurea	Purple cone-flower	Pink	1.2 m (4 ft)	45–60 cm (18–24 in)					■	■	■		P

Latin	Common or varietal name	Colour	Height	Spread or p.d.	Spring			Summer			Aut		Reminders
					E	M	L	E	M	L	E	M	
Echinops ritro	Globe thistle	Steel-blue	1.2 m (4 ft)	60 cm (2 ft)					■	■			P, F/A, Conceal bare stems with other plants
Endymion hispanicus	Bluebell	Blue, lilac, pink, white	30 cm (12 in)	15 cm (6 in)		■	■	■					B, Plant 10–15 cm (4–6 in) deep
Epimedium grandiflorum	Bishop's hat	White, pink, violet, yellow	30 cm (12 in)	30 cm (12 in)				■					R
E. perralderianum		Yellow	30 cm (12 in)	38 cm (15 in)				■					R, Good foliage
Eremurus robusta	Giant foxtail lily	Salmon yellow	3 m (10 ft)	1.2 m (4 ft)			■	■					P, Needs a sheltered site
E. robusta	'Shelford Hybrids'	Pale pink, copper	2.1 m (7 ft)	90 cm (3 ft)				■	■				P
E. stenophyllus bungei	Foxtail lily	Golden yellow	90 cm (3 ft)	60 cm (2 ft)				■					P
Erigeron speciosus		Lilac	45 cm (18 in)	30 cm (12 in)					■	■			P, Prefers moisture-retentive soil
E. speciosus	'Darkest of All'	Violet blue	45 cm (18 in)	30 cm (12 in)					■	■			P, Prefers moisture-retentive soil
E. speciosus	'Charity'	Light pink	45 cm (18 in)	30 cm (12 in)					■	■			P, Prefers moisture-retentive soil
E. speciosus	'Gaiety'	Bright pink	45 cm (18 in)	30 cm (12 in)					■	■			P
E. speciosus	'Prosperity'	Blue	45 cm (18 in)	30 cm (12 in)					■	■			P
E. speciosus	Quakeress'	Pale mauve-pinks	45 cm (18 in)	30 cm (12 in)					■	■			P
Eryngium alpinum		Blue	60 cm (2 ft)	38 cm (15 in)					■	■	■		P, F/A
E. giganteum		Silver-blue	1.2 m (4 ft)	60 cm (2 ft)						■	■		Bi
E. variifolium		Blue	75 cm (2½ ft)	30 cm (12 in)					■	■			P, E
Eschscholzia californica	Californian poppy	Orange and mixtures	38 cm (15 in)	15 cm (6 in)					■	■	■	■	A, Does best in poor hot soil
Euphorbia griffithii		Orange-scarlet	75 cm (2½ ft)	60 cm (2 ft)			■	■					P, A 'traveller'
E. myrsinites		Lime-yellow	15 cm (6 in)	38 cm (15 in)	■	■							P, Slightly tender
E. wulfenii		Lime-green	1.2 m+ (4 ft+)	1.2 m+ (4 ft+)			■	■	■	■	■		P, Must have a hot, sheltered site
E. polychroma		Acid-yellow	45 cm (18 in)	60 cm+ (2 ft+)		■	■						P, Best in full sun
Festuca glauca		Purple	15 cm (6 in)	30 cm (12 in)				■	■				P, Good as a 'contrast' plant
Foeniculum vulgare	Fennel	Yellow	1.5–2.4 m (5–8 ft)	30–60 cm (12–24 in)					■	■			P, Good emerald foliage
F. vulgare	'Purpureum'	Yellow	1.5–2.4 m (5–8 ft)	30–60 cm (12–24 in)					■	■			P, Good purple-bronze foliage

Latin	Common or varietal name	Colour	Height	Spread or p.d.	Spring			Summer			Aut		Reminders
					E	M	L	E	M	L	E	M	
Fritillaria imperialis	Crown imperial	Orange, rust, yellow	90 cm (3 ft)	38 cm (15 in)		■							B, Set bulbs 23 cm (9 in) deep on their sides
Gaillardia aristata	Blanket flower	Yellow and red	75 cm (2½ ft)	45 cm (18 in)					■	■	■	■	P
G. aristata	'Goblin'	Yellow and red	35 cm (14 in)	15–20 cm (6–8 in)					■	■	■	■	P
G. aristata	'Mandarin'	Flame-orange	90 cm (3 ft)	38 cm (15 in)					■	■	■	■	P
G. aristata	'Burgundy'	Wine-red	60 cm (2 ft)	60 cm (2 ft)					■	■	■	■	P
Galega officinalis	Goat's rue	Lilac	1.5 m (5 ft)	75 cm (2½ ft)						■	■		P
Galanthus nivalis	Snowdrop	White and green	8–20 cm (3–8 in)	8–15 cm (3–6 in)	■								B, Needs moisture retentive soil and humus
Galtonia candicans	Summer hyacinth	White	1.2 m (4 ft)	18 cm (7 in)					■	■	■		B, Plant 15 cm (6 in) deep
Gaura lindheimeri		Pinkish white	1.2 m (4 ft)	40 cm (16 in)						■	■	■	P, Best in front of dark backgrounds
Gazania × hybrida		Orange	23 cm (9 in)	30 cm (12 in)					■	■	■	■	A, Very tender
G. splendens		Orange	23 cm (9 in)	30 cm (12 in)					■	■	■		A
Geranium endressii		Pink	45 cm (18 in)	90 cm (3 ft)			■	■	■	■			P, Evergreen in mild winters
G. endressii	'Rose Clair'	Salmon pink	45 cm (18 in)	90 cm (3 ft)			■	■	■	■			P
G. hybrid	'Claridge Druce'	Lilac-pink	45 cm (18 in)	90 cm (3 ft)			■	■	■	■			P
G. ibericum		Blue-purple	60 cm (2 ft)	45 cm (18 in)					■	■			P
G. macrorrhizum		Pink or white	38 cm (15 in)	90 cm (3 ft)			■	■	■				P, Aromatic foliage
G. pratense	Meadow crane's bill	Deep blue	75 cm (2½ ft)	75 cm (2½ ft)				■	■	■			P
G. pratense	'Mrs Kendall Clarke'	Pale blue	75 cm (2½ ft)	75 cm (2½ ft)				■	■	■			P
G. pratense	'Johnson's Blue'	Blue	38 cm (15 in)	75 cm (2½ ft)				■	■	■			P
G. psilostemon		Magenta	75 cm (2½ ft)	60 cm (2 ft)				■	■				P, May need support
G. sanguineum	Bloody crane's bill	Magenta	23 cm (9 in)	45 cm + (18 in +)				■	■	■	■		P, Trails
G. sanguineum	'Album'	White	23 cm (9 in)	45 cm + (18 in +)				■	■	■	■		P, Trails
G. phaeum	Dusky crane's bill	Very dark maroon	45 cm (18 in)	60 cm (2 ft)				■	■	■			P, Does not mind some shade
Geum chiloense	'Mrs Bradshaw'	Red	60 cm (2 ft)	45 cm (18 in)				■	■	■	■		P

Latin	Common or varietal name	Colour	Height	Spread or p.d.	Spring E	Spring M	Spring L	Summer E	Summer M	Summer L	Aut E	Aut M	Reminders
G. chiloense	'Fire Opal'	Orange–vermilion	60 cm (2 ft)	45 cm (18 in)				■	■	■	■		P
G. chiloense	'Lady Stratheden'	Yellow	60 cm (2 ft)	45 cm (18 in)				■	■	■	■		P
Gilia capitata		Pale blue	45 cm (18 in)	15 cm (6 in)				■	■	■	■		A
G. tricolor		Pale lilac	60 cm (2 ft)	23 cm (9 in)					■				A
Gladiolus	hybrid varieties	All except blue	60 cm–1.2 m (2–4 ft)	10–15 cm (4–6 in)					■	■	■		C, Plant 15 cm (6 in) deep (see text)
G. byzantinus		Magenta or wine red	60 cm (2 ft)	10–15 cm (4–6 in)				■					C, Hardy in most areas
Godetia grandiflora	hybrid varieties	Pink, crimson, mauve, salmon, etc.	30–38 cm (12–15 in)	15 cm (6 in)				■	■	■			A
Gypsophila elegans		Pink or white	60 cm (2 ft)	30 cm (12 in)			■	■	■	■	■		A
G. paniculata	Baby's breath	Pink or white	90 cm (3 ft)	60–90 cm (2–3 ft)				■	■	■			P
Helenium autumnale		Red, yellow, orange, bronze	to 1.8 m (to 6 ft)	45 cm (18 in)						■	■	■	P
Helianthemum nummularium	Rock rose, sun rose	Pink, white, red, crimson, yellow	10–25 cm (4–10 in)	to 60 cm (2 ft)				■	■				P, Tender in cold winters
H. nummularium	'Ben Afflick'	Orange, yellow	10–25 cm (4–10 in)	to 60 cm (2 ft)				■	■				P, Tender in cold winters
H. nummularium	'Ben Heckla'	Bronze-gold	10–25 cm (4–10 in)	to 60 cm (2 ft)				■	■				P, Tender in cold winters
H. nummularium	'Ben Hope'	Crimson-pink	10–25 cm (4–10 in)	to 60 cm (to 2 ft)				■	■				P, Tender in cold winters
H. nummularium	'Ben Nevis'	Yellow and orange	10–15 cm (4–6 in)	to 45 cm (to 18 in)				■	■				P, Tender in cold winters
H. nummularium	'The Bride'	White	10–25 cm (4–10 in)	to 60 cm (to 2 ft)				■	■				S, Grey foliage
H. nummularium	'Mrs Croft'	Pink and orange	10–25 cm (4–10 in)	to 60 cm (to 2 ft)				■	■				S, Grey foliage
Helianthus annuus	Sunflower	Yellow	to 3 m+ (to 10 ft+)	45 cm (18 in)					■	■	■		A, Needs strong support and responds to feeding
Helichrysum angustifolium	Curry plant	Mustard yellow	45 cm (18 in)	60 cm (2 ft)				■	■	■			S, Aromatic grey foliage
H. bracteatum	Strawflower	Yellow, red, pink, white etc.	30 cm–1.2 m (12 in–4 ft)	30 cm+ (12 in+)					■	■	■		A
H. petiolatum			30 cm+ (12 in+)	to 1.2 m (to 4 ft)									S, Tender and trailing (foliage only)
Helleborus corsicus		Green	60 cm (2 ft)	90 cm (3 ft)	■	■							P, Needs space
H. orientalis	Lenten rose	Green, white, pink, maroon	60 cm (2 ft)	45 cm (18 in)	■								P, Feed after flowering

Latin	Common or varietal name	Colour	Height	Spread or p.d.	Spring			Summer			Aut		Reminders
					E	M	L	E	M	L	E	M	
Hemerocallis dumortieri		Yellow	60 cm (2 ft)	60 cm (2 ft)			■	■					P, Scented, needs space
H. dumortieri	hybrids	Orange, rust, pink, yellow, maroon, etc.	75 cm (2½ ft)	45 cm (18 in)				■	■	■			P
Hesperis matronalis	Dame's violet, sweet rocket	White, lilac or mauve	105 cm (3½ ft)	45 cm (18 in)				■					P, Short-lived, but seeds well
Heuchera sanguinea	Coral-flower	Coral-red	30–45 cm (12–18 in)	45 cm (18 in)				■	■	■	■		P
H. sanguinea	'Pearl Drops'	White	30–45 cm (12–18 in)	45 cm (18 in)				■	■	■	■		P
H. sanguinea	'Red Spangles'	Blood red	30–45 cm (12–18 in)	45 cm (18 in)				■	■	■	■		P
H. sanguinea	'Scintillation'	Pink	30–45 cm (12–18 in)	45 cm (18 in)				■	■	■	■		P
H. sanguinea	'Sunset'	Bright red	30–45 cm (12–18 in)	45 cm (18 in)				■	■	■	■		P
Hosta elata		White to pale violet	90 cm (3 ft)	60 cm (2 ft)				■	■				P, Best in semi-shade
H. fortunei		Lilac	90 cm (3 ft)	45 cm (18 in)					■				P, Best in semi-shade
H. fortunei	'Albopicta'	Mauve	60 cm (2 ft)	45 cm (18 in)					■				P, Best in semi-shade, yellow variegated leaves
H. fortunei	'Aureo-marginata'	White	60 cm (2 ft)	45 cm (18 in)					■				P, Shade, gold-edged green leaves
H. lancifolia		Lilac	60 cm (2 ft)	60 cm (2 ft)					■	■	■		P, Shade, narrow green leaves
H. sieboldiana		Whitish mauve	60 cm (2 ft)	60 cm (2 ft)						■			P, Shade
H. sieboldiana	'Elegans'	Lilac	60 cm (2 ft)	60 cm (2 ft)					■	■			P, Shade
H. undulata		Pale lilac	60 cm (2 ft)	60 cm (2 ft)						■			P, Shade, green and white leaves
Hyacinthus (hybrids)		Pink, white, blue, cream, etc.	to 30 cm (to 12 in)	23 cm (9 in)		■	■						B, Plant 13–15 cm (5–6 in) deep, 15 cm (6 in) apart
Iberis gibraltarica		Lilac	30 cm (12 in)	45 cm (18 in)		■	■						P, E short-lived and tender
I. sempervirens	Candytuft	White	23 cm (9 in)	60 cm (2 ft)			■	■					P, E
I. umbellata	Annual candytuft	Pink, white, red, mauve, etc.	to 38 cm (to 15 in)	23 cm (9 in)				■	■	■	■		A
Impatiens sultani	Busy Lizzie	Red, white, pink, purple, etc.	23–60 cm (9 in–2 ft)	23–60 cm (9 in–2 ft)			■	■	■	■	■	■	P, Best grown as A, shade
Incarvillea delavayi		Pink	60 cm (2 ft)	38 cm (15 in)			■	■					P, Vanishes completely in winter
Inula hookeri		Pale yellow	60 cm (2 ft)	60 cm (2 ft)						■	■		P, Does better in damp soil

A fine example of a mixed border, with trees, roses and climbers providing a permanent framework for seasonal colour. Rose 'Florence May Morse' phlox and penstemons.

A wide-paved path is both practical and attractive, its edges here are softened by alchemilla, hostas, dwarf bamboo and silene. The border plants are chosen for form and foliage-colour as well as for their flowers.

Latin	Common or varietal name	Colour	Height	Spread or p.d.	Spring			Summer			Aut		Reminders
					E	M	L	E	M	L	E	M	
I. magnifica		Golden yellow	1.8 m (6 ft)	90 cm + (3 ft +)						■	■		P, Does better in damp soil
Iris (species and hybrids)		All colours				■	■	■					R, Plant to face south (or north in southern hemisphere)
Kniphofia (hybrids) Gp. 1	'Alcazar'	Orange	90 cm (3 ft)	60 cm (2 ft)				■	■				P, Rather tender
K. (hybrids) Gp. 1	'Modesta'	Ivory and rose	60 cm (2 ft)	45 cm (18 in)				■	■				P, Rather tender
K. (hybrids) Gp. 1	'Gold Else'	Yellow	75 cm (2½ ft)	50 cm (20 in)				■	■				P, Rather tender
K. (hybrids) Gp. 2	'Bee's Lemon'	Lemon yellow	105 cm (3½ ft)	60 cm (2 ft)				■	■	■	■		P, Substantial foliage
K. (hybrids) Gp. 2	'Maid of Orleans'	Ivory cream	75 cm (2½ ft)	60 cm (2 ft)				■	■	■	■		P, Substantial foliage
K. (hybrids) Gp. 2	'Samuel's Sensation'	Scarlet	1.5 m (5 ft)	75 cm (2½ ft)				■	■	■	■		P, Substantial foliage
K. nelsonii major		Flame-red	75 cm (2½ ft)	45 cm (18 in)							■	■	P, Grassy leaves
K. n. rufa		Yellow and red	60 cm (2 ft)	38 cm (15 in)							■	■	P, Grassy leaves
Kochia scoparia	*Trichophylla*, burning bush	Foliage only	to 90 cm (to 3 ft)	60 cm (2 ft)									A, Green foliage, scarlet autumnal colour
Lamium galeobdolon	'Variegatum'	Yellow	30 cm (12 in)	infinite				■	■				P, Invasive, will grow in shade
L. maculatum		Pink	30 cm (12 in)	30–60 cm (12 in–2 ft)			■						P
L. maculatum	'Album'	White	30 cm (12 in)	30–60 cm (12 in–2 ft)			■	■					P
L. maculatum	'Aureum'	Pink	15 cm (6 in)	15–45 cm (6–18 in)			■	■					P, Tender, needs semi-shade, grown for foliage colour
Lampranthus aurantiacus		Flame orange	30 cm (12 in)	to 45 cm (to 18 in)				■	■	■	■		A (or P)
L. spectabilis	(species)	Magenta	30 cm (12 in)	30 cm (12 in)				■	■	■	■		A (or P), Needs an arid site and full sun
L. spectabilis	varieties	Amber, pink, cerise, purple etc.	30 cm (12 in)	30 cm (12 in)				■	■	■	■		A (or P), Needs an arid site and full sun
Lathyrus latifolius	Everlasting pea	Pink or magenta	to 3 m+ (to 10 ft+)	45 cm (18 in)				■	■	■	■		P
L. latifolis	'White Pearl'	White	to 3 m+ (to 10 ft+)	45 cm (18 in)				■	■	■	■		P, More tender
L. odoratus	Sweet pea	All except yellow	38 cm–3 m (15 in–10 ft)	25–38 cm (10–15 in)				■	■	■	■		A, Scented climber or dwarf border plant
Lavatera trimestris	Mallow	Pink	to 90 cm (to 3 ft)	to 60 cm (to 2 ft)					■	■	■		A, Very quick growing
L. trimestris	'Splendens Alba'	White	to 90 cm (to 3 ft)	to 60 cm (to 2 ft)					■	■	■		A, Very quick growing

Latin	Common or varietal name	Colour	Height	Spread or p.d.	Spring E	Spring M	Spring L	Summer E	Summer M	Summer L	Aut E	Aut M	Reminders
Liatris callilepis	Gay feather	Carmine-pink	to 90 cm (to 3 ft)	45 cm (18 in)					■	■	■		P
L. callilepis	'Kobold'	Carmine-pink	60 cm (2 ft)	45 cm (18 in)					■	■	■		P, Good on poor soils
L. spicata		Pink, white, or purple	90 cm (3 ft)	45 cm (18 in)							■		P, Good on damp soils
Ligularia dentata	'Desdemona'	Orange	1.5 m (5 ft)	90 cm (3 ft)					■	■			P, Best in damp soils
L. przewalskii		Yellow	1.8 m (6 ft)	75 cm (18 in)					■	■			P, Best in damp soils
Lilium auratum	Golden-rayed lily of Japan	White and yellow	2.4 m (8 ft)	30 cm (12 in)						■	■		B, Plant 15–30 cm (6–12 in) deep, shade lower stem
L. candidum	Madonna lily	White	1.5 m (5 ft)	25 cm (10 in)				■	■				B, Plant 5 cm (2 in) deep in sun, lime tolerant
L. henryi		Apricot-yellow	2.4 m (8 ft)	30 cm (12 in)					■	■			B, Plant 20 cm (8 in) deep, partial shade
L. regale	Royal lily	Pink and white	1.8 m (6 ft)	30 cm (12 in)					■				B, Plant 15–23 cm (6–9 in), sun
L. pumilum		Red	1.2 m (4 ft)	15 cm (6 in)				■					B, Plant 10 cm (4 in) in ordinary soil, sun
L. tigrinum	Tiger lily	Orange, red	1.8 m (6 ft)	23 cm (9 in)						■	■		B, plant 15 cm (6 in) in lime-free soil, sun
Limnanthes douglasii	Poached egg flower	White and yellow	15 cm (6 in)	10 cm (4 in)				■	■	■			A, Scented, damp or dry soil, (best in damp) full sun
Limonium latifolium		Lilac-blue	60 cm (2 ft)	45 cm (18 in)				■	■	■			P, F/A
L. sinuatum	Statice	Blue and mixtures	45 cm (18 in)	30 cm (12 in)					■	■	■		A, F/A
L. suworowii	Pink pokers	Carmine	45 cm (18 in)	30 cm (12 in)					■	■	■		A, F/A
Linum flavum		Yellow	45 cm (18 in)	23 cm (9 in)				■	■	■			P, Sometimes shy flowering
Linum grandiflorum	Scarlet flax	Rose or crimson	45 cm (18 in)	10–15 cm (4–6 in)				■	■	■			A
L. narbonense	Flax	Blue	30–60 cm (12–24 in)	30 cm (12 in)			■	■	■	■	■		P, A little tender
Lobelia erinus	Bedding lobelia	Purple, blue, white and pink	10–23 cm (4–9 in)	10 cm (4 in)			■	■	■	■	■	■	A
L. fulgens		Scarlet	90 cm (3 ft)	38 cm (15 in)						■	■	■	HHP
Lobularia maritimum	Sweet alyssum	Pink, white, or mauve	15 cm (6 in)	30 cm (12 in)				■	■	■	■		A
Lunaria annua	Honesty	Magenta	90 cm (3 ft)	30 cm (12 in)		■	■	■					Bi
L. annua	'Variegata'	Paler pink	90 cm (3 ft)	30 cm (12 in)		■	■	■					B, Variegated foliage in second year
Lupinus arboreus	Tree lupin	Mauve, white, or yellow	1.2 m (4 ft)	90 cm (3 ft)				■	■	■			P. Short-lived, prefers acid soil

Latin	Common or varietal name	Colour	Height	Spread or p.d.	Spring E	Spring M	Spring L	Summer E	Summer M	Summer L	Aut E	Aut M	Reminders
L. polyphyllus	(hybrids) 'Russell Lupins'	Many bi-colours	60–90 cm (2–3 ft)	75 cm (2½ ft)			■	■	■				P
Lychnis chalcedonica	Jerusalem cross	Red	90 cm (3 ft)	38 cm (15 in)					■	■			P
L. coronaria	Rose campion	Carmine or white	60 cm (2 ft)	20 cm (8 in)					■	■	■		P, Short-lived
Lysimachia nummularia	Creeping Jenny	Yellow	4 cm (1½ in)	60 cm (2 ft)				■	■				P
L. nummularia	'Aurea'	Yellow	4 cm (1½ in)	60 cm (2 ft)				■	■				P. Golden yellow leaves
L. punctata	Yellow loosestrife	Yellow	90 cm (3 ft)	30 cm (12 in)				■	■	■			P, Invasive
Lythrum salicaria	Purple loosestrife	Pink, crimson or magenta	1.8 m (6 ft)	60 cm (2 ft)				■	■	■	■		P
Macleaya cordata		White	2.4 m (8 ft)	60 cm (2 ft)				■	■	■			P
M. microcarpa	Plume poppy	Buff apricot	2.4 m (8 ft)	60 cm (2 ft)				■	■				P, Invasive, beautiful foliage
Malcomia maritima	Virginian stock	Pink, mauve, white, crimson	20 cm (8 in)	Sow direct, thin out later				■	■	■			A, Day-scented
Malva moschata	Musk mallow	Pink	60 cm (2 ft)	45 cm (18 in)				■	■	■	■		P
M. moschata	'Alba'	White	60 cm (2 ft)	45 cm (18 in)				■	■	■	■		P
Matthiola bicornis	Night-scented stock	Pink	38 cm (15 in)	23 cm (9 in)					■	■			A, Evening and night-scented
M. incana	Ten-week stock	'Stock' colours	30–75 cm (12 in–2½ ft)	20–38 cm (8–15 in)				■	■				Bi
M. incana	Perpetual flowering or 'All-year-round' stock	White	38 cm (15 in)	30 cm (12 in)			■	■	■				A or B
M. incana	Brompton stock	'Stock' colours	45 cm (18 in)	30 cm (12 in)			■	■	■				Bi
M. incana	Trysomic stock	Mixed colours	38 cm (15 in)	30 cm (12 in)			■	■	■				HHA, Flowers seven weeks from sowing
Meconopsis cambrica	Welsh poppy	Yellow or orange	30 cm (12 in)	30 cm (12 in)				■	■	■	■		P, Prefers damp soil
Mesembryanthemum criniflorum	Livingstone daisy	All colours except blue	15 cm (6 in)	23 cm (9 in)				■	■	■			A
Moluccella laevis	Bells of Ireland	Green	60 cm (2 ft)	23 cm (9 in)					■				A, F/A
Monarda didyma	Bergamot	Scarlet	90 cm (3 ft)	38 cm (15 in)					■	■	■		P, Fragrant leaves
M. didyma	'Croftway Pink'	Rose pink	90 cm (3 ft)	38 cm (15 in)					■	■	■		P, Fragrant leaves
M. didyma	'Melissa'	Pale pink	90 cm (3 ft)	38 cm (15 in)					■	■	■		P, Fragrant leaves
M. didyma	'Prairie Night'	Purple	90 cm (3 ft)	38 cm (15 in)					■	■	■		P, Fragrant leaves

Latin	Common or varietal name	Colour	Height	Spread or p.d.	Spring			Summer			Aut		Reminders
					E	M	L	E	M	L	E	M	
M. didyma	'Snow Maiden'	White	90 cm (3 ft)	38 cm (15 in)					■	■	■		P, Fragrant leaves
Muscari botryoides	Grape hyacinth	Blue	10–20 cm (6–8 in)	8–10 cm (3–4 in)	■	■	■						B, Leaves remain until mid-summer
M. botryoides	'Album'	White	15–20 cm (6–8 in)	8–10 cm (3–4 in)		■	■	■					B
Myosotis alpestris	Forget-me-not	Blue	20 cm (8 in)	15 cm (6 in)			■	■					Bi
Myrrhis odorata	Sweet Cicely	White	90 cm (3 ft)	1.2 m (4 ft)			■	■					P, Aromatic, ferny foliage. Grows almost anywhere
Narcissus	'February Gold'	Yellow	30 cm (12 in)	10 cm (4 in)	■								B Plant all narcissus as early as possible, though this is not always easy in late summer borders
Narcissus	'February Silver'	White and lemon	30 cm (12 in)	10 cm (4 in)	■								B
Narcissus	'Tête-à-tête'	Yellow	15 cm (6 in)	8 cm (3 in)	■								B
Narcissus	'Peeping Tom'	Golden yellow	40 cm (16 in)	10 cm (4 in)	■								B
Narcissus	'March Sunshine'	Yellow and orange	30 cm (12 in)	10 cm (4 in)		■	■						B
Narcissus	'Pepper'	Yellow, orange-red	30 cm (12 in)	10 cm (4 in)		■	■						B
Narcissus	'Quince'	Yellow	18 cm (7 in)	8 cm (3 in)		■	■						B
Narcissus	'Rip van Winkle'	Green-yellow	15 cm (6 in)	5 cm (2 in)		■	■						B
Narcissus	'Sweetness'	Yellow	35 cm (14 in)	10 cm (4 in)		■	■						B
N. triandrus albus	'Angel's Tears'	White	10 cm (4 in)	4 cm (1½ in)		■	■						B
N.	'Woodcock'	Yellow	30 cm (12 in)	10 cm (4 in)		■	■						B
N.	'Golden Harvest'	Yellow	45 cm (18 in)	10 cm (4 in)		■	■						B
N.	'Mount Hood'	White	45 cm (18 in)	10 cm (4 in)		■	■						B
N.	'Fortune'	Yellow and orange	45 cm (18 in)	10 cm (4 in)		■	■						B
N.	'Ice Follies'	White and Yellow	45 cm (18 in)	10 cm (4 in)	■	■							B
N.	'Yellow Cheerfulness'	Yellow	45 cm (18 in)	10 cm (4 in)	■	■	■						B
N.	'Thalia'	Cream and white	45 cm (18 in)	10 cm (4 in)	■	■	■						B Very beautiful
N.	'Geranium'	Cream and orange	45 cm (18 in)	10 cm (4 in)	■	■	■						B

(*Opposite*) Good, humus-rich soil is important for these fine astilbes, hostas and the lilies.

Latin	Common or varietal name	Colour	Height	Spread or p.d.	Spring E	Spring M	Spring L	Summer E	Summer M	Summer L	Aut E	Aut M	Reminders
N.	'Actaea'	White, red and yellow	45 cm (18 in)	10 cm (4 in)			■						B
Nemesia strumosa	Poor man's orchid	Mixed	45 cm (18 in)	10–15 cm (4–6 in)					■	■			A, Feed
Nepeta faassenii	Catmint	Blue-mauve	45 cm (18 in)	38 cm (15 in)			■	■	■	■	■		P, Needs protection from cats, tender
N. faassenii	'Six Hills Giant'	Blue-mauve	60 cm (2 ft)	38 cm (15 in)			■	■	■	■	■		P
Nerine bowdenii	Naked nannies	Pink	60 cm (2 ft)	15 cm (6 in)							■	■	B, Plant 15 cm (6 in) deep, needs warm site
Nicotiana affinis	Tobacco flower	Mixed	90 cm (3 ft)	30 cm (12 in)				■	■	■	■		A, Night-scented
Nigella damascena	Love-in-a-mist	Blue or mixed	60 cm (2 ft)	15 cm (6 in)				■	■	■			A, F/A
N. damascena	'Moody Blue'	Blue	20 cm (8 in)	20 cm (8 in)				■	■	■			A
Oenothera erythrosepala	Evening primrose	Yellow	1.2 m (4 ft)	38 cm (15 in)				■	■	■	■		Bi
O. missouriensis		Yellow	15 cm (6 in)	45 cm (18 in)					■	■			P, Trails
O. tetragona		Yellow	90 cm (3 ft)	30 cm (12 in)					■	■	■		P, Red-purple foliage
Onopordum acanthium	Scotch thistle	Purple	2.4 m (8 ft)	90 cm (3 ft)					■	■			Bi, Handsome silver foliage, best in groups
Origanum vulgare aureum	Golden marjoram	Pink	23 cm (9 in)	30 cm (12 in)				■	■	■			P, Golden, aromatic foliage
Paeonia lactiflora	'Bowl of Beauty'	Soft pink	60 cm (2 ft)	90 cm (3 ft)				■	■				P, Dislikes disturbance
Paeonia	'La Cygne'	White	60 cm (2 ft)	90 cm (3 ft)				■	■				P, Dislikes disturbance,
Paeonia	'Sarah Bernhardt'	Pink	60 cm (2 ft)	90 cm (3 ft)				■	■				P Protect in winters, feed after flowering
Paeonia	'Solange'	Cream-buff to white	60 cm (2 ft)	90 cm (3 ft)				■	■				P
P. mlokosewitschii	'Molly the Witch'	Pale yellow	60 cm (2 ft)	90 cm (3 ft)		■	■						P
P. officinalis		Crimson	75 cm (2½ ft)	90 cm (3 ft)			■	■					P
P. officinalis	'Rubra plena'	Crimson	75 cm (2½ ft)	90 cm (3 ft)			■	■					P
Papaver nudicaule	Iceland poppy	Mixed	75 cm (2½ ft)	30–45 cm (12–18 in)					■	■			A, Bi, sometimes P
P. somniferum	Opium poppy	Shades of pink, mauve, crimson and white	90 cm (3 ft)	30 cm (12 in)					■	■			A, Seed-heads very decorative
P. rhoeas	'Shirley Poppy'	Mixed	60 cm (2 ft)	30 cm (12 in)				■	■	■			A

Latin	Common or varietal name	Colour	Height	Spread or p.d.	Spring			Summer			Aut		Reminders
					E	M	L	E	M	L	E	M	
P. orientale	Oriental poppy	Mixed	90 cm (3 ft)	90 cm (3 ft)			■	■					P, Leaves a gap after flowering
Pelargonium	'Geranium' zonal pelargonium	Mixed	to 60 cm (2 ft)	45 cm (18 in)			■	■	■	■			P, Tender, very good for gap filling
Penstemon barbatus		Pink to cerise	90 cm (3 ft)	60 cm (2 ft)				■	■	■			P, Tender, needs winter protection
P. hartwegii		Scarlet	60 cm (2 ft)	30–45 cm (12–18 in)				■	■	■			P, More hardy
P. × *gloxinioides*	hybrids	Mixed	60 cm (2 ft)	30–45 cm (12–18 in)				■	■	■			P, Very tender
Perovskia atriplicifolia	Turkish sage	Violet-blue	1.5 m (5 ft)	45 cm (18 in)						■	■		P, Cut down to 45 cm (18 in) in spring
Petunia hybrids		Mixed	23–38 cm (9–15 in)	30 cm (12 in)					■	■	■	■	P, (HHA), Dead-head often, spray against aphids
Phacelia campanularia		Blue	23 cm (9 in)	15 cm (6 in)					■	■	■		A, Protect against slugs
Phalaris arundinacea	'Picta', gardener's garters	Purplish	60 cm (2 ft)	infinite				■	■				P, Good striped folage, very invasive
Phlomis samia		Creamy-yellow	90 cm (3 ft)	60 cm (2 ft)				■	■				P, E, F/A
Phlox drummondii		Pinks, white, purples, crimson	38 cm (15 in)	23 cm (9 in)					■	■	■		A
P. paniculata		As above with salmon and scarlet	45 cm–1.2 m (1½–4 ft)	45–60 cm (18 in–2 ft)					■	■	■		P
P. paniculata	'Norah Leigh'	Lilac-pink	45 cm–1.2 m (18 in–4 ft)	45–60 cm (18 in–2 ft)					■	■	■		P, Not constitutionally strong
Phuopsis stylosa		Pink	23 cm (9 in)	60 cm (2 ft)					■	■	■		P, Good ground cover
Phygelius aequalis		Coral-range	75 cm (2½ ft)	60 cm (2 ft)					■	■	■	■	P or S, Can be grown as a wall shrub or border plant
P. capensis	Cape fuchsia	Rust or red	1.8 m (6 ft)	60 cm (2 ft)					■	■	■	■	P or S, Best in light soil
P. capensis	'Coccineus'	Scarlet	1.8 m (6 ft)	60 cm (2 ft)					■	■	■	■	P or S
Physalis alkekengi	Chinese lantern	White	38 cm (15 in)	60 cm + (2 ft +)					■	■			P, F/A, Grown for its orange 'lanterns'
P. franchettii	Chinese lantern	White	60 cm (2 ft)	60 cm (2 ft)					■	■			P, F/A, Roots are invasive
P. franchettii	'Gigantea'	White	90 cm (3 ft)	60 cm (2 ft)					■	■			P. F/A, Roots are invasive
Phystostegia virginiana	Obedient plant	Pink, white, mauve	75 cm–1.2 m (2½–4 ft)	60 cm (2 ft)					■	■			P, Prefers good moisture
P. virginiana	'Vivid'	Deep pink	75 cm–1.2 m (2½–4 ft)	60 cm (2 ft)					■	■			P, retentive soil, mulch
P. virginiana	'Summer Show'	White	75 cm–1.2 m (2½–4 ft)	60 cm (2 ft)					■	■			P in spring
P. virginiana	'Summer Spire'	Lilac-purple	75 cm–1.2 m (2½–4 ft)	60 cm (2 ft)					■	■			P

Latin	Common or varietal name	Colour	Height	Spread or p.d.	Spring			Summer			Aut		Reminders
					E	M	L	E	M	L	E	M	
Platycodon grandiflorum	Balloon-flower	Blue-mauve	60 cm (2 ft)	38 cm (15 in)				■	■	■			P
P. grandiflorum	'Album'	White	60 cm (2 ft)	38 cm (15 in)				■	■	■			P
P. grandiflorum	'Mariesii'	Blue-mauve	38 cm (15 in)	30 cm (12 in)				■	■	■			P
Polemonium coeruleum	Jacob's ladder	Blue or white	60 cm (2 ft)	30 cm (12 in)		■	■	■	■				P, Self-seeds
P. foliosissimum		Mauve-blue	90 cm (3 ft)	45 cm (18 in)				■	■	■	■		P
Polygonatum × *hybridum*	Solomon's seal	Green and white	1.2 m (4 ft)	30–45 cm (12–18 in)				■					R, Prefers semi-shade, watch for saw-fly larvae
Polygonum amplexicaule atrosanguineum		Red	1.2 m (4 ft)	90 cm + (3 ft +)				■	■	■	■	■	P, Invasive, likes damp soil
P. bistorta	'Superbum'	Pink	90 cm (3 ft)	90 cm (3 ft)			■	■					P, Invasive, likes damp soil
Potentilla (garden hybrids)	'Gibson's Scarlet'	Red	30 cm (12 in)	45 cm (18 in)				■	■	■	■		P, Mulch in spring
Potentilla	'Glory of Nancy'	Crimson to maroon	45 cm (18 in)	45 cm (18 in)				■	■	■	■		P, Mulch in spring
Potentilla	'Yellow Queen'	Yellow	38 cm (15 in)	38 cm (15 in)				■	■	■	■		P, Mulch in spring
Primula spp.	Polyanthus	Mixed	8–23 cm (3–9 in)	20 cm (8 in)		■	■						P, Incorporate peat and old manure before planting
Primula spp.	'Wanda'	Violet-cerise	8 cm (3 in)	15 cm (6 in)	■	■	■						P, Divide after flowering
Prunella grandiflora	Self-heal	Purple	15 cm (6 in)	45 cm (18 in)			■	■	■	■	■	■	P, Does not mind partial shade
P. webbiana	'Pink Loveliness'	Pink	23–30 cm (9–12 in)	38 cm (15 in)			■	■	■	■	■	■	P
P. webbiana	'Loveliness'	Lilac	23–30 cm (9–12 in)	38 cm (15 in)			■	■	■	■	■	■	P
P. webbiana	'Rosea'	Rose-pink	23–30 cm (9–12 in)	38 cm (15 in)			■	■	■	■	■	■	P
P. webbiana	'Alba'	White	23–30 cm (9–12 cm)	38 cm (15 in)			■	■	■	■	■	■	P
Pulmonaria officinalis	Lungwort	Pink/purple, blue	30 cm (12 in)	30 cm (12 in)		■	■						P. Good foliage, best in partial shade
P. saccharata		Pink to blue	30 cm (12 in)	30 cm (12 in)	■	■							P, Even better foliage
Pulsatilla vulgaris	Pasque flower	Amethyst	15 cm (6 in)	15 cm (6 in)		■	■						P, Good in chalk gardens
P. vulgaris	'Budapest'	Reddish-purple	15 cm (6 in)	15 cm (6 in)		■	■						P
P. vulgaris	'Rubra'	Red	15 cm (6 in)	15 cm (6 in)		■	■						P
Puschkinia scilloides		Pale blue	10–20 cm (4–8 in)	5–8 cm (2–3 in)	■	■	■						B

Latin	Common or varietal name	Colour	Height	Spread or p.d.	Spring			Summer			Aut		Reminders
					E	M	L	E	M	L	E	M	
Ranunculus asiaticus		Mixed	38 cm (15 in)	15 cm (6 in)			■	■	■				T, Needs rich soil and regular watering
Reseda odorata	Mignonette	Green/yellow, orange	30 cm (12 in)	15–23 cm (6–9 in)				■	■	■	■	■	A, Sweet-scented
R. odorata	'Goliath'	Green, red, yellow	30 cm (12 in)	15–23 cm (6–9 in)				■	■	■	■	■	A, Sweet-scented
Ricinus communis	Castor-oil plant	Greenish	1.5 m (5 ft)	90 cm (3 ft)					■				A, Foliage good, poisonous
R. communis	'Gibsonii'	Reddish	1.5 m (5 ft)	90 cm (3 ft)					■				A, Even better foliage, poisonous
R. communis	'Impala'	Creamy	1.5 m (5 ft)	90 cm (3 ft)					■				A, Better still, poisonous
Rudbeckia fulgida	var. *deamii*, black-eyed Susan	Yellow	60 cm (2 ft)	30 cm (12 in)					■	■	■		P
R. fulgida	'Goldsturm', black-eyed Susan	Yellow	60 cm (2 ft)	60 cm (2 ft)						■	■	■	P
R. nitida	Coneflower	Yellow	2.1 m (7 ft)	60 cm (2 ft)						■	■	■	P, Protect foliage from slugs
R. nitida	'Herbstonne'	Yellow	2.1 m (7 ft)	60 cm (2 ft)						■	■	■	P, Protect foliage from slugs
Ruta graveolens	'Jackman's Blue'	Yellow	60 cm (2 ft)	40 cm (16 in)					■				P, E, Striking blue foliage
Salpiglossis sinuata	Painted tongue	Mixed	60 cm (2 ft)	30 cm (12 in)					■	■	■		A, Needs good soil and support
S. sinuata	'Splash'	Mixed	60 cm (2 ft)	30 cm (12 in)					■	■	■		A, Does better on poor soil
S. sinuata	'Grandiflora'	Mixed	90 cm (3 ft)	30 cm (12 in)						■	■	■	A
Salvia horminum		Blue, pink or white bracts	45 cm (18 in)	20 cm (8 in)			■	■	■	■	■		A
S. splendens	'Salvia'	Scarlet and mixed	38 cm (15 in)	25 cm (10 in)					■	■	■	■	A
S. virgata nemorosa		Purple-blue	60 cm (2 ft)	45–60 cm (18–24 in)					■	■	■		P, Rather tender
Saponaria ocymoides		Rose pink	8 cm (3 in)	30 cm (12 in)					■	■	■		P
S. officinalis	Bouncing Bet	Pale pink	90 cm (3 ft)	considerable					■	■	■		P, Invasive, flopping
Saxifraga moschata	'Mossy' saxifrage	Cream or white	8 cm (3 in)	45 cm (18 in)		■	■						P Can get bare in the middle
S. moschata	'Atropurpurea'	Red	8 cm (3 in)	45 cm (18 in)		■	■						P
S. moschata	× 'Peter Pan'	Pink	8 cm (3 in)	45 cm (18 in)		■	■						P
S. moschata	× 'Pixie'	Red	5 cm (2 in)	30 cm (12 in)		■	■						P
S. umbrosa	London pride	Pale pink	30 cm (12 in)	45 cm (18 in)			■						P, E, Prefers partial shade and good soil

Latin	Common or varietal name	Colour	Height	Spread or p.d.	Spring			Summer			Aut		Reminders
					E	M	L	E	M	L	E	M	
Scabiosa atropurpurea	Sweet scabious	Crimson or mixed	90 cm (3 ft)	23 cm (9 in)					■	■	■		A, Scented
S. caucasica		Blue-mauve	60 cm (2 ft)	45 cm (18 in)				■	■	■	■		P
S. caucasia	'Clive Greaves'	Deep mauve	60 cm (2 ft)	45 cm (18 in)				■	■	■	■		P
S. caucasica	'Moonstone'	Light blue	60 cm (2 ft)	45 cm (18 in)				■	■	■	■		P
S. caucasica	'Moorheim Blue'	Dark violet-blue	60 cm (2 ft)	45 cm (18 in)				■	■	■	■		P
Schizanthus pinnatus	Butterfly flower	Mixed	15 cm–1.2 m (6 in–4 ft)	23–45 cm (9–18 in)					■	■	■	■	A, Taller varieties need support
Schizostylis coccinea	Kaffir lily	Scarlet	90 cm (3 ft)	considerable								■	R Do not allow to dry out in hot summers; divide
S. coccinea major		Darker red	90 cm (3 ft)	considerable								■	R congested clumps every three years
S. c. major	'Mrs Hegerty'	Pink	90 cm (3 ft)	considerable							■	■	R
S. c. major	'Viscountess Byng'	Pale pink	90 cm (3 ft)	considerable							■	■	R
Scilla siberica		Blue	15 cm (6 in)	8–10 cm (3–4 in)	■								B
S. siberica	'Spring Beauty'	Brilliant blue	15 cm (6 in)	8–10 cm (3–4 in)	■								B
Sedum spectabile	Ice plant	Pink-mauve	45 cm (18 in)	45 cm (18 in)							■	■	P, F/A, Good foliage
S. spectabile	× 'Autumn Joy'	Pink to crimson	60 cm (2 ft)	45 cm (18 in)							■	■	P, F/A, Good foliage
Senecio maritima	'Diamond'	Generally removed	60 cm (2 ft)	30 cm (12 in)									A, (P), Grown for foliage contrast
S. maritima	'Silver Dust'	Generally removed	60 cm (2 ft)	30 cm (12 in)									A, (P), Whiter and more dissected leaves
Sidalcea malvaeflora		Pink	1.3 m ($4\frac{1}{2}$ ft)	60 cm (2 ft)				■	■	■	■		P Slightly tender, may need staking, cut down after flowering to encourage secondary bloom
S. malvaeflora	'Croftway Red'	Red	90 cm (3 ft)	60 cm (2 ft)				■	■	■	■		P
S. malvaeflora	'Rose Queen'	Rose-pink	75 cm ($2\frac{1}{2}$ ft)	45 cm (18 cm)				■	■	■	■		P
Sisyrinchium striatum	Satin flower	Creamy yellow	45 cm (18 in)	15–30 cm (6–12 in)				■	■				P, Does not like good soil, needs sun and sharp drainage
Smilacina racemosa	False spikenard	Cream	90 cm (3 ft)	60 cm (2 ft)			■	■					P, Scented, prefers semi-shade
Solidago canadensis	Golden rod	Yellow	1.8 m (6 ft)	90 cm (3 ft)						■	■	■	P, Good in poorer soil, watch for mildew
S. canadensis	'Golden Wings'	Yellow	1.8 m (6 ft)	90 cm (3 ft)						■	■	■	P, Good in poor soil, watch for mildew

Latin	Common or varietal name	Colour	Height	Spread or p.d.	Spring E	Spring M	Spring L	Summer E	Summer M	Summer L	Aut E	Aut M	Reminders
Stachys lanata	Lamb's ears, flannel flower	Mauve	45 cm (18 in)	30 cm (12 in)					■				P, E
S. lanata	'Silver Carpet'	No flowers	13 cm (5 in)	30 cm (12 in)									P, E, May be killed in cold winters, keep reserve stocks
S. macrantha		Rose-purple	75 cm (2½ ft)	38 cm (15 in)			■	■	■				P
Tagetes erecta hybrids	African marigold	Lemon, orange or golden	30–90 cm (12 in–3 ft)	20–45 cm (8–18 in)					■	■	■	■	A, Protect young plants from slugs
T. patula hybrids	French marigold	Yellow through red to brown	15–36 cm (6–14 in)	20–30 cm (8–12 in)					■	■	■	■	A, Protect young plants from slugs
Tellima grandiflora		Green	45–60 cm (18–24 in)	45 cm (18 in)		■	■	■					P, Semi-shade, best in moist soil
T. grandiflora	'Purpurea'	Green	45–60 cm (18–24 in)	45 cm (18 in)		■	■	■					P, Has purple leaves in winter
Thalictrum aquilegifolium		Mauve	90 cm (3 ft)	45 cm (18 in)				■					P. Resents disturbance, blue grey fern-like foliage
T. aquilegifolium	'Album'	White	90 cm (3 ft)	45 cm (18 in)				■					P, Foliage fern-like
T. dipterocarpum		Mauve and cream	1.2–1.5 m (4–5 ft)	45 cm (18 in)				■	■	■			P, Foliage fern-like
T. dipterocarpum	'Album'	White	1.2–1.5 m (4–5 ft)	45 cm (18 in)				■	■	■			P, Foliage fern-like
T. dipterocarpum	'Hewitt's Double'	Mauve	1.2–1.5 m (4–5 ft)	45 cm (18 in)				■	■	■			P. Foliage fern-like
Thymus × citriodorus	Lemon-scented thyme	Lilac	30 cm (12 in)	to 38 cm (15 in)				■	■	■			S, Can be killed in cold, wet winters
T. × citriodorus	'Aureus'	Lilac	30 cm (12 in)	to 38 cm (15 in)				■	■	■			S, Golden foliage
T. × citriodorus	'Silver Queen'		30 cm (12 in)	to 38 cm (15 in)				■	■	■			S, Variegated foliage
T. drucei		Pink, white or mauve	30 cm (12 in)	to 38 cm (15 in)				■	■	■			S
T. drucei	'Coccineus'	Crimson	30 cm (12 in)	to 38 cm (15 in)				■	■	■			S
Tiarella polyphylla		Pinkish white	60 cm (2 ft)	30 cm (12 in)				■	■	■			P, Best in semi-shade
T. trifoliata		White	50 cm (20 in)	30 cm (12 in)				■	■	■			P
Tigridia pavonia	Tiger flower	Red, yellow, white	60 cm (2 ft)	10 cm (4 in)					■	■	■		C Do not plant before end of April, needs rich well drained soil, do not allow to dry out in hot weather
T. pavonia	'Alba'	White	60 cm (2 ft)	10 cm (4 in)					■	■	■		C
T. pavonia	'Red Giant'	Scarlet	60 cm (2 ft)	10 cm (4 in)					■	■	■		C
T. pavonia	'Rubra'	Orange red	60 cm (2 ft)	10 cm (4 in)					■	■	■		C

Roses provide form, structure and colour in a border, with echinops as an excellent contrast. Bergenias add year-round value.

A border backed by a warm stone wall is a perfect place for a satisfying collection of flower and foliage shapes. Achilleas, phormium and kniphofias.

Latin	Common or varietal name	Colour	Height	Spread or p.d.	Spring E	Spring M	Spring L	Summer E	Summer M	Summer L	Aut E	Aut M	Reminders
Tolmeia menziesii	Pick-a-back plant	Greenish rust	60 cm (2 ft)	40 cm (16 in)				■					R
T. menziesii	'Variegata'	Greenish rust	60 cm (2 ft)	40 cm (16 in)				■					R, Not for sunny borders
Tradescantia virginiana	Spider flower	Purple	60 cm (2 ft)	45 cm (18 in)				■	■	■	■		P Prefers moist soils, protect young leaves from slugs
T. virginiana	'Blue Stone'	Blue	60 cm (2 ft)	45 cm (18 in)				■	■	■	■		P
T. virginiana	'Isis'	Royal blue	60 cm (2 ft)	45 cm (18 in)				■	■	■	■		P
T. virginiana	'Osprey'	White and blue	60 cm (2 ft)	45 cm (18 in)				■	■	■	■		P
Tropaeolum majus	Nasturtium	Red, salmon, cream, yellow	25–38 cm (10–15 in)	38 cm (15 in)				■	■	■	■		HHA Best in poor hot soil. Watch for aphis and caterpillars, good foliage plant
T. majus	'Alaska'	Red, cream, yellow, salmon	20 cm (8 in)	30 cm (12 in)				■	■	■	■		HHA Good foliage plant
Tulipa	'Pink Beauty'	Pink	15–38 cm (6–15 in)	15 cm (6 in)		■							B Best in free-draining slightly alkaline soils; plant deeply to 23–30 cm (9–12 in) in November; lift after flowering and replant elsewhere to die down, or leave in border, siting so that emerging herbaceous plants conceal fading leaves; add lime 85–115 g per sq. m (3–4 oz per sq. yd) to acid soils
Tulipa	'Bellona'	Yellow	15–38 cm (6–15 in)	15 cm (6 in)		■							B
Tulipa	'Keizerskroon'	Red and yellow	15–38 cm (6–15 in)	15 cm (6 in)		■							B
Tulipa	'Diana'	White	15–38 cm (6–15 in)	15 cm (6 in)		■							B
Tulipa	'Marechal Niel'	Yellow	30–38 cm (12–15 in)	15 cm (6 in)		■							B
Tulipa	'Schoonoord'	White	30–38 cm (12–15 in)	15 cm (6 in)		■							B
Tulipa	'Electra'	Cherry red	30–38 cm (12–15 in)	15 cm (6 in)		■	■						B
Tulipa	'Athleet'	White	38–50 cm (15–20 in)	15 cm (6 in)		■	■						B
Tulipa	'Van der Eerden'	Red	38–50 cm (15–20 in)	15 cm (6 in)		■							B
Tulipa	'Garden Party'	Pink and white	50 cm (20 in)	20 cm (8 in)		■							B
Tulipa	'Pax'	White	50 cm (20 in)	20 cm (8 in)		■							B
Tulipa	'Dreaming Maid'	White and pink	50 cm (20 in)	20 cm (8 in)		■							B
Tulipa	'Orange Wonder'	Orange	50 cm (20 in)	20 cm (8 in)		■							B
Tulipa	'Apeldoorn'	Red	60–75 cm (2–2½ ft)	20 cm (8 in)		■	■						B
Tulipa	'Gudoschnik'	Yellow and red	60–75 cm (2–2½ ft)	20 cm (8 in)		■	■						B

Latin	Common or varietal name	Colour	Height	Spread or p.d.	Spring			Summer			Aut		Reminders
					E	M	L	E	M	L	E	M	
Tulipa	'Clara Butt'	Salmon pink	60–75 cm (2–2½ ft)	20 cm (8 in)			■						B Best in free-draining slightly alkaline soils; plant deeply to 23–30 cm (9–12 in) in November; lift after flowering and replant elsewhere to die down, or leave in border, siting so that emerging herbaceous plants conceal fading leaves; add lime 85–115 g per sq. m (3–4 oz per sq. yd) to acid soils
Tulipa	'La Tulipe Noire'	Maroon black	60–75 cm (2–2½ ft)	20 cm (8 in)			■						B
Tulipa	'The Bishop'	Violet-mauve	60–75 cm (2–2½ ft)	20 cm (8 in)		■	■						B
Tulipa	'Niphetos'	Yellow	60–75 cm (2–2½ ft)	20 cm (8 in)			■						B
Tulipa	'Arkadia'	Yellow	45–60 cm (18–24 in)	15 cm (6 in)		■							B
Tulipa	'Queen of Sheba'	Red and yellow	45–60 cm (18–24 in)	15 cm (6 in)		■							B
Tulipa	'White Triumphator'	White	45–60 cm (18–24 in)	15 cm (6 in)		■							B
Tulipa	'Artist'	Green and pink	90 cm (3 ft)	15–20 cm (6–8 in)		■	■						B
Tulipa	'Dillenburg'	Orange	90 cm (3 ft)	15–20 cm (6–8 in)		■	■						B
Tulipa	'Mrs John T Scheepers'	Yellow	90 cm (3 ft)	15–20 cm (6–8 in)		■	■						B
Tulipa	'Viridiflora'	Green	90 cm (3 ft)	15–20 cm (6–8 in)		■	■						B
Tulipa	'Absalon'	Yellow, brown, crimson	60–75 cm (2–2½ ft)	20 cm (8 in)			■						B
Tulipa	'May Blossom'	Cream and purple	60–75 cm (2–2½ ft)	20 cm (8 in)			■						B
Tulipa	'Black Parrot'	Dark purple	45–60 cm (18–24 in)	20 cm (8 in)		■	■						B
Tulipa	'Blue Parrot'	Blue-mauve	45–60 cm (18–24 in)	20 cm (8 in)		■	■						B
Tulipa	'Orange Parrot'	Orange	45–60 cm (18–24 in)	20 cm (8 in)		■	■						B
Tulipa	'White Parrot'	White	45–60 cm (18–24 in)	20 cm (8 in)		■	■						B
Tulipa	'Red Parrot'	Red	45–60 cm (18–24 in)	20 cm (8 in)		■	■						B
Tulipa	'Brilliant Fire'	Red	45–60 cm (18–24 in)	15 cm (6 in)		■							B, Scented
Tulipa	'Eros'	White	45–60 cm (18–24 in)	15 cm (6 in)		■							B, Scented
Tulipa	'Gold Medal'	Deep yellow	45–60 cm (18–24 in)	15 cm (6 in)		■							B
T. kaufmanniana hybrids	'Johann Strauss'	Cream, white, red	10–25 cm (4–10 in)	15 cm (6 in)	■	■							B
T. kaufmanniana	'Shakespeare'	Yellow, red, salmon	10–25 cm (4–10 in)	15 cm (6 in)	■	■							B
T. kaufmanniana	'The First'	Pale yellow and red	10–25 cm (4–10 in)	15 cm (6 in)	■	■							B

Latin	Common or varietal name	Colour	Height	Spread or p.d.	Spring E	Spring M	Spring L	Summer E	Summer M	Summer L	Aut E	Aut M	Reminders
T. kaufmanniana	Water-lily tulip	White, red, yellow	10–25 cm (4–10 in)	15 cm (6 in)		■							B Best in free-draining slightly alkaline soils; plant deeply to 23–30 cm (9–12 in) in November; lift after flowering and replant elsewhere to die down, or leave in border, siting so that emerging herbaceous plants conceal fading leaves; add lime 85–115 g per sq. m (3–4 oz per sq. yd) to acid soils
T. fosteriana hybrids	'Easter Parade'	Yellow	30–45 cm (12–18 in)	15 cm (6 in)		■							B
T. fosteriana	'Cantata'	Red	30–45 cm (12–18 in)	15 cm (6 in)		■							B
T. fosteriana	'Princeps'	Red	30–45 cm (12–18 in)	15 cm (6 in)		■							B
T. fosteriana	'Purissima'	Creamy-yellow	30–45 cm (12–18 in)	15 cm (6 in)		■							B
T. greigii hybrids	'Red Riding Hood'	Scarlet	30–45 cm (12–18 in)	15 cm (6 in)		■							B
T. greigii	'Pandour'	Red and white	23–30 cm (9–12 in)	15 cm (6 in)	■	■							B
T. tarda		Yellow and white	15 cm (6 in)	8 cm (3 in)	■								B
T. turkestanica		Cream, white and green	25 cm (10 in)	10 cm (4 in)	■	■							B
Veratrum album		Greenish white	1.2 m (4 ft)	38 cm (15 in)					■				P, Protect handsome foliage from slugs
V. nigrum		Blackish red	1.2 m (4 ft)	45 cm (18 in)						■			P, Best in semi-shade in moist soil
V. viride		Green yellow	2.1 m (7 ft)	60 cm (2 ft)				■	■				P
Verbascum bombyciferum		Yellow	1.2–1.8 m (4–6 ft)	45–60 cm (18–24 in)				■	■				P, Silver stems and leaves
V. chaixii		Yellow	90 cm–1.5 m (3–5 ft)	45 cm (18 in)					■	■			P, Woolly white foliage
V. chaixii	'Album'	White	90 cm–1.5 m (3–5 ft)	45 cm (18 in)					■	■			P, Woolly white foliage
V. × *hybridum*	'C. L. Adams'	Deep yellow	1.8 m (6 ft)	50 cm (20 in)				■	■	■			P
V. × *hybridum*	'Cotswold'	Mixed	1.2 m (4 ft)	45 cm (18 in)				■	■	■			P
V. × *hybridum*	'Gainsborough'	Lemon yellow	1.2 m (4 ft)	45 cm (18 in)				■	■	■			P, Grey leaves
Verbena bonariensis		Rosy-lavender	1.2–1.5 m (4–5 ft)	60 cm (2 ft)				■	■	■	■	■	P, Water well and give liquid feeds
V. × *hybrids*		Mixed	to 45 cm (18 in)	30 cm (12 in)				■	■	■	■	■	P, but grown as annuals
Veronica exaltata		Pale blue	1.5 m (5 ft)	60 cm (2 ft)					■	■			P, Rich well-drained soil
V. gentianoides		Pale blue	40 cm (16 in)	23 cm (9 in)			■	■					P
V. gentianoides	'Variegata'	Pale blue	40 cm (16 in)	23 cm (9 in)			■	■					P, Cream and green leaves
V. incana		Blue	40 cm (16 in)	25 cm (10 in)				■	■	■			P

Latin	Common or varietal name	Colour	Height	Spread or p.d.	Spring			Summer			Aut		Reminders
					E	M	L	E	M	L	E	M	
V. spicata		Pale to dark blue	15–45 cm (6–18 in)	15–30 cm (6–12 in)				■	■	■			P
V. spicata	'Crater Lake Blue'	Ultramarine	15–45 cm (6–18 in)	15–30 cm (6–12 in)				■	■	■			P
V. spicata	'Pavane'	Pink	60 cm (2 ft)	15–30 cm (6–12 in)				■	■	■			P
V. spicata	'Alba'	White	45 cm (18 in)	15–30 cm (6–12 in)				■	■	■			P
Vinca minor	Lesser periwinkle	Blue	10 cm (4 in)	1.2 m (4 ft)	■	■	■	■	■				S
V. minor	'Alba'	White	10 cm (4 in)	1.2 m (4 ft)	■	■	■	■	■				S
V. minor	'Albo-plena'	White	10 cm (4 in)	1.2 m (4 ft)	■	■	■	■	■				S
V. minor	'Aurea variegata'	Blue	10 cm (4 in)	1.2 m (4 ft)	■	■	■	■	■				S, Yellow and green leaves
V. minor	'Burgundy'	Wine-red	10 cm (4 in)	1.2 m (4 ft)	■	■	■	■	■				S
V. minor	'La Grave'	Blue purple	10 cm (4 in)	1.2 m (4 ft)	■	■	■	■	■				S
Viola cornuta		Lavender blue	10–30 cm (4–12 in)	40 cm (16 in)				■	■				P, Usually short-lived
V. cornuta	'Alba'	White	10–30 cm (4–12 in)	40 cm (16 in)				■	■				P, Usually short-lived
V. labradorica		Blue-mauve	13 cm (5 in)	40 cm (16 in)		■	■						P, Purple leaves, self-seeds
V. odorata	Sweet violet	Purple, mauve or white	15 cm (6 in)	30 cm (12 in)	■	■							P, Scented flowers
V. tricolor	Heartsease	Yellow, cream, purple	5–15 cm (2–6 in)	23 cm (9 in)			■	■	■	■	■		A
V. × wittrockiana	Garden pansy	Mixed	to 15 cm (6 in)	30 cm (12 in)			■	■	■	■	■		P, Short-lived
V. × wittrockiana	'King of the Blacks'	Black-purple	to 15 cm (6 in)	30 cm (12 in)			■	■	■	■	■		P
Zantedeschia aethiopica	Arum lily	White	90 cm (3 ft)	90 cm (3 ft)			■	■					R
Z. aethiopica	'Crowborough'	White	90 cm (3 ft)	90 cm (3 ft)			■	■					R, The hardiest form
Zinnia elegans		Mixed	18–75 cm (7 in–2½ ft)	13–45 cm (5–18 in)				■	■	■	■	■	A
Z. elegans	'Envy'	Lime-green	60 cm (2 ft)	30 cm (12 in)				■	■	■	■	■	A

(*Opposite*) This border will still be interesting when the main colours are over: Poppies have fine seed-heads, macleayas and verbascums will remain until cut down by frost

INDEX

Numbers in **bold** refer to main entries in Chapter 5 where the reader will also find more varieties described than listed here.